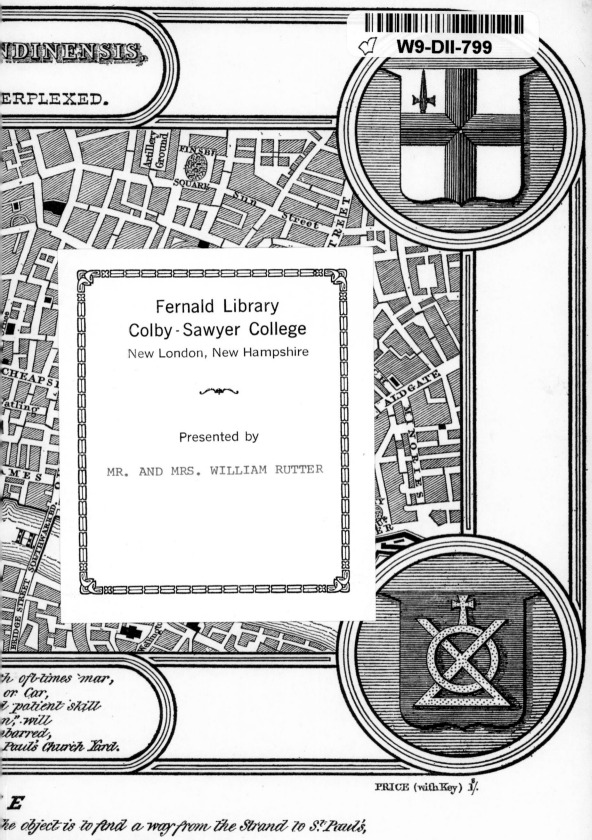

HISTORIANS
OF LONDON

The Monument of M.ʳ JOHN STOW; now standing in the Parish Church of S.ᵗ Andrew Undershaft

STANLEY RUBINSTEIN

HISTORIANS OF LONDON

An account of the many Surveys,
Histories, Perambulations, Maps and
Engravings made about the
City and its Environs,
and of the dedicated Londoners
who made them

ARCHON BOOKS
1968

SBN 208 00660 5

This edition published 1968
in the United States of America
by Archon Books, Hamden, Connecticut 06514

© Stanley Rubinstein 1968

Printed in Great Britain

With pleasure and with his permission
I dedicate this book to

otherwise known as
Alderman Sir Gilbert Inglefield
Lord Mayor of London
and a Member of the Court of Assistants of
the Worshipful Company of Musicians,
con amore

FOREWORD

by the Right Honourable the Lord Mayor
Sir Gilbert Inglefield

The late Mr Henry Ford, during the hearing of a libel suit, asserted that 'History is bunk'. He was wrong, of course, and had he consulted Herodotus, Gibbon or Trevelyan, he might well not have made this derisory comment. As that astute scholar Francis Bacon put it: 'Reading maketh a full man . . . histories make men wise'.

One is very much the wiser for having read *Historians of London*. For my part I feel exhilarated, as if I have just left a successful party at its apogee. The host, my old friend Stanley Rubinstein, replenishing my glass as it were from the Pierian spring, introduced me to a splendid gathering: antiquarians, artists, littérateurs, wits and buffoons spanning more than four hundred years, and to others who, like Mr Pickwick, enjoyed 'ruminating on the strange mutability of human affairs'. There I met John Stow, nodded to John Strype, shook hands with the earnest and somewhat long-winded John Noorthouck who deplored the habit among historians of extending 'their details with abundance of frivolous particulars', and chatted with the noted Victorian writer and critic Peter Cunningham. I was glad, too, to encounter Dr Lettsom, whose well-known illiteracy was said to have rivalled his callousness. As I remember it, my version of the epigram written on him differs a little from Stanley Rubinstein's, and perhaps mine helps accentuate his legendary foibles:

> When patients ill, they comes to I,
> I physics, bleeds and sweats 'em:
> Sometimes they live, sometimes they die,
> What's that to I? I Lettsom.

Many and varied are the subjects of such epitaphs, whom one would like to meet—John Spong the carpenter, for instance, who 'liv'd by railing, though he was not wit'.

What a vital duty the literary host performs! But for Boswell, my long-standing friendship with Samuel Johnson might never have transpired. Now, stimulated and encouraged by Stanley Rubinstein's fund of knowledge

—drawn in large measure from lifelong research in his unique private library—I am eager among other things to discover the engaging, vivacious letters of that trenchant chronicler the Marquis de Verment, following his visit to England in the early nineteenth century. And when I have occasion as Lord Mayor to perform the picturesque ceremony of placing a new quill pen in the cold hand of John Stow's effigy in the Church of St Andrew Undershaft, St Mary Axe, I shall do so with particular reverence and gratitude.

Gilbert Inglefield

The Mansion House, London
1968

CONTENTS

LIST OF ILLUSTRATIONS

List of Illustrations

List of Illustrations

Preface

Years ago, in search of a short cut to the merits (and demerits) of London Histories, I wrote to Mr Raymond Smith, then Librarian of the Guildhall Library, asking him to refer me to a book which would give me the information for which I was looking. He replied that a critical bibliography of London Histories had not yet been written, and that it was a project which he had been long intending to carry out himself. I then realized that I should have to learn the History of London the hard way, and began enthusiastically to prowl round the second-hand bookshops—and to write. . . .

When I had worked for some months, and the pages were growing in number, I had a check. I attended the Annual Meeting of the members of the London Topographical Society when the chairman (a distinguished Fellow of the Society of Antiquaries) expressed the willingness of himself and his colleagues on the council to 'jot down' for any member of the society, a list of books relating to the aspect of Old London in which that member was particularly interested. He stipulated, however, that before such a bibliography could be published, it must be complete—a never-ending task; in other words, such a published work would have to be perfect.

At that moment I might well have torn up what I had written, had I not, on second thoughts, realized that half a loaf is better than no bread to the student of London History, hungry for information, and I decided to continue with my self-imposed task. The resulting book could have been very much longer; to be of any real use it could not have been any shorter.

To be interested in, and to collect books about Old London and, it follows, the people who lived in it (which may be even more exciting), one should be endowed with a strong streak of sentiment; a love of, and reverence for, old things which have stood the test of time. Too many of the moderns can think of London in no other way than as an anachronism in this modern world of hurry and noise, fit only to be covered, buried under, and obliterated by masses of precast shapeless concrete.

Having determined to write about books on Old London I realized I must define more precisely what I was proposing to do; and I very soon decided to limit my work to old books, interpreting 'old' as meaning books about London before I could remember it. My memory goes back to the late 1890s—but only just, and when required to make a borderline decision I have never failed to decide in favour of the book in question; it is better to regret having bought one book too many, than one too few.

I am told that the Guildhall Library has the most complete collection of books on London in existence, but Volume One of the Members' Library Catalogue of the Greater London Council, *London History and Topography* which was published in 1939, is, I believe, the fullest printed bibliography of London. It contains the titles of some 3,000 books, but it is neither complete nor up-to-date. There are several hundred books in the catalogue which the private collector can never hope to own, but there are hundreds which, by the judicious expenditure of a few shillings a week, he may, in time, come to possess; similarly there are a number which can be ignored. No book on London can be wholly bad, but it is advisable to concentrate on the 'better' ones, and not to emulate the magpie who collects only for the sake of possession, although there is certainly a thrill in acquiring a book which is not listed in the G.L.C. catalogue.

There are, of course, some books one is never likely to see: for instance, *London's Deliverance Predicted: in a short Discourse, Showing the Causes of Plagues in General, and the Probable Time (God Not Contradicting the Course of Second Causes) When This Present Pest may Abate, Etc.*, by John Gadbury and referred to in William Thomas Lowndes' *Bibliographer's Manual of English Literature*, as 'this notorious astrological imposter', published in London, 1665. And another, *A True and Faithful Account of the Several Informations Exhibited to the Honourable Committee Appointed by the Parliament to Inquire into the Late Dreadful Burning of the City of London. Together with other Information Touching the Insolency of Popish Priests and Jesuits; and the Increase of Popery, Brought to the Honourable Committee Appointed by the Parliament for that Purpose.* Printed in the year 1667, this is the pamphlet referred to by Samuel Pepys in his Diary, under the date 14th September 1667: 'Here I saw a printed account of the examination taken touching the burning of the City of London, shewing the plot of the Papists therein; which it seems has been ordered to be burned by the hands of the common hangman in Westminster Palace.'

But for every unattainable book there are dozens of attainable ones. One cannot hope to *read* through every book one buys, but one should know what it is about, which is why I am constantly changing my bedside books, and am able to claim at least a nodding acquaintance with every book I have ever bought. Inevitably some books are in no fit condition to be introduced into a bedroom. Many collectors are concerned about the condition of the books which they buy; they will cheerfully pay for a beautiful binding without so much as a thought for what lies (!) between the covers. On the other hand, I, remembering that beauty is but skin deep, concentrate on the contents of the book. It is all to the good if the binding is sound, and if any part of the original binding remains, so much the better, but unless it is an old scarce book I will not touch a 'dirty book'—with the 'sere, the yellow leaf'—which offends one's every sense, and cries aloud to be retired to salvage.

Bed seems to me the best place in which to read a book's Preface, or Advertisement, as it used to be called. I like to know what was in the author's mind when he wrote his book, and the preface, which is so often the last thing an author writes, not only frequently tells us what he set out to do, but relates it in the light of what, in his view, he has achieved. Mention of the preface, which opens a book, emphasizes the importance of the index, which closes it.

Many of the books to which I shall later refer must be regarded as reference books, rather than narratives to be read through from cover to cover. No one will ever claim to know everything about London, and no one can be expected to carry everything which he reads in his head; the next best thing is to know where to turn for facts when they are wanted, which is the more easily achieved by cultivating the habit of remembering where one has seen them indexed.

For entertainment I read the dedication, if there is one; the more servile it is, the more it amuses me. Dedications have an old world charm of their own—and the flowery language in which they were composed imparts a fragrant bouquet, reminiscent of sun-drenched days and spacious gardens.

Such dedications, evolved in the hope of attracting the favour of a patron, are no longer written. Dr Samuel Johnson's failure, in the middle of the eighteenth century, to interest Lord Chesterfield in his *Dictionary* is well known. Less known, perhaps, is the letter which Horace Walpole wrote to the Rev. William Beloe in reply to the latter's request to accept the dedication of his translation of *Aulus Gellius*. Walpole wrote, from his beloved Strawberry Hill (on 2nd Dec. 1794):

'I do beg and beseech you, good Sir, to forgive me, if I cannot possibly consent to receive the dedication you are so kind and partial as to propose to me. I have in the most positive, and almost uncivil manner, refused a dedication or two lately. Compliments on virtues which the persons addressed, like me, seldom possessed, are happily exploded and laughed out of use. Next to being ashamed of having good qualities bestowed on me to which I should have no title, it would hurt to be praised on my erudition, which is most superficial; and on my trifling writings, all of which turn on most trifling subjects. They amused me while writing them; may have amused a few persons; but having nothing solid enough to preserve them from being forgotten with other things of as light a nature. I would not have your judgment called in question hereafter, if somebody reading your *Aulus*

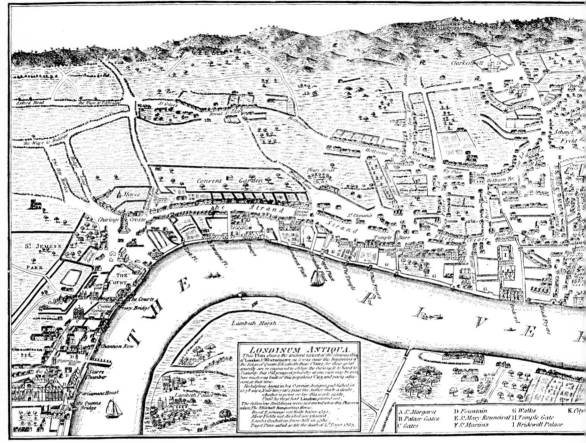

LONDINUM ANTIQUA.
This Plan shews the ancient extent of the famous City
of London & Westminster as it was near the beginning of
the Reign of Queen Elizabeth these Plates are thus great
scarcely are so engraved to oblige the curious & to hard to
Posterity this old prospect whereby at one view may be seen
how much was built of this populous City, and parts adia
none at that time.
Radulphus Aona in his Oxonia Antiqua published in
1578 does Now ten years past the Author made a doubt
whether to print or lay this work aside,
Until he first had London platted out.
The following Buildings were not erected when this Plan was
taken, The Whitehall Banqueting house,
Royal Exchange not built before 1570,
More Fields not divided nor planted
Lambs Conduit on Snow hill in 1589,
Paget Place called so till the death of L.d Paget 1563.

A S.t Margaret	D Fountain	G Walks	K City
B Palace Gates	E S.t Mary Rouncival	H Temple Gate	
C Gates	F S.t Martins	I Bridewell Palace	

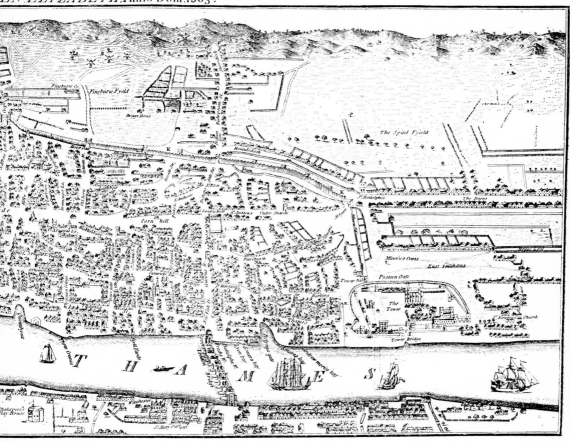

Gellius should ask, "What were those writings of Lord O. which Mr Beloe so much commends? Was Lord O. more than one of the *mob of gentlemen who wrote with ease?*" Into that class I must sink; and I had rather do so imperceptibly, than to be plunged down to it by the interposition of the hand of a friend, who could not gainsay the sentence.

'For your own sake, my good Sir, as well as in pity to my feelings, who am sore at your offering what I cannot accept, restrain the address to a mere inscription. You are allowed to be an excellent translator of classic authors; how unclassic would a dedication in the old-fashioned manner appear! If you had published a new edition of *Herodotus* or *Aulus Gellius*, would you have ventured to prefix a Greek or Latin dedication to some modern lord with a Gothic title? Still less, had those addresses been in vogue at Rome, would any Roman author have inscribed his work to Marcus, the incompetent son of Cicero, and told the unfortunate offspring of so great a man, *of his high birth and declension of ambition?* which would have excited a laugh on poor Marcus, who, whatever may have been said of him, had more sense than to leave proofs to the public of his extreme inferiority to his father.'

Nowadays, if a book is dedicated to anybody, it is usually to a wife or a sweetheart (and I pray to be pardoned for using such an old fashioned word), and is very terse.

As, in the early stages, a collection of old books will probably be made up of treasures garnered out of the sixpenny and shilling boxes, the odd volume is not to be ignored. Apart from the facts that a book labelled Volume One may not infrequently be found to contain Volumes One and Two bound in one volume, or, less frequently, to be the only volume which was published, an incomplete set gives the collector something for which to search, transforming the entry into a second-hand bookshop from an aimless quest into a voyage of discovery.

My first London book was a copy of the Fourth (1633) Edition of John Stow's *Survey of London*, minus the covers, the title page, T. Porter's map of London and Westminster, the first couple of pages of *The Epistle Dedicatorie* and the last couple of pages of *The Second Table*, but with the original spine, and otherwise in perfect condition . . . it cost four shillings and sixpence—in 1910!

The first volume of my *London Past and Present* by Henry B. Wheatley and Peter Cunningham came, spotless inside and out, from a sixpenny box in Berkhamsted; the second volume, with a battered cover, cost me seven shillings and sixpence at a rather smart shop in Eastbourne, whilst the (odd) third volume has yet to be found. But a set would cost three or four guineas, an unnecessary expenditure as the books are not scarce, and can be referred to in most public libraries. It is pleasant to own such reference and encyclopaedic books, but the beginner should, for the time being, concentrate on a foundation of the 'classics' of London topography.

A word of warning against bargaining: I am not interested in bargains, in the money sense. I do not buy to sell; I do not buy what I cannot afford, and I prefer to pay what the bookseller asks, rather than incur his ill will, his scorn or his displeasure. It was not always so: very many years ago I offered half a crown for a book marked three shillings—and for which I would willingly have paid four. I have never forgotten the stone-cold polite-ness with which the bookseller took the book out of my hand and replaced it on his shelf; there was nothing more to be said—the incident was closed— the relationship between buyer and seller had been determined, and had I attempted to reopen the matter he would no doubt have told me exactly what he thought of me—as man to man.

Conversely, I claim that I am entitled to buy a book at its marked price, and there are a number of occasions when I have replaced a book on the shelf, or left it in the bookseller's hand, because he has tried to add to the marked price—on the excuse that it is an old or out-of-date one, or somebody else's figures.

Twice I have written to booksellers, gently remonstrating against these catchpenny methods: on one occasion, when I was asked to pay four shillings and sixpence for a book marked three shillings and sixpence, on the ground that the price of his books hadn't been changed since the last stock-taking, I received a polite letter of apology and a request to call for the book at the marked price. On the other occasion I had selected a really handsome birthday present for myself—marked four pounds—and was asked seven pounds ten shillings for no apparent reason at all, leaving me with the only possible explanation that it was because I had taken a fancy to the book. My protest, written more in sorrow than in anger, was ignored—so I wrote the shop off as a place to be avoided. One day I shall find that the shop has changed hands—and I shall be able to restore it to my visiting list.

London is a vast province; it has been growing for centuries and its boundaries cannot be precisely defined. Similarly the ambit of a collection will inevitably spread as different facets of the subject fascinate. Owning Laurence Hutton's *Literary Landmarks of London*, it was only curiosity which made me take down from a bookseller's shelf *Literary London, its Lights and Comedies* by W. P. Ryan, but I should have been less than human had I resisted the temptation to acquire it—for six shillings—since it was the author's presentation copy to Coulson Kernahan, and contained a four-page letter breathing defiance at a threat of libel proceedings by Marie Corelli!

Then, how could I refuse to pay half a crown for J. O. Halliwell-Phillipps' *Outlines of the Life of Shakespeare*, which I came across in an old bookshop in Chiswick—even if it was the Fifth, instead of the complete Seventh Edition?

And what matter if the cover *had* apparently been attacked by a rat, the inscription: 'H. S. Harper Esq. With the Author's kind regards. Hollingbury Copse, Brighton, Nov. 1885.' (the year of publication), was intact. The book is a mine of information on London in the time of Shakespeare.

I paid even less, in the Farringdon Road, for the two volumes (bound in one) of *Athenae Oxonienses. An Exact History of all the Writers and Bishops Who have had their Education in the Most ancient and famous University of Oxford from the Fifteenth year of King Henry the Seventh, Dom. 1500, to the End of the Year 1690. Representing the Birth, Fortune, Preferment, and Death of all those Authors and Prelates, the great Accidents of their Lives, and the Fate and Character of their Writings. To which are added, The FASTI or Annals, of the said University, for the same time.* In other words, a *Who's Who*, published in two folio volumes in 1691 and 1692, containing the history of 1,491 people, distinguished and otherwise (including, of course, many notable Londoners), but written in such an entertaining manner that it can be read by the hour. Anthony Wood, the author, was expelled from the University at the instance of Henry Hyde for a libel which the work contained on his father, the first Earl of Clarendon. He, according to Wood, had taken bribes from men who, after the restoration of Charles II sought public office in order to retrieve their reputations and their fortunes.

A sample of the tittle-tattle to be found in the work is the epitaph on William Prynne, who, living and writing in the seventeenth century, was surely as eccentric a bencher as Lincoln's Inn can ever have harboured:

> Here lies the corpse of William Prynne,
> A Bencher late of Lincoln's Inn,
> Who restless ran through thick and thin.
>
> This grand scripturient paper-spiller,
> This endless, needless margin-filler,
> Was strangely tost from post to pillar.
>
> His brains career were never stopping,
> But pen with rheume of gall still dropping,
> Till hand o're head brought ears to cropping.
>
> Nor would he yet surcease such theams,
> But prostitute new virgin-reams
> To types of his fanatick dreams.
>
> But whilst he this hot humour bugs,
> And for more length of tedder tugs,
> Death fang'd the remnant of his lugs.

Anthony Wood. 12 Dec. 1670

Odd numbers of old periodicals, such as *The Gentleman's Magazine* are not to be despised; they can be picked up for a few shillings.

Sir George Laurence Gomme, a former clerk to the London County Council, and an enthusiastic Londoner, combed through *The Gentleman's Magazine* from 1731 to 1868 to produce a number of volumes on English topography, including three on London which were published in 1904–5, but he could not, for obvious reasons, include every item from *The Gentleman's Magazine*, and the odd volumes contain innumerable paragraphs which will add to the picture of old London. Thus, in Volume Eight, for the year 1738 (I paid sixpence for its 700-odd pages), I find in the *Historical Chronicle* for Tuesday, the 8th August: 'At a Jackmaker's in *Breadstreet*, as the Journeyman and Apprentice were beating a hot Piece of Iron, a Spark flew into a Hole punched in a Bomb that had been purchas'd among old Iron, and fir'd it; in an instant it burst and flew into a thousand Splinters, tearing the Forge and Staircase all to pieces, shatter'd the back Windows, cutting their wood-work, as if done by a Saw, and did other considerable Damage in the Shop; some of the Splinters flew across the Way into the Dining-Room Windows of a Tobacconist, but it did no other Hurt than breaking the Glass; but what is most strange, the Journeyman and Apprentice received no Harm.' It is a little difficult to believe that that paragraph was written over two hundred years ago.

Or, in the odd volume—for 1761—is a plan for street improvements in London which, if carried out, would have involved moving the Monument.

The *Gentleman's*, the first and best of the eighteenth-century magazines, is only one of many such: *The Annual Register* is another. Many years ago I bought a run from Volume One to Sixty-One—1758 to 1819—for four pounds and discovered, when I had sorted out my purchase, that the volume for 1797 was missing. I picked up the missing volume ten years later. Later still I bought—for four shillings and sixpence—the general index for the whole period.

Another purchase of the same description was Volumes One to Fifteen of *The Antiquary* (January 1880—June 1887), a periodical which contains articles of every description, many of them on various aspects of London, by such authorities as Henry Wheatley, Cornelius Walford, Sir Laurence (then G. L.) Gomme and many others, upon whose accuracy one may rely.

A book—a battered calf bound octavo—(for which I paid twopence in Farringdon Road) is entitled *The Present State of Britain* and bound up with it is *A General List, or Catalogue, of all the Offices and Officers Employed In the several Branches of his Majesty's Government, Ecclesiastical, Civil, Military, etc. I. In South-Britain, or England. II. In North-Britain, or Scotland. And The Subordinate Offices and Officers, placed under the Grand Offices, to whose Direction and Disposal they immediately appertain.* It was published in London in 1736, and its 893 pages are full of information about the London of King George II. The lists of 'The King's Officers and Servants in Ordinary above Stairs, under the *Lord-Chamberlain*,' contain such obsolete offices as, for instance, an *Embellisher of Letters to the Eastern Princes*, a *Laundress of the Body-Linnen*, who was assisted by a *Necessary Woman*, and a *Semstress* and a *Starcher*, both of whom received 'in lieu of all Bills, £400 per ann'. Then there was a *Master of the Revels*, but he could not have been very active, for the compiler of the list left his christian name blank. There were twenty-five musicians, each earning £40 per ann., in addition to the *Master of Musick*, who received £200 per ann. There was a *Court-Drummer*, who earned £24 per ann., a *Master of the Tennis Court*, a *Card-maker* (Mrs Cope), an *Operator for the teeth*, a *Chocolate-Maker*, a *Yeoman Arras-Worker*, a *Stewer of Herbs*—Mrs Alice Bill, who received £24 per ann., and a *Rat-killer*, in the person of Mrs Eliz. Stubbs, who was paid £48. 3s. 4d. per ann.

The *Present State of Britain* also recorded the daily pay and allowances of the personnel of His Majesty's Garrisons, including the Tower of London, where the *Constable* and *Chief Governor* received £2. 14s. 9d., the *Yeoman Warders* 1/6d., the *Gentleman-Gaoler* and the *Physician* 1/1d. each, the *Water Pumper* 7d., the *Apothecary* 61/2d., the *Scavenger* 4d., and the *Clock-Keeper* and *Bell-Ringer* 25/8d.

In contrast there is food for thought in a little book published in 1778 entitled *Addresses presented from the Court of Common Council to the King, on his Majesty's Accession to the Throne. . . . Resolutions of the Court, Granting the Freedom of the City to several Noble Personages, with their answers. . . .* Thus at 'A Common Council holden in the Chamber of the *Guildhall* of the City of *London*, on *Tuesday*, the Fifth Day of *May*, 1761. A Motion was made, and Question put, that the Freedom of this City be presented to the Right Honourable *Arthur Onslow*, Speaker of the House of Commons, in five successive Parliaments, as a grateful and lasting Testimony of the respectful Love and Veneration which the Citizens of *London* entertain of his Person and distinguished Virtue; for the many eminent Qualifications he displayed; the unwearied and disinterested Labours he bestowed; and the impartial and judicious Conduct he maintained in the Execution of that arduous and important Office, during a Course of three and thirty Years; and for that exemplary Zeal, which, upon all proper Occasions, he exerted with so much Dignity and Success, in Support of the Rights, Privileges, and constitutional Independence of the Commons of *Great Britain*.' The same was unanimously resolved in the affirmative.

And another motion was resolved that a copy of the Freedom 'be delivered by the Chamberlain . . . in a Gold Box, of the Value of One Hundred Guineas.'

But on 16th June Mr Chamberlain informed the Court that he had waited on the Right Honourable *Arthur Onslow*, with the copy of his Freedom in a gold Box, 'but that the said Mr Onslow could not be prevailed upon to accept the said Box', which was to be deposited with Mr Chamberlain, 'till the further Order of this Court'.

In the meantime, on 5th June 1761, the Freedom of the City was presented to His Royal Highness *Edward Augustus*, Duke of York and Albany, Rear Admiral of the Blue Squadron of his Majesty's Fleet, 'in a Gold Box, of the Value of One Hundred and Fifty Guineas'. Said His Royal Highness, some seven weeks later, 'It is with Pleasure I receive this Compliment from the Court of Common Council of *London*, as a fresh Instance of their Duty to the King, and as a distinguishing Mark of their Attention to me. I shall think myself happy in any Opportunity of shewing my Regard to the City of *London*, and in promoting its Trade and Prosperity; and I shall always exert my best Endeavours in that Profession to which I belong, and which is essentially connected with the Reputation and Independence of this commercial Country.'

Much the same thing was said by His Royal Highness the Duke of Gloucester on 6th June 1765, when he acknowledged the Freedom of the City which was voted to him in a similarly priced gold box on the 23rd March 1765.

His Serene Highness, the Hereditary Prince of Brunswick Lunenburg, was less voluble. His Freedom was voted, in what would seem to have been the standard gold box, on 15th October 1765. His Serene Highness's answer, delivered on 18th December 1766, was, perhaps, intended to be sarcastic: 'My Lord Mayor and Gentlemen,' he said, 'I accept your Present with great Pleasure, and I look upon it as a particular Honor conferred on me by this great and opulent City.'

His Royal Highness the Duke of Cumberland received his Freedom in a gold box on 16th December 1767, and replied modestly enough three months later.

But the Right Honourable Charles Townshend, Chancellor and Under Treasurer of his Majesty's Exchequer, died before the Freedom, voted to him on 23rd June 1767, could be presented, and the gold box, 'of the Value of One Hundred Guineas', was ordered to be deposited with Mr Chamberlain.

The last of the Freedoms recorded was voted, on 10th October 1768, to 'the most illustrious Prince *Christian* the Seventh, by the Grace of God, King of *Denmark, Norway*, the *Vandals* and *Goths*, Duke of *Sleswick, Holstein, Stormarn*, and the *Dithmarches*, Count of *Oldenburg* and *Delmenhorst* &c., &c.' His gold box was 'of the Value of Two Hundred Guineas', and two days later the Lord Mayor reported that the King had 'signified his Pleasure that it should be delivered to Baron *Dieden*, his Majesty's Minister at this Court'.

Amongst other items in the little book are the 'Humble' Addresses to

King George III on the births, 'and the safe Delivery of the Queen', of six children born between 1762 and 1768.

Pamphlets and books, equally interesting, crop up from time to time, and topographical articles turn up in unexpected places. Some years ago, I was browsing round an old second-hand bookshop in Gloucester, looking for something light to read in the train, when, on the shilling tray, I came across Volume Twenty-seven (May to August 1902) of *The Pall Mall Magazine*, containing a charmingly illustrated article by Hugh B. Philpott and Hedley Fitton on the widening of the western end of Piccadilly, to relieve the traffic congestion at the bottom of Hamilton Place!

My thanks are due to the Oxford University Press for kindly permitting me to quote the extracts on page 164 from their publication *The Life and Times of Anthony À Wood*, abridged from Andrew Clark's edition, which I recently came across in a second-hand bookseller's catalogue.

At this point perhaps, we can with advantage remember and apply something Horace wrote in his *Art of Poetry*:

> Hearing excites the Mind by slow Degrees;
> The Man is warm'd at once by what he sees.

And, before buying any books it is a good idea to wander round the confines of the Old London Wall; it is not possible to trace its course with precision, but one can start at Blackfriars and stroll round by the site of the Wall's several gates, still commemorated by their names—Ludgate, Newgate, Aldersgate, Cripplegate, Moorgate, Bishopsgate, Aldgate, down to the Tower, 'two English miles and more, by 608 feet' wrote Stow in 1598, and back via the river gates, Billingsgate and Dowgate.

The Wall enclosed a space of 380 acres—within which there were, at the time of the Great Fire in 1666, more than 100 Parish Churches for the 350,000 inhabitants of the City. 86 Churches were burnt down in the Fire—but some were rebuilt by Sir Christopher Wren, and before the second world war there were over 50, of which 19 (16 of them Wren's) were destroyed during the war.

The map of 'London and Westminster in the Reign of Queen Elizabeth Anno Dom: 1563', reproduced from Thomas Pennant's *Some Account of London*, showing the City Wall and the Gates, helps to set the scene on the stage upon which the History of London has been enacted (see pp. 16 and 17).

1

John Stow

An hour or two at a local library, handling their books on Old London, and at a few second-hand bookshops will help the would-be collector to recognise the 'common' ones. Having done which he should invest in Stow's *Survey of London*.

John Stow was a tailor, who became London's first historian and topographer. The reader of his *Survey* will acquire a detailed description of the City of London, ward by ward, as well as information about its inhabitants and the manner of their living and dying; it is the foundation stone upon which everybody who hopes to make an intelligent study of Old London and Londoners must build.

The First Edition of Stow's *Survey* was published in 1598 by John Wolfe, who entered it at Stationer's Hall, (that being the only way in those days by which a work could be protected against literary pirates) on 7th July in that year.

'The Epistle Dedicatorie' in the *Survey* begins: 'To the Right Honourable, the Lord Maior of the City of LONDON, to the Communalty, and Citizens of the same, JOHN STOW Citizen wisheth long Health and Felicity', and having explained at some length why he undertook the work, Stow concluded: 'Touching the Dedication, I am not doubtful where to seek my Patron, since you be a Politick Estate of the City; as the Walls and Buildings be the Material Parts of the same. To you therefore do I address this my whole Labour, as well that by your Authority I may be protected, as warranted by your own Skill and Understanding of that which I have written. I confess that I lacked my desire to the Accomplishment of some special Parts: but I trust hereafter that shall be supplied; and I profess (if more touching this work come unto me) to afford it in all Duty. In the mean time I recommend this to your View, my Labours to your Consideration, and my self to your Service (as I have professed during Life) in this or any other.'

The Rt Hon John Burns (1858–1943), one of the first three independent Labour MPs, made a magnificent collection of London books, and bought a copy at its remarkably low catalogue price of ten guineas. It is in the 'original brown calf panelled with gold and blind lines; flowers at angles, and ARMS of the CITY OF LONDON in centre', as described by the bookseller, who added: 'No doubt the DEDICATION COPY to the Lord Mayor (Sir Stephen Soame) and corporation of London.'

This book now has a little label inside the cover which reads 'Ex Libris The John Burns Library. Presented by the Right Hon. Lord Southwood to the London County Council in trust for the people of London. December 1943'. A truly munificent gesture.

A reprint of the *Survey* was called for only a year after publication, and such copies have the date 1599 on the title page. A presentation copy to Elizabeth Stow, with her name printed within an ornamental border on the verso of the title page, and her initials and the City arms stamped on the covers, is in the British Museum.

The Second Edition, with slight variations and some new matter, was published in 1603 by John Windet, 'Printer to the honourable Citie of London'. The epistle to the Second Edition is the same as to the First, but the dedication is to 'ROBERT LEE, Maior, and the Commonalty', and a few words were inserted in the last paragraph.

Thereafter the First Edition of 1598 was not reprinted until 1842, when it was edited by William John Thoms, a noted antiquary, who added some of the variations of the 1598 text with notes. This edition was published again with illustrations in 1876. I have a copy of both editions.

Professor Henry Morley, LL.D. edited an edition in 1889 (reprinted in 1890, and again in 1893) which contained, in addition to the 1603 text, some of the matter which Stow cut out of his original 1598 edition. It is in octavo, and is therefore more portable than the Thoms in Royal 8vo. A copy of the 1603 edition was published in Everyman's Library, edited and with an introduction by Henry B. Wheatley, in 1912. I have a specially bound copy of this book, with three special leaves bound in; the first, headed with the crest of the City, contains the message, 'With the Best Wishes of Sir William Henry Dunn, Lord Mayor, the Mansion House, London, Christmas, 1916', the second, a title page, is headed 'The Mansion House Edition', whilst the third contains an explanation of 'City Mottoes'. A revised reprint was published in Everyman's Library in 1956.

The historian and topographer Charles Lethbridge Kingsford (1862–1926) said the last word on the 1598–1603 Stow, and his two volumes, published in 1908, and republished with additional notes, in 1927 at thirty shillings, contain all the variations between the two versions, with a number of notes; everything, apparently, that is known about Stow and his works, and a map of London circa 1600.

Stow died on the 5th April 1605, and was buried in St Andrew Undershaft Church, St Mary Axe. There is a Stow Commemoration Service in this church every year, arranged by the London and Middlesex Archaeological Society, which is attended by the Lord Mayor who removes last year's quill pen from Stow's hand and replaces it with a new one.

The frontispiece shows a picture of his monument, reproduced from the life of Stow which John Strype wrote and included in his edition of the *Survey* which was published in 1720. It was engraved by *John Sturt* (a fact not noted by Horace Walpole in his *Anecdotes of Painting in England*). The monument as one sees it today, is not as Sturt saw it in 1720, for it was restored by the Merchant Taylors Company in 1905.

John Wolfe, the publisher of the First Edition died, and on 27th April 1612 the work was transferred by his widow to John Pyndley, whose widow in turn transferred it, on 2nd November 1613, to George Purslowe.

The title page of the Third Edition published by Purslowe 'dwelling at the East end of Christs Church', records that the *Survey* was 'written in the yeere 1598, by John Stow, Citizen of London. Since then, continued, corrected and much enlarged, with many rare and worthy Notes, both of Venerable Antiquity, and later memorie; such, as were never published before this present yeere 1618.'

'The Epistle Dedicatorie' is addressed 'To the Right Honourable, George Bolles, Lord Maior of the Citie of London; Sir Anthony Benn, Knight, Recorder of London: and to all the Knights and Aldermen, Brethren—Senatours in the State of so Famous a Citie: all of them being my Honourable Masters: A.M. wisheth the fruition of all tempor all felicities in this life; and the never-failing fulnesse of blessednesse in the life to come,' and a paragraph, with the marginal note *A perpetuall glory to London, to produce her own native sons to be her majistrates*, commences—'For being a Citie-child my selfe, I hold it an attribute of credite for me to record it, though much more honour to you (being of the same worthy Ranke) to read it—'. 'A.M.' was Anthony Munday, a playwright and a poet, and John Stow's literary executor.

Kingsford does not mention an edition in 1617, but I have seen a copy so dated, and near the end of the enlarged Fourth (folio) Edition of 1633, 'Printed by Elizabeth Purslow', (was she the wife, widow or daughter of George?) 'to be sold by Nicholas Bourne, at his Shop at the South Entrance of the Royall Exchange', is the following notice:

TO THE READER

We are here to give you notice (gentle Reader) that the Monuments, Epitaphs, and Inscriptions, that in this collection of Churches (Builded, Repaired, and Beautified) are here (with their Churches) inserted, are onely such as have beene raised, composed, and added, since the last imprinting of this Booke, called THE SURVEY OF LONDON, that Impression being in the yeere 1617. Those of greater times and antiquity, are to be turned to as they stand before in their severall Wards and Parishes.

Perhaps the Edition *was* published in *1617*—destroyed by fire, after only a few copies had been distributed—necessitating a second impression in 1618.

An interesting 'curiosity' is the insertion, between pages 20 and 21, of four unnumbered pages, ('Let this halfe sheete be placed between Folio 20 and 21' is the instruction [to the binder] at the foot of the first of them). It relates how 'Master Hugh Middleton' bought the New River Water to London, and includes 'The Speech at the Cesterne, according as it was delivered to mee'. The water had in fact been let into the New River Head at Clerkenwell five years earlier—on 29th September 1613.

And the 1633 edition proclaims that the *Survey* (previously it had been spelt Survay) was 'Begunne first by the paines and Industry of John Stow, in the yeere 1598. Afterwards inlarged by the care and diligence of A.M. in the yeere 1618. And now completely finished by the study and labour of A.M. H.D. and others, this present yeere 1633.'

'H.D.' is identified in a marginal note as Humphry Dyson, and the 'and others' include one 'W.W.', whose initials thus appear in the margin of 'The Epistle Dedicatorie' 'to The Right Honourable Ralph Freeman, now Lord Maior of the City of London', and a number of other dignitaries.

Combing through the *Dictionary of National Biography* I came across the name William Wyrley, an antiquary—and Rouge Croix pursuivant who made a collection of arms and monumental inscriptions in Leicestershire and other counties, as well as in churches in and near London. He died in 1618, but he may well have contributed anonymously to the 1618 edition, and his contribution reproduced as a matter of course in the 1633 edition.

No amount of combing through the *Dictionary of National Biography*, however, produces a name for 'C.I.', another of the 'and others', who thus signed the 'To the Reader' which followed 'The Epistle Dedicatorie', and in which he apologized that the 'Worke' is 'not so absolutely Methodicall as he could wish it were'. He explains that this is due to the book's 'Bulke, and Mortality of the AUTHORS who have spent [two of them now] their lives in the disquisition of venerable ANTIQUITY concerning this CITY'. Munday had died on 10th August of that year, aged eighty, and William Wyrley may have been the other deceased author referred to.

'C.I.' is not content to let the matter rest there; he continues to apologize and explain that the want of method is due to the delay in obtaining information 'since every dayes Experience teaches, how unstable oftentimes and incertaine Friendship is, when she promises Information in this kinde'.

There is another acid tone prefacing 'The Remaines or Remnants of Divers Worthy Things' which fill the last 180 (out of 939) pages 'which should have had their due place and honour in this Worke, if promising friends had kept their words. But they failing, and part of them comming to my hands by other good means, they are here inserted, to accompany my Perambulations foure miles about *London*'.

This 1633 edition also contains a great deal of new material: further notes on churches, Acts of Parliament and, in particular, the Coat of Arms of the Mayors and City Companies. This will, no doubt, be the edition which Samuel Pepys, thirty years later, on 10th December 1663, saw at his bookseller's in St Paul's Church Yard but did not buy; odd, as Pepys was so essentially a Londoner.

The book includes such up-to-the-minute news as: 'A briefe Relation of the six children drowned at the Ducking-pond, 19 January, 1633', 'A briefe Relation of that lamentable Fire, that hapned on London Bridge the 13 of February, 1633'. Also the epitaph on Munday himself, who had not died until 10th August 1633, so the edition must have been published late in the year. All these three items are referred to in the index at the end of the book.

But the paging shows signs of a harassed sub-editor: the eight pages following 534 are numbered 527 through to 534 although the text is different. There are no pages numbered 653, 654, 771, or 772.

Kingsford confirms that Munday's additions were considerable, but he repeats Strype's remark that 'they consist very largely of copies of monumental inscriptions from churches and extracts from the *Summarie* and *Annales*', which Stow had been publishing for over thirty years. However, many of these inscriptions are of great interest, and they certainly help to build up a mental picture of the Londoners of the sixteenth century and earlier. And the interest is the greater as Munday inserted original verses in praise of various Dear Departed, which never found their way on to monuments.

He also recorded monuments in some of the churches which were destroyed in the fire of 1666. For instance, in the Parish Church of St John Zachary in 'Engaine lane, or Maiden lane, and at the North-west corner thereof,' there was 'A very goodly Monument in the East end in the Chancell,' which read:

This monument is erected to the memory of Sir JAMES PEMBERTON, *Knight; who being Sheriffe of this City at the comming in of King* JAMES, *entertained neere 40. Earles and Barons in his House, on the day of the King's being proclaimed. Afterwards,* ANN *1612. was elected Maior of this most honourable Citie of* LONDON. *Hee erected a Free-schoole in the Parish of* ECLESTON *in*

LANCASHIRE, *sixteene yeeres before his death; and gave fifty Pounds by the yeere, to the maintaining thereof for ever. Hee gave also five hundred Pounds to Christs Hospital, and two hundred Pounds to the Company of Goldsmiths; besides many liberal Gifts to the poore of his Kindred, and many other most charitable Uses. He died the eighth day of September, 1613. aged, 68. yeeres.*

> Marble nor Touch, nor Alabaster can
> Reveale the Worth of the long buried Man:
> For oft (we see) Mens Goods, when they are gone,
> Doe pious Deeds, when they themselves did none.
> Mine (while I liv'd) my Goodness did expresse,
> 'Tis not Inscriptions make them more or lesse:
> In Christ I hope to rise amongst the Just,
> Man is but Grasse, all must to Wormes and Dust.

*

> *Vertue and Death, being both enamoured*
> *On worthy* PEMBERTON. *In heat of Love,*
> *To be possest of that each coveted,*
> *Thus did they dialogue, and thus they strove.*

Vertue. What Vertue challengeth, is but her Right.
Death. What Death layes claims to, who can contradict?
Vert. Vertue, whose power exceeds all other Might.
Dea. Where's Vertues Power, when Death makes all submit?
Vert. I gave him life; and therefore he is mine.
Dea. That life he held no longer than I list.
Vert. I made him more than mortall, meere Divine.
Dea. How hapt he could not then Deaths Stroke resist?
Vert. Because (by Nature) all are borne to dye.
Dea. Then thine owne Tongue yeelds Death the Victory.
Vert. No, Death, thou art deceiv'd, thy envious stroke
     Hath given him Life immortal, 'gainst thy Will:
Dea. What Life can be, but vanisheth as Smoake?
Vert. A Life that all thy Darts can never kill.
Dea. Have I not lock'd his Body in my Grave?
Vert. That was but Dust, and that I pray thee keepe.
Dea. That is as much as I desire to have,
     His comely Shape in my eternall Sleepe.
Vert. But where's his honourable Life, Renowne and Fame?
Dea. They are but Breath, them I resigne to thee.
Vert. Them I most covet.

31

Dea.   I preferre my claime,
           His Body mine.
Vert.   Mine his Eternity.

> *And so they ceast, Death triumphs o'er his Grave,*
> *Vertue o'er that which Death can never have.*

And as faire Trophees, fit to beautifie
His Hearse, Vertue hangs up these Ornaments;
His justice, Wisedome, and Integritie,
His Courage, dreadlesse of what are events,
His upright Soule in that high Dignitie,
Which *London* gives her chiefest Presidents.
Free from compare with such as went before,
Or should succeed. It was his sole desire
Truth might report those Actions, lesse or more,
Which honest Thoughts did in his heart inspire.
His Care of Learning, and his liberal minde
Unto the poore, love to his Company,
Kindred and Friends, to whom he was most kinde,
And whom he dealt with truly bounteously.
These Graces better doe become his Grave,
Than wastfull Words of fruitlesse Flattery;
And their due Merit (doubtlesse) he shall have,
Among the Blessed in Eternity.

> Whereto faire *Vertue* now hath brought her sonne,
> Worthily honour'd Sir *James Pemberton.*   *A.M.*

And it is the only 'Poem' in the book with Anthony Munday's initials. But Munday was better known as a dramatist than as a poet (in *Wits Treasury* written by Francis Meres in 1598 he is spoken of as 'our best plotter') and as around the turn of the century he was living in St Giles, Cripplegate, at the same time as Shakespeare was residing with the Mountjoys in the corner house at the intersection of Muggle (Mugwell or Monkwell) Street and Silver Street on the boundary between Farringdon and Cripplegate Wards, it is probable that Munday and Shakespeare knew each other, and met—frequently.

Munday had, in 1584, translated *The Two Italian Gentlemen*, which may have been consulted by Shakespeare when he was writing *Two Gentlemen of Verona*, some six or seven years later, and some enthusiasts have professed to see Munday's hand in *Titus Andronicus*, which is thought to have been one of the earliest dramas on which Shakespeare worked.

In 1602 Munday was working for Philip Henslowe's Company with John Webster, Thomas, Middleton and Michael Drayton on a play, *Caesar's Fall* (which has not come down to us). It has been suggested that this was written as a counter-attraction to Shakespeare's *Julius Caesar*, which some authorities believe to have been acted about 1599–1600, although it was not printed until 1623.

Anthony Munday records a poem, reminiscent of Mark Antony's speech over the body of Julius Caesar, as 'Intended to be hung in a Faire Table by the Tombe' of Sir Thomas Sutton in the Charterhouse. It is headed 'An Epitaph written by a Friend to Goodnesse'.

> When bad men dye, the memory remaines
> Of their corruptions and ungodly wayes:
> As merit to their mis-applyed paines,
> Out of ill actions forming as ill prayse.
> For Vertue wounded by their deep disgrace,
> Leaves shame to their Posterity and Race.
>
> When good men dye, the memory remaines
> Of their true Vertues, and most Christian waies;
> As a due guerdon to their godly paines,
> Out of good actions forming as good praise:
> For Vertue cherished by their deeds of grace,
> Leaves Fame to their Posterity and Race.
>
> Among those good (if goodness may be sayd
> To be among the seede of mortall men)
> In upright ballance of true merit weigh'd
> Needs must we recken famous *Sutton* then.
> In whom, as in a mirror doth appeare,
> That faith with workes did shine in him most cleere.
>
> And let us not, as is a common use,
> Measure him by a many other more;
> In death, to cover their bad lifes abuse,
> To launch out then some bounty of their store.
> No, *Sutton* was none such, his Hospitall;
> And much more else beside, speakes him to all.
>
> For as God blest him with abundant wealth,
> Like to a carefull Steward he imploy'd it,
> And ordered all things in his best of health,
> As glad to leave it, as when he enjoyed it.
> And being prepared every houre to dye,
> Disposed all his gifts most Christianly.

In *Abrahams* bosome sleeps he with the blest,
His works, they follow him, his worth survives,
Good Angels guide him to eternall rest,
Where is no date of time, for yeares or lives.
You that are rich, do you as he hath done,
And so assure the Crown that he hath won.

FINIS

Sir Thomas Sutton died on 12th December 1611; his funeral was solemnized at Christ Church on 28th May 1612, and in March 1616 his remains were buried in a vault beneath 'a very costly and beautiful Tombe' (Stow) erected in the hospital Chapel 'in the West side of the Quire' (Stow), or 'on the North syde of the chapell' (J. R. Malcolm, quoting Memorabilia from the Governor's books), but 'in a most inappropriate situation in respect of light' (E. W. Brayley), which may be the reason why the epitaph had not, in 1633, and indeed has never been, 'hung in a faire Table by the Tombe'.

Who was the writer of the 'Friend to Goodnesse'? It might have been Anthony Munday himself—perhaps it is a fragment from *Caesar's Fall*! But then why did not Munday append his initials?

It might have been Ben Jonson who, it has been suggested, intended, in *Volpone*, to satirize Sir Thomas Sutton, and to whom Sutton allowed a 'constant pension'.

It might have been Francis Beaumont, whose cousin, of the same name, was appointed Master of the Charterhouse by James I in 1617, the year after the poet's death.

It might have been Francis Bacon, who wrote of the Charterhouse as this 'triple good'.

It might even have been Shakespeare! Shakespeare had friends outside the theatre—neighbours and people whom he respected as much as they respected him. There is no reason why, when one of them died, he should not have consoled the surviving relatives with an epitaph. Both Edmund Malone and Nicholas Rowe refer in their writings to an epitaph alleged to have been written by Shakespeare. The style is admittedly different, but he might have been experimenting, particularly if writing anonymously. Speculation is more than half the excitement of antiquarian research.

Turn to 'A Remembrance of M. John Banester, Chirurgion and Licentiate in Physicke,' which is printed inconsequently in the middle of the description of Aldersgate Ward, immediately following a reference to two monumental stones in the Parish Church of St Olave in Silver Street, and followed by a reference to the Parish Church of St Leonards in Foster Lane—

34

both Churches being within a stone's throw of the house in which Shakespeare was living from 1598 to 1604.

The *Dictionary of National Biography* suggests that the 'Remembrance' was written by Banester's old friend William Clowes, a surgical author, whom he had met in 1563, when surgeon to the forces sent under the Earl of Warwick to relieve Le Havre.

But William Clowes, who was born in or about 1540 (the year in which John Banester [or Banister] was born) died in 1604—and Banester survived him by six years. So, unless the obituary had been commissioned before his death, which was sometimes done, we must look elsewhere for the author. Before leaving Clowes, however, it is interesting to note that he was the author, inter alia of *A Prooved Practice for all Young Chirurgians concerning Burnings with Gunpowder, and Wounds made with Gunshot, Sword, Halbard, Pike, Launce or such other*, published in 1591, whilst in 1602 he wrote *A Right Frutefull and Approved Treatise for the Artificiall Cure of the Struma or Evill, cured by the Kinges and Queenes of England* and which, says the *Dictionary of National Biography*, 'besides their surgical interest are full of pictures of daily life in the reign of Queen Elizabeth.'

John Banester had studied at Oxford, and he could have met Shakespeare when the latter made one of his return visits there. Or Shakespeare might have met him at a banquet at Barber Chirurgians Hall, whichw as also within a few steps of Mountjoy's house; they might even have walked home together afterwards, for Banester was living round the corner, in Silver Street.

As we have seen Banester was at Le Havre in 1563, as surgeon to the Earl of Warwick's forces (which suggests another—very tenuous—link with Shakespeare), and he served in the Earl of Leicester's expedition to the Low Countries in 1585 (a stronger link for Shakespeare was a member of a group of actors which, taking its name from their patron, was known as 'the Earl of Leicester's servants').

The muster-master general of the English forces in the Netherlands in the following year (1586) was Thomas Digges, and the Earl of Leicester may well have introduced Shakespeare both to Digges and Banester.

Then Leonard, Thomas Digges' son, wrote two poems in praise of Shakespeare after his death: indeed, he is one of the few contemporary poets who mentions Shakespeare.

Thomas Digges had died in 1595, and was buried in St Mary Aldermanbury, the Parish Church of Cripplegate Ward, so it is fair to assume that he and his son, who, at the date of his father's death, was only seven years old, were living in the Ward, and that Shakespeare already knew the family when he, too, came to live there.

There is thus nothing so improbable in the thought that Shakespeare and Banester remained friends till the latter's death in 1610 and I leave it to Shakespearian scholars to ponder on whether the following epitaph might possibly be from his pen:

A Remembrance of M. *John Banester, Chirurgion and Licentiate in Physicke.*

Great men that ne're did good in all their dayes,
    But at the very instant of their death,
Finde yet no meane commenders of their prayse,
    Although it lasts no longer then a breath:
    Shall then good men, though lesser in degree,
    Finde none to give them right and equitie?

If one shall say, The great mans life was such,
    So good, so full of hospitality:
When God doth know, he ne're did halfe so much,
    Though thus he must be grac'd with flattery.
    Shall meane men, who such workes truly did,
    Be nothing spoken of? Oh God forbid.

Not then, as equalling with any Great,
    My fatherly good friend, *John Banester*:
No more but truth of thee let me repeate,
    A Sonnes Love-teares, thy body to interre.
    That such as knew thee better farre then I;
    May say, Thy vertues did not with thee dye.

Thy Skill and Practice, that it selfe commends,
    Some of the best have truely found the same,
Not partially employed to wealthy friends,
    But even the poorest wretch, the sicke and lame
    Felt of the best. Some difference there might be:
    The rich pay'd somewhat, poore men had it free.

Thy care and cost layd out for common good,
    In greater measure then came in againe:
But that heavens blessing with thy bounty stood,
    Hardly had stretcht so many to sustaine.
    But it is true: The liberall heart God leaves,
    And from him still all cause of lacke removes.

Thy weekly charity given to the poore
    In Bread, beside, in money from thy Purse:
Even in the hardest yeeres dealt at thy doore,

36

When some repin'd that every day did worse;
Makes poore men say: Our good relief is gone,
Let them goe to thy find-faults and have none.

Poore maymed Souldiers, sore-sicke hearted men,
 That under miseries hard Crouch did bow,
Were freely cur'd, me thinks they cry: Lord, when,
 Where shall we find our good Physicion now?
 I doubt not, but some others will as much:
 Yet (in these dayes) we find not many such.

Sleepe then, thou happy Soule, in endlesse rest,
 All good mens grones be powred on the grave:
Live thou in *Abrahams* bosome with the blest;
 Where Faith and Workes due recompence shall have.
 My Sight growes dimme, fighting my hart makes sore:
 Teares blot my paper. I can write no more.

There is nothing like an epitaph to help conjure up a vision of the Dear Departed. Thus, Elizabeth Lucar, whose epitaph was, says Munday, 'A very faire Stone, and fairely plated in the South Ile and body of the Parish Church of St Lawrence Poultney', which was destroyed in the fire of 1666 (and was not rebuilt), was referred to in the chapter heading in John Strype's 1720 edition as 'Elizabeth Lucar *qualified to a Wonder*'. whilst a marginal note laconically records: *Elizabeth Lucar*, an accomplished woman'. The Epitaph reads:

Every Christian heart seeketh to extoll
 The glorie of the Lord, our onely Redeemer:
Wherefore Dame Fame must needs enroll
 Paul Withypoll his child, by love and nature
Elizabeth, the wife of *Emmanuel Lucar*,
 In whom was declared the goodnesse of the Lord,
 With many high vertues, which truely I will record.

She wrought all Needle-workes, that women exercise,
 With Pen, Frame, or Stoole, all Pictures artificiall,
Curious Knots, or Trailes, what fancie would devise,
 Beasts, Birds, or Flowers, even as things naturall:
Three manner Hands could she write, them faire all.
 To speake of Algorisme, or accounts, in every fashion,
 Of women, few like (I thinke) in all this Nation.

Dame Cunning her gave a gift right excellent,
 The goodly practice of her Science Musicall,
In divers Tongues to sing, and play with Instrument,
 Both Viall and Lute, and also Virginall;
Not onely upon one, but excellent in all.
 For all other vertues belonging to Nature,
 God her appointed a very perfect creature.

Latine and *Spanish*, and also *Italian*,
 She spake, writ, and read, with perfect utterance;
And for her *English*, she the Garland wan,
 In Dame *Prudence* Schoole, by Graces purveyance,
Which clothed her with Vertues, from naked Ignorance:
 Reading the Scriptures, to judge Light from Darke,
 Directing her faith to Christ, the onely Marke.

> *The said* Elizabeth deceased 29. *day of*
> *October,* Anno Domini 1537. *Of yeeres not*
> *fully 27. This Stone, and all hereon*
> *contained, made at the cost of the said*
> Emmanuel, *Marchant-Taylor.*

Curious that the name of 'Withypoll' appears in the index, whilst 'Lucar' does not.

Another epitaph is of Sir Henry Kebyll (variously spelt) who died in 1518 and which, Munday tells us, was 'On the out-side of the folding tables which hang in the upper end of the Chauncell' of Aldermarie Church, in Cordwayner Streete Ward also destroyed in the Fire of 1666.

Kebyll was a munificent benefactor to the Church, notwithstanding which, Stow tells us, his 'bones were unkindly cast out, and his Monument pulled downe', to make room for Sir William Laxton and Thomas Lodge, Mayors who died in 1556 and 1583 respectively.

Heere is fixt the Epitaph of Sir Henry Kebyll *Knight,*
Who was sometime of London *Maior, a famous worthy wight,*
Which did this Aldermarie *Church erect and set up right.*

Though death prevaile with mortal wights, and hasten every day,
Yet vertue overlives the Grave, her fame doth not decay:
As memories doe shew reviv'd, of one that was alive,
Who being dead, of vertuous fame, none should seeke to deprive,
Which so in life deserv'd renowne, for facts of his to see,
That may encourage other now, of life good minde to be.

Sir *Henry Keble*, Knight, Lord Maior of *London*, here he sate,
Of Grocers worthy Companie, the chiefest in his state,
Which in this City grew to wealth, and unto worship came,
When *Henry* raign'd, who was the seventh of that redoubted name:
But he to honor did atchive the second golden yeere
Of *Henries* raigne, so call'd the 8. and made his fact appeare.
Whê he this Aldermary Church gan build with great expence,
Twice 30. yeeres agon, no doubt, counting the time fro hence:
Which work began the yere of Christ, well known of Christenmen
One thousand and five hundred just, if ye will adde but ten.
But lo, when man purposeth most, God doth dispose the best,
And so before this work was don God cald this Knight to rest.
This Church as then not fully built, he died about the yeere, 1516
whê *Ill May day* first took his name, which is down fixed here:
Whose works became a Sepulcher, to shroud him in that case.
God took his soule, but corps of his was laid about this place.
Who when he died, of this his worke, so mindful, still he was,
That he bequeath'd 1000 pound, to have it brought to passe.
The execution of whose gift, or where the fault should be,
The worke as yet unfinished shall shew you all for me.
Which Church stands there, if any please to finish up the same,
As he hath well begun, no doubt, and to his endlesse fame,
They shall not onely well bestow their Talent in this life,
But after death, when bones be rot, their fame shall be most rife:
With thankfull praise and good report of our Parochians here,
Which have of right Sir *Henries* fame afresh renewed this yere.
God move the minds of wealthy men, their works so to bestow
As he hath done, that though they die, their vertuous fame may flow.

> *Inclita perpetuo durabit tempore Virtus,*
> *Et floret fato non violanda truci.*

This epitaph is interesting, not only for the reference to the Ill—or Evil May day of 1517, (Munday erroneously says 1516 here, but gives the right date in another reference) 'so called', Stow wrote, 'of an insurrection made by Prentises, and other young persons against Aliens', but also because of the line 'But lo, when man purposeth most, God doth dispose the best', from Thomas à Kempis' *Of the Imitation of Christ*, which had been translated into English only in 1501. The more commonly quoted version of this quotation is 'Man proposes, God disposes,' and some years ago I asked in *Notes and Queries* to be informed who first substituted 'proposes' for 'purposeth'. But answer came there none. Actually in the relevant paragraph in an

(1894) edition of the *Imitation* the word 'purpose' appears three times, 'purposeth' twice and 'purposes' once.

Then there is the epitaph written by Christopher Brooke, of whom Anthony Wood, in his *Athenae Oxonienses*, writing of Samuel Broke, or Brooke D.D. adds:

> He had an ingenious Brother named *Christop. Brooke*, a *Yorkshire* man born, who after he had left the University (whether this, or *Cambridge*, I cannot yet tell, notwithstanding several of his Sirname and time have studied in *University Coll.*) he setled in *Lincolns* Inn, purposely to advance himself in the municipal Law, where he became known to, and admired by, *Joh. Selden, Ben. Jonson. Mich. Drayton, Will Browne, George Withers* and *Joh. Davies* of *Hereford*, especially after he had published *An Elegy consecrated to the never dying memory of Henry Prince of Wales.* Lond. 1613. qu. In the yeare following, he being then a Bencher, was elected Summer Reader of his House, became a Benefactor to the Chappel there, and wrot another book ent. *Eglogues; dedicated to his much loved friend Mr Will. Browne of the Inner Temple.* Lond. 1614 oct. He hath also Verses put before the first part of *Britannia's pastorals*, pen'd by the said *Browne*, also before a poetical piece called *The legend of Great Cromwell*, written by *Mich-Drayton*, and had a considerable hand in dishing out *The Odcombian Banquet*, an. 1611.

There must have been a reason why Shakespeare was not mentioned in this company of poets and playwrights; and why he was mentioned by so few of his contemporaries. Was it because they took him so very much for granted? Had he a sense of humour which did not amuse some of his colleagues? One of his contemporaries was John Weever—who had written appreciations of Shakespeare and some of his contemporaries in his *Epigrammes* published in 1599, and it may be that Shakespeare was sufficiently ungrateful as to make a joke at the expense of Weever in his creation of Bottom the Weaver with his ass's head in *A Midsummer Night's Dream*?

But here is the epitaph:

> *In obitum Generosissimae, charissimose;* Elizabethae
> Croftes, nuper uxoris *Caroli Croftes*, Armigeri:
> Christoph. Brooke *devotissimus, hoc memoriae pignus posuit.*
> *obiit 20. Decemb. 1597.*

> Gentle beholder of these dolefull lines,
> With carefull mutes and mournfull accents sounding,
> Resolve to teares, viewing these sad designes
> Of dreiry sorrow, and hearts deepest wounding.

Consuming Time, abridging world desire,
Insulting death, fearefull, prodigious strange,
Eclipsing, waxing heate of Natures fire,
With wayning forc'd and necessary change:
Since you have done your worst to date her dayes.
Whilome the worlds, now heavens gracious ghest:
I, this sad memory of her lifes prayse
Presume to write, in skilfull Arts the least.
She was descended of right gentle blood,
Kinde, courteous, affable and mild by nature,
Modest her thoughts, her disposition good,
Her mind Exchequers store to every creature,
Her Conscience spotlesse, her Religion pure,
Her life sincere, her studie contemplation:
Her hope was heaven, with life aye to endure,
Her faith was constant in her Soules salvation.
Her vertuous care her children to direct,
Conform'd to reason in her husbands will:
Her bounty to her servants, friends respect
Desire to helpe, and with no neighbour ill.
Thrice happy then (breath-lesse) in Tombe that lyest:
Earth hath but earth, thy better part survives:
From worldly warefare, summoned to the highest,
Whose death from life, a second life derives,
Death life confirmes, Heaven earth unites in one:
Her life in death, and blisse when world is done.

There are several other significant little touches in Stow's *Survey*. For instance:

'... This parish of saint *Buttolph* is no great thing notwithstanding diverse strangers are there harboured, as may appear by a presentment, not many yeres since made of strangers, inhabitantes in the warde of Belinsgate in these wordes: "In Belinsgate warde were one and fiftie households of strangers, whereof thirtie of these householdes inhabited in the parish of saint *Buttolph*, in the chiefe and principall houses, where they give twentie pounde the yeare for a house lately letten for foure markes: the nearer they dwell to the water-side the more they give for houses, and within thirtie yeares before there was not in the whole warde above three Netherlanders; at which time there was within the said parish levied, for the helpe of the poore, seaven and twentie pound by the yeare; but since they came so plentifully thither, there cannot bee gathered above eleven pounds, for the stranger will not contribute to such charges as other Citizens doe".'

We find idiomatic expressions which one would hardly have thought went back to Shakespeare's day: there is a lengthy reference (in the 1618, Third Edition) to 'William Jones, Merchant, and free of the Worshipful Company of Haberdashers', of whom amongst a number of other good deeds, Munday relates:

'Let mee commend that truely religious man, who perceiving the heavy want of divers honest householders, laboriously endeavouring (night and day) to maintaine their charge; but that the worlds extremity frowned too fiercely on them. I know the man, and oftentimes (in teares) hath he sayd to me: Here is true poverty indeed, too modestly silent in speaking their mighty neede and miserie, and therefore justly deserving pitie. To two, three, foure, and many times more of these, hath hee bin, and is a liberall Benefactor (weekly) with his owne hands: yet not in his owne name, or as comming from himselfe (hee being so meanly disguised at such times of his comming to them, and so sudden also in departing from them, that they were not able to distinguish him) but alledging, that the reliefe was sent them from some, who understood their need (almost) as well as themselves, and willed them to bee thankfull only to God for it.'

A marginal note informs us, in language which might almost be used today, 'This man blew no Trumpet of his charitable actions.' This marginal note was omitted in the enlarged Fourth Edition. Why?

2

John Strype

Interest in Stow's *Survey of London* will extend to the *Survey of the Cities of London and Westminster* ... 'brought down from the Year 1633 ... by JOHN STRYPE, M.A. a Native also of the said CITY', and 'Printed for A. Churchill, J. Knapton, R. Knaplock, J. Walthee, E. Horne, B. Tooke, D. Midwinter, B. Cowse, R. Robinson and T. Ward, MDCCXX', in two folio volumes. In the preface to his edition of Stow, Henry Morley records that Strype's edition included a two-sheet plan of the City of London, Westminster and Southwark, a map of London in Elizabeth's time and forty-one plates. My copy contains sixty-seven plates.

Kingsford mentions a design to reprint Stow's *Survey* in 1694, with large additions and improvements, and, referring to a broadsheet in the Bodleian Library, conjectures that it was apparently projected by Awnsham Churchill and other London publishers, but does not refer to an advertisement, printed at the back of the title page of Edward Hatton's *New View of London* (published in 1708) which reads as follows:

'In a short time *Proposals* will be published for Reprinting Mr Stow's large Survey of *London*, improv'd; with very great Additions throughout, and illustrated with about 100 large Copper Cutts, viz. of the City in general, and of several of the Wards thereof: Of *Westminster, Southwark*, and all the Out-Parts of the City as they now are: and also several Ornamental Plates of Churches, and other Publick Buildings, in *Folio*.

'*Note*, this Work has been long preparing, the Cutts requiring much Time and Great Expences, but they are now all finished, and may be seen at the Undertakers,

R. *Chiswell*, at the *Rose* and *Crown* in St *Paul's* Church-Yard. *A* and *J. Churchill*, at the *Black Swan* in *Pater-Noster-Row. Tho. Horne*, under the *Royal Exchange* in *Cornhill. John Nicholson*, at the *King's Arms* in *Little Britain;* and *R. Knaplock*, at the *Bishop's Head* in St *Paul's* Church-Yard.' These same 'undertakers' had published the *New View of London*, and when we compare their names with the publishers of the 1720 edition it is reasonable to suppose that the latter succeeded to the enterprise as and when the 'undertakers', one by one, dropped out, and that it was the Fifth Edition published in 1720 which was being advertised in 1708. This would appear to be borne out by Strype who writes, in his preface ('Dated from LOW LEYTON in the County of ESSEX this 16th Day of April, 1720') that a new edition of the *Survey* having been determined upon, the preparation of it had 'by the desire of those concerned' fallen to him. He also mentions that he was working on the new edition before 1703; he details the steps taken to collect up-to-date information, and refers to an order of the Court of Aldermen, dated the 19th May 1702, which directed 'Mr. Town Clerk' to peruse certain notes which he had compiled so that nothing detrimental to the City might be published.

In search of facts he had 'recourse unto a Parochial Visitation Book Anno 1693, in the Bishop of London's Registry'. He prints a letter which, at his request, the Bishop wrote 'To the Reverend the CLERGY of the City of *London*, and the Suburbs'—'Gentlemen, A new Edition of Stow's SURVEY OF LONDON being now preparing, and in a good forwardness for the Press...' and he requests them to assist by sending Strype particulars respecting bene-factions, monumental inscriptions and so forth, and concludes 'Brethren, I do approve of Mr. *Strype's* undertaking in setting forth a new Edition of STOW's *Survey*. And the Matters propounded to you in this Paper, being so conducive to the Improvement of it, I cannot but recommend it unto you, the Clergy of *London*, and of the Suburbs. H. LONDON.'

There is evidence, in the work itself, that it was prepared years before it was published: Strype includes 'An Account of the Aldermen and their Deputies in the year 1706, when this Book was first prepared for the Press', adding, at the end of the list, 'The Alterations of the Aldermen since (divers of them being since dead) will be seen under each Ward.'

Then he prints 'An exact List of all the Stage Coaches and Carriers, with the Names of the Towns they come from, and their respective Inns in London, and the Days they go out; Very useful for Shopkeepers and Tradesmen'—the list itself being followed by the following notification: 'This is transcribed from a List printed An. 1707: Since which Time there may be some Altera-tion in Days and Inns. And therefore, if any such be met with, it will be excusable.'

Kingsford records that Thomas Hearne, the antiquarian, on hearing of the project in 1707 wrote: 'Stow should have been simply reprinted as a venerable original, and the additions given in a different character', which is what W. H. Thoms did 135 years later.

But if the Fifth Edition was in the process of being completed in 1708 why was it not published until 1720? What happened to the rest of the 100 'Copper Cutts'? and why was there no mention of Strype in the 1708 ad-vertisement? He certainly was not altogether unknown because he had al-ready published his lives of Cranmer (1694) and Sir John Cheke (1705).

G. Vertue Sculp.

JOHANNES STRYPE *M.A.*

LONDINENSIS; Natus Anno Christi MDCXLIII. *Ad huc in vivis.*

Philalethes, & Philarchæus.

Hatton has quite a lot to say about Stow in his preface, but ignores Strype, who (turning the other cheek—as befits a clerical author) refers those of his readers 'minded to know the architecture . . . of the new built churches' to the *New View of London*.

In the preface Strype acknowledged his indebtedness for information received from a long list of persons, 'Beseeching their Excuse, if in haste I have not set them down in that Order and Precendency that their respective Qualities require'. Twelve years should have been long enough to settle the order of that 'Precendency'! George Vertue's engraving of John Strype would seem to suggest that he cannot have had much sense of humour; which may perhaps in part account for his amazing industry in compiling those two stupendous volumes.

In the 'CHAPTERS and CONTENTS of the Six Books of the SURVEY of the Cities of LONDON and WESTMINSTER' Strype, in general, follows Stow, but there are considerable additions in every chapter, and a number of new chapters on a variety of subjects are added.

One notes a curious error in sub-editing: There is no Chapter XX in the Fifth Book: in the 'Chapters and Contents' it is followed by the word 'Blank', but in the book itself the end of Chapter XIX is followed by Chapter XXI. There is not a missing Chapter, because Chapter XXI, dealing with foreigners, continues where Chapter XIX left off.

The index refers to several things, both interesting and amusing: for instance, an Act of Common Council was passed in 1671 dealing with the streets, lanes and common passages, and which was prefaced as follows:

'Veneris *primo die* Martii, $167\frac{1}{2}$ By the Commissioners for Sewers, Pavements, etc. *in* LONDON.

'The Commissioners willing that all Persons concerned may take Notice of a late Act of Common Council, and of several ancient Customs, and other Statutes, Rules, and Orders relating to the paving and cleansing of the Streets and Sewers, and preventing other Inconveniences to the common Passages in and about the City of LONDON, and Liberties thereof; and that due Conformity may be yielded thereunto, and the Penalties for Breach thereof may be avoided: Have *agreed* and *ordered*, That the same can be forthwith printed in a small Book, and delivered to, or left for, every Householder within this City and Liberties; and which are as follows, That is to say:'

Then follow the Act, and 'Rules, Orders, and Directions'—thirty-nine of them—and whilst some of them are, thanks to improved sanitation, out-of-date, others might be enforced, even today, with advantage to the community.

This house to house distribution has a modern ring about it, and the last rule proves that the delivery of a parcel by C.O.D. is no new thing. It reads as follows:

'*Lastly*, That every Householder do pay to the Person delivering this Book, *three Pence* at least, for and towards the Charge of Printing and Delivery of the same.'

One wonders why the 'at least', and whether anybody ever paid more!

Amongst a host of other facts Strype records 'the Gifts and Benefactions of well disposed Persons, for the Relief of the Poor, in Money, Bread, Fewel, Harbour, Education of Youth', etc. that they might, thus recorded, 'remain to Posterity, and not be lost in Oblivion; and also, that such Lands, Houses, Rents, or Money given and bequeathed for such and such good Uses, might not be embezzelled or misapplied, or swallowed up by any unjust Means, and the Poor defrauded for ever'.

There was nothing new in such an allegation: Stow had expressed the wish that generous citizens might do their good deeds in their lifetime, 'not forgetting the olde Proverbe:

> *Women be forgetful, children be unkind,*
> *Executors be covetous, and take what they find.*
> *If any body aske where the deads goods became,*
> *They answere, So God me help & holydome, he died a poore man.*

And Stow refers to some specific instances of broken trusts 'for Executors of our time having no conscience, (I speake of my own knowledge) prove more testaments then they performe'.

Strype is prosy and, topographically, very factual, and he is not so easy to read as Stow. But he cannot be ignored: he is as necessary to one's knowledge of the eighteenth, as Stow is of the earlier centuries.

He had an irritating habit of clipping an epitaph short—thus, he records the following epitaph in St Anne's Church, Soho, on 'Gresham Hakewel, Son of Gresham Hakewel of Weston Turvile in the County of Bucks, Gent. 1692. Aged 16. Also Katherine Hakewel, his Daughter, 1692 aged 18.

> Farewel my only Comfort, Prop and Stay
> Of my Family, wrapt and wound in Clay;
> Would I had not liv'd to have known this Day, etc.
> Written by their Father.'

Although Stow does not mention Shakespeare his *Survey* did contain a chapter entitled 'Sports and pastimes of old time used in this Citie' in which, after quoting Fitzstephen (who wrote in the twelfth century) at some length, and writing a few words about stage plays in 1391 and 1409, Stow brings Fitzstephen's recital more up-to-date, writing 'Of late time in place of those Stage plays, hath been Comedies, Tragedies, Enterludes, and Histories, both true and fayned: For the acting whereof certaine publike places as the

Theater, the Curtine, etc. have been erected.'—the marginal note being 'Theater and Curten for Comedies and other shewes.'

Again, in a later chapter entitled 'The Suburbes without the Walles' Stow writes of the pulling down of the Priory of St John Baptist at Holywell and the erection of many houses 'for the lodgings of noble men, of strangers borne and other', and finishes off 'And neare thereunto are builded two publike houses for the acting and shewe of Comedies, Tragedies, and Histories, for recreation. Whereof the one is called the Courtein, and the other the Theatre: both stand on the southwest side towards the field.'

The Theatre was pulled down voluntarily in December 1598 and January 1599, and the Curtain should have been demolished in 1600, by Order of the Lords of the Council. In fact it was not, but the Order must have been known to Stow, and the carrying out of it assumed by him, because in the Second Edition (1603) of his *Survey* he omitted the sentence in the chapter dealing with the Suburbs (which I have quoted) containing the reference, by name—and using different spellings—to 'the Courtein' and 'the Theatre', and in the chapter dealing with 'Sports and Pastimes' he omitted 'as the Theater, the Curtine etc. . . .', he changed '&' into 'and', and retained the marginal note, as did Munday in the 1618 and 1633 editions, printing '*Theater & Curten*' in italics, in the latter.

These little differences invite speculation as to why they were made, particularly when one considers that the Curtain was still standing in 1633, and that when the references to the Curtain and the Theater were deleted from the text it would have been more logical to revise the marginal note. And as the materials from the Theater were used to build the Globe Theatre, across the water, in 1599, Stow might, in his Second Edition, and Munday should in the Third and Fourth, have mentioned the Globe; perhaps the more particularly as he referred—briefly—to the two Beare Gardens, and—at some length—to the Bordello or Stewes on Bankside.

John Strype reinserted both *The Theatre* (spelt thus) and the Curtain (ditto) into his text, and he refers, inter alia, to The Globe on the Bankside, as well as to the two Beare Gardens. Then he proceeds:

'For the foulness of these rude Sights, and for that these beastly Combats were usually performed on *Sundays*, and that so much Money was idly thrown away, that might have been better given to the Poor, a Poet in the latter time of *Hen* VIII. made and printed these homely Verses, more commendable for his Zeal than his Poetry:

> *What Folly is this to keep with danger*
> *A great Mastive Dog, and a fowle ougly Bear?*
> *And to this one Ende, to see them two fight*
> *With terrible tearings; a ful ougly sight.*

And yet methinks those Men be most Fools of al,
Whose store of Money is but very smal:
And yet every Sunday they wil surely spend
One Peny or two, the Bearward's Living to mend.
At Paris Garden each Sunday a Man shall not fail
To find two or three hundred for the Bearward's Vale.
One halfpeny a piece they use for to give,
When some have not more in their Purses, I believe.
Wel, at the last Day their Conscience will declare,
That the Poor ought to have all that they may spare.
If you therefore it give, to see a Bear fight,
Be sure God his Curse upon you will light.'

His marginal note to this is 'Certain Rhimes against Sports. *Crowly* the Printer his Epigram.'

Robert Crowley (Croleus or Crule), who was born in 1534, was a preacher as well as a bookseller and a writer. Amongst other things, mostly religious, he wrote *One and Thirty Epigrams,* 'wherein are briefly touched so many abuses, that may, and ought to, be put away.' This book he printed in his house in '*Ely rents* in *Holbourn* near to *London*' in 1550.

In his chapter dealing with the River Thames, Strype records a dispute between the City and King Charles I about certain privileges concerning the river, which lead to an 'incident' on the publication of the 1633 edition, (curiously referred to as the Second Edition) and which can only be explained by quoting in full:

'But it seems, these Privileges and Jurisdictions in the *Thames,* thus claimed by the City, were not allowed by the Court in K. *Charles* I. his Time, but thought to encroach upon the Prerogative of the King's High Court of Admiralty: Some Passages in the foregoing Discourse giving such Offence, that it had like to have hindred the Sale of the Second Edition of this Book, *An.* 1633. being then newly Printed. For K. *Charles* I. as soon as he heard of it, commanded Sir *Henry Marten,* the Judge of the Court of Admiralty, either to obliterate certain Passages out of the said Book, before it came forth, or else to stop the Publishing of it. For which Purpose, Secretary *Coke,* by that King's Command, wrote a special Letter to the said Judge. But it being somewhat too late to make these Corrections, (the Book being now compleately Printed off) the said Sir *Henry Marten* ordered the Company of *Stationers* to Print the Secretaries Letter to him at the End of the Book, and his own Letter and Order to them thereupon. Which was accordingly done: And they were as follows:

To my Honorable Friend Sir HENRY MARTEN, *Knight, Judge of the High Court of the Admiralty.*

Sir, His Majesty understanding that there is a second Edition of *Stowes Survey* of the City of *London*, new put to Sale, wherein there are some Passages prejudicial to his Majesties Right in his Admiralty, and Derogatory to the just Power belonging thereunto; He doth therefore require you his Judge in that High Court to examine the said Book, and to cause the said Passages inserted in prejudice of the Admiral Jurisdiction, and in support of any other Pretence against the same, to be left out; or else to prohibit the Publishing and Sale of the said Book. And for so doing, this Signification of his Majesty's Pleasure may be your sufficient Warrant. So I rest

Your assured Friend to serve you,

Garlicke Hith. 21.
Dec. 1633.   JOHN COKE.

Further Execution of the Letter above mentioned could not be made, for that it came after the Impression was finished and published.

HENRY MARTEN

To the Master and Wardens of the Company of STATIONERS.

You may understand by the Contents of the Letter above mentioned, directed unto me, what is required at my Hands to perform. I am therefore to require you upon your Receipt hereof, forthwith to cause the Book to be brought unto you, and to take Order that all the Words, together with the Copy of the Letter, and for my Answer thereunto, as above made for this Impression, to be imprinted *Page 939.* Col. *prima, verbatim* in all the said Books, as well sold, as hereafter to be sold, before any further Sale of the said Books be made; and this shall be your Warrant in this behalf.

Doctors Commons,   HENRY MARTEN'
24 Dec. 1633.

There is no page 939 in the book, and the letter is printed on page 39. Strype prefixes a second appendix to his 1720 Edition with the following paragraph:

'Sundry matters of Note coming to Hand, since the finishing of this work, being of Use, and tending to the farther Improvement of it; it was necessary to add an *Appendix*, for the repositing and preserving of them; and likewise for the supplying any Omissions or rectifying any Errors. Which is done with References to the proper Places, whereunto they do belong.'

Strype lists 273 pre-publication subscribers, of whom 37 were described as Booksellers, and the work was sold at six guineas.

Kingsford lists a *Survey* by Robert Seymour (of which I have a copy); 'The whole being an Improvement of Mr Stow's and other *Surveys*', 'Printed for J. READ in White-Fryars, Fleet Street' in two folio volumes in 1734–5, and another two-folio volume edition, with Sir William Dugdale's *History of St Paul's* added, 'By a Gentleman of the Inner Temple', in 1753.

I have also a poor and truncated copy of Seymour's *Survey* in large octavo, 'Printed and Sold by the Booksellers in City, Town and Country. MDCCXXXVI'.

The *Survey* has been attributed to John Mottley (writing in the name of Elijah Jenkins, of *Joe Miller's Jests*, or *The Wit's Vade Mecum* published in 1739, the year after Miller's death), on the authority of William Upcott, a literary antiquarian, though William Oldys, another well-known antiquary, wrote in his diary on 29th June 1737: '. . . Mr Ames told me that Mr Cook is the author of Seymour's *Survey of London*, in two vols. fol.'.

Thomas Cooke (not Cook), commonly called Hesiod Cooke, after one of his plays, was a dramatic poet and miscellaneous author, who died in great poverty on 29th December 1756. Mottley and Cooke had collaborated in writing a dramatic opera, entitled *Penelope*, so the *Survey* may have been a joint effort.

There is no clue as to whose 'other *Surveys*' Mottley (or Cooke) was referring, but presumably Strype's was one of them. Strype died in 1737, but a Second Edition of his *Survey* was published in 1754–5, containing 132 plates.

Nearly a hundred years later, there is a reference to a projected edition of Stow in the preface to the Second, corrected and enlarged, Edition of Peter Cunningham's *Hand-Book of London Past and Present* published in 1850. Amongst the numerous correspondents to whom that author gave thanks is 'T. Edlyne Tomlins', and Cunningham adds: '(who is engaged, I am glad to find, on a new edition of Stow)'. I do not know what happened to that projected edition, but T. Edlyne Tomlins did write a book about Islington, to which I refer in Chapter Four.

Towards the end of the last century Henry A. Harben projected an edition of Stow's *Survey*, and spent many years in research and accumulation of material. His feelings when Kingsford's Edition appeared in 1908 can be better imagined than described. Fortunately he decided that his labours should not be wasted and, although he did not live to see the work completed, *A Dictionary of London* arose out of the ashes—metaphorically speaking—of his proposed Stow, and was published in 1918.

It is a topographical work; and maybe it owes something to Hatton, whose *New View* contained a very full alphabetical list of 'the Streets, Squares, Lanes, Markets, Courts, Alleys, Rows, Rents, Yards, and Inns in London, Westminster and Southwark,' and who, in his preface, had referred to 'a small Treatise called A GUIDE THROUGH PARIS; an Inspection of which gave somewhat of Birth to the General Heads in the following Book . . .'

Harben dealt systematically with the streets and buildings of the City, where they are (or were), the origin and derivation of their names and how they developed—by reference to a formidable list of records, books, and maps.

There is another mystery which may not be apparent on a first perusal of these books. In Stow's *Survey* there is a chapter entitled 'Honour of Citizens and Worthiness of Men in the same'. In the First Edition the benefactions of some twenty-seven worthy citizens are very shortly detailed in some semblance of chronological order; they are followed by a mention of the charitable gifts of two ladies, and the name of each benefactor is set out in the margin opposite the paragraph referring to him (or her).

In the Second Edition (1603) Stow added forty-two men and three ladies. The eighteenth of the men added, and the twenty-eighth of the citizens mentioned, is Sir John Percivall, and the following paragraph refers to the good deeds of Lady Thomasine, his wife—but in the margin opposite that paragraph is the name 'Rich. Carew'.

There was a Richard Carew, an antiquary who was still alive in 1603; in the previous year he had published his *Survey of Cornwall*, the county with which he was associated as Justice of the Peace in 1581, Member of Parliament for Saltash, 1584, High Sheriff in 1586 and Member of Parliament for Michell, in 1597. Why did Stow intend to publicize him? And why were the good deeds of Lady Thomasine substituted for his? The *Survey* tells us that she was born in Cornwall; she may have been an ancestress of Richard Carew. 'Rich.' might have been a misprint for 'Nich'. which suggests that Stow might have intended to glorify Sir Nicholas Carew of Beddington in Surrey, Knight of the Garter, a zealous papist who was beheaded in 1538 for plotting with the Marquis of Exeter, Lord Montacute and Sir Edward Neville to set Cardinal Pole on the throne in the place of Henry VIII. Stow himself had been reported to the Queen's Council as a suspicious person in 1558, and accused before the Ecclesiastical Commission in 1570, and a friend may have hinted to him that it would be a trifle dangerous to glorify a noted papist!

I continue to speculate: amongst Sir Nicholas Carew's seven great grandchildren were a Nicholas and an Elizabeth and in 1592—six years before the publication by Stow of his *Survey*—Queen Elizabeth had discovered that Elizabeth Carew, one of her maids of honour, was carrying on an intrigue with Sir Walter Raleigh (whom she regarded as her property) and had committed him to the Tower of London—so Stow's reluctance to glorify a *Carew* is very understandable.

Another possible—and perhaps simpler—explanation is that the Star Chamber, which exercised a strict authority over the Press, censored the paragraph.

The error was repeated in the 1618 and 1633 editions, whilst Strype, in 1720, expanded the marginal reference into 'Richard Carew'. Kingsford included 'Richard Carew' in his index of names, but did not query this curious instance of perpetuated error.

Remarks on London: 'being an Exact Survey of the Cities of London and Westminster, Borough of Southwark, and the Suburbs and liberties contiguous to them, by shewing where every street, Lane, Court, Alley, Green, Yard, Close, Square, or any other Place, by what Name soever called, is situated . . .' by W. Stow was 'Printed for T. Norris at the Looking-glass, and H. Tracy at the Three Bibles, on London Bridge. 1722'. It was dedicated 'To His Royal Highness, GEORGE, Prince of Wales', and in 'The Epistle Dedicatorie' the author modestly confesses that his survey 'is too mean a Trifle to make a Present of to your most Illustrious Person; but as an indubitable Right of Succession (except an Act of Contingency, which God forbid, should deprive these three Kingdoms of so great a blessing) will bring these most Populous Places under your Dominion, the humble Offering claims your Royal Patronage'. There is no evidence that W. Stow was related to John Stow; indeed the book appears to be the only evidence that he ever existed!

The author recalls 'the dreadful Conflagration, which in 1666, laid the most famous Metropolis of *Great Britain* in Ashes', and explains that 'the ever-wakeful Eye of Providence, having always a tender regard of preserving this Nation from the Fury of Papery, Slavery, and arbitrary power, in setting your sacred Father on the *British* Throne, it is my Presumption to think, that Fate contriv'd the Magnificence of this great City by Fire, for the better Reception of a King, who may justly claim the Title of *Defender of the Faith*.'

There is a reference 'to all who esteem you the Darling of Mankind, when your Royal Highness was left sole Regent of the Land; and at a Time too, when a vile Rabble attempted (but in vain) to eclipse the Glory of glorious *Augusta* with Anarchy and Confusion'.

And the author ends his dedication wishing 'You, your Royal Consort and Illustrious Issue, long life, Health and Prosperity, mounted by Guardian-Angels above the Reach of Inconstancy and Envy'. The author describes his pocket book (which contains 180 pages) as 'Multum in parvo', and in the preface writes: 'to take the Description of every Place in it, and Places contiguous or adjacent thereto, required some weeks . . .', explaining that the places 'cannot be less than 25 miles in Circumference; which Spot contains about 70,000 Dwelling Houses . . . so that there is no Occasion to fortify it with Stone-Walls, Bulwarks, and Towers; for as its Inhabitants are computed to be about 1,500,000 Souls, among which are about 100,000 Men fit to bear Arms, they are able to give a Field Battle to the greatest Monarch or Potentate on Earth'. And he ends his seven-page preface: 'So if this Piece finds a favourable Acceptance among my Countrymen, it is all the Favour the

Author expects for his extream labour, of traversing 2,175 Streets, Lanes. Courts, and other Places; which tracing backwards and forwards, comprehended near 250 miles; a Perambulation never yet performed by any other Man besides myself, in any Age past, nor this wherein we live'.

It is charitable to suppose that W. Stow had not come across Hatton's *New View of London.*

Included in the many interesting facts in the book are the addresses of post offices, Inns and 'Cathedrals, Collegiate and Parochial Churches, Chapels and Tabernacles', 'A Table of Rates for Hackney Coaches in London, settled by Parliament, by Stat. 5 and 6. Will and Mary,' wherein, after the rates, the reader is advised:

'And if any Coachman shall refuse to go at, or exact more Hire than the Rates hereby limited he shall for every such Offence forfeit 40 shillings; if you give Information against him at the Office for Licensing Hackney Coaches in *Surrey Street* in the *Strand.*

'What is related about Coachmen, will serve for Directions in the Affairs of Chairmen: Let the Weather be Wet or dry, or the Time be Day or Night, it's the same; get into the Chair, and order the Chairmen to carry you as you design; and if they behave themselves unmannerly, take the Number of the Chair, as you do of a Hackney Coach, and complaining at the Office abovementioned, the Commissioners will correct their Insolence.'

Plus ça change, plus c'est la même chose!

The book is recorded, without comment, in Lowndes's *Bibliography*, but it had been advertised on a fly-leaf at the end of another pocket-sized book published that same year (1722), entitled *The Antiquities of London and Westminster*, written 'By N.B.' and 'Printed for *H. Tracy*, at the *Three Bibles* on *London Bridge*'.

In 1730 a book was published and 'Printed for *A. Bettesworth* and *Charles Hitch*, at the *Red Lion*; and *J. Batley*, at the *Dove*; in *Pater-noster-Row*' under the title of *A New View, and Observations on the Ancient and Present State of London and Westminster*, under the authorship of Nathaniel Crouch in the name of Robert Burton, and, although he did not die until 1736, 'Continued by an Able Hand'. This was the Fourth Edition (with some modifications) of *Historical Remarques on London and Westminster*, which had been published in 1681, the other editions appearing in 1703 and 1722.

In the previous century a poet by the name of Nicholas Breton had signed some of his work 'N.B.' but it is very arguable that 'N.B.' of *The Antiquities* was Nathaniel (Crouch Robert) Burton, for *The Antiquities*, published in 1722, was reproduced almost word for word in Burton's Fourth Edition of *Historical Remarques*. The first paragraph of N.B.'s *Antiquities* reads: 'LONDON, the Metropolis and Glory of the Kingdom of *England*, the Seat of the *British* Empire, may boast itself to be the largest in Extent, the fairest built, the most populous, the best inhabited of any in the whole World, and for a general Trade throughout the Universe all others must give her Precedence.' Whilst the Fourth Edition of Burton's *Historical Remarques* (sub. nom. *A New View* . . .) began: 'LONDON, the Metropolis of *England*, and Seat of the *British* Empire, may boast itself of being the largest in Extent, the fairest built, the most populous and best inhabited of any in the European World; nay probably, in the Universe; and for a general Trade throughout the known World, all others must give her the Precedence'.

The same fly-leaf which advertised W. Stow's book also advertised N.B's *Antiquities*, but as 'Printed for John Tracy' instead of H. Tracy, at the same address.

While there were 244 pages in *The Antiquities* which did not contain any *Historical Remarks*, the Fourth Edition of the *Historical Remarques* contained 312 pages, and then brought the first edition's Historical Remarks from 1681 to the year 1730 (so numbered).

There is plenty of quotable material, but two extracts must suffice: 'The magnificent and abundant Plenty of the King's Tables, hath caused Amazement in Foreigners. In the Reign of King *Charles* I. there were daily in his Court 86 Tables well furnished each Meal, whereof the King's Tables had 28 Dishes, the Queen's 24, 4 other Tables 16 Dishes each, 3 other 10 Dishes, 12 other 7 Dishes, 17 other 5 Dishes, 3 other 4, 32 had 3, and 13 had each 2, in all about 500 Dishes each Meal, with Bread, Beer, Wine, and all other things necessary. There was spent Yearly in the King's House of *Gross Meat*, 1500 *Oxen*, 7000 *sheep*, 1200 *Veals*, 300 *Porkers*, 400 *Sturks*, or young Beefs, 6800 *Lambs*, 300 Flitches of *Bacon*, and 26 *Boars*. Also 140 dozen of *Geese*, 250 dozen of *Capons*, 470 dozen of *Hens*, 750 dozen of *Pullets*, 1470 dozen of *Chickens;* for Bread 36400 Bushels of *Wheat*, and for Drink 600 Tun of *Wine*, and 1700 Tun of *Beer*. Moreover of *Butter* 46640 l. together with the *Fish*, and *Fowl, Venison, Fruit, Spice* proportionably. This prodigious Plenty in the King's Court, caused Foreigners to put a higher Value upon the King, and was much for the Honour of the Kingdom. The King's Servants being Men of Quality, by his Majesty's special Order went to *Westminster-hall* in Term time, to invite Gentlemen, to eat of the King's *Acates* or *Viands*, and in Parliament-time, to invite the Parliament-men thereto'.

And at the other end of the social stratum: 'On the *Thursday* before *Easter*, called *Maunday Thursday*, the King, or his Lord *Almoner*, was wont to wash the Feet of as many poor Men, as his Majesty had Reigned Years; and then to wipe them with a Towel, (according to the Pattern of our *Saviour*) and then to give every one of them two Yards and a Half of *Woollen Cloth*, to make a Suit of Cloaths; also *Linnen Cloth* for two Shirts, and a pair of *Stockings*, and a pair of *Shoes*, three Dishes of *Fish* in Wooden platters, one of *Salt Salmon*, a second of Green *Fish* or *Cod*, a third of *Pickle*

Herrings, *Red-Herrings*, and *Red Sprats*, a Gallon of *Beer*, a Quart Bottle of *Wine*, and four six-penny Loaves of *Bread*, also a Red Leatherpurse with as many single Pence as the King is Years old, and in such another Purse, as many Shillings as the King had Reigned Years. The Queen doth the like to divers poor Women'.

Plus c'est la même chose, plus ça change!

3

Hatton, Maitland, Ilive, Chamberlain and Others

Robert Burton's *New View and Observations* is not to be confused with Edward Hatton's *New View of London*, to which I have referred in passing. In his introduction Hatton notes 'As to the Figure or Shape of *London*, some authors have compared it to that of a Laurel Leaf, in these words:

> LONDON *is like a Laurel Leaf, may She*
> *Be verdant still, and flourish like the Tree.*

And then, after recording that '*London*, with *Westminster*, by reason of the turning of the River. . . . Some have compared it to a Carpenter's Rule,' he pointed out that 'it much resembles the Shape (including *Southwark*) of a great *Whale*, *Westminster* being the under jaw, *St James's Park* the Mouth; the *Pall Mall* etc. Nd. the upper jaw; *Cock and Pye Fields*, or the meeting of the 7 *streets*, the Eye; and the rest of the City and *Southwark* to *East Smithfield*, the Body; and thence Ed. to *Limehouse* the Tail; and 'tis probably in as great a proportion, the largest of Towns, as that is of Fishes.'

The 'meeting of the 7 *streets*' is thus explained by Hatton in the first section of his book: '*Seven streets*, so called, tho there be but 4, viz. *white lyon str.* from the Dyals N.W. and S.E. *St. Andrews str.* N. and S. *Queen str.* N.E. *Earl str.* near E. and W. for all except Queen str. do cross that space in Center, whereof is placed a Pillar with 7 Dyals, and from thence appear 7 streets. These are built in *Cock* and *Pye Fields*, near *St Giles str.* and from *Cha* X N. 780 yds to the said Pillar'.

The Oxford Dictionary of Quotations, on Matthew Henry's authority, credits Philip Henry, the nonconformist minister (1631–1696) with 'They are not *amissi sed praemissi* (Not lost but gone before)', but Hatton records the following inscription on 'a gray Marble plated Grave-Stone', in Alhallows Barking Church:

> *Here lyeth the Body of* Margaret, *the Wife* of Abraham Ash, Russia
> *Merchant, who was the daughter* of Arthur Dee, *Dr in Physick; 14 years*

Physician to the Emperor of all Russia. *She had issue by her said Husband* 10 *children, and dyed in Childbed at the Age of 33 Years,* 21 January Anno 1638.

> Thou Bed of rest preserve for him a Room,
>> Who lives a Man divorc'd from his dear Wife;
> That as they were one Heart so this one Tomb,
>> May hold them near in Death as link'd in Life.
> She's gone before, and after comes her Head,
> To sleep with her among the blessed dead.

And still on the same subject: Hatton records a grave-stone in St Dunstan Stepney Church bearing this inscription:

Here lyeth the Body of MARY ANGEL, *Widow, who departed this life the 29th of* November *1693. Aged 72 years.*

> To say, an Angel here interr'd doth lye,
> May be thought strange, for Angels never dye.
> Indeed some fell from Heav'n to Hell,
>> Are lost, and rise no more:
> This only fell by Death to Earth,
>> Not lost, but gone before,
> Her Dust lodg'd here, her Soul perfect in Grace
> 'Mongst Saints and Angels now hath took its place.

And finally, if only as a pathetic reminder of infant mortality in those days—'In the Sly Ile', (of Allhallows Barking Church) 'a gray Marble Grave Stone', with this Inscription.

Here lye 5 *Sons* and 3 *Daughters of* John Pym and Elizabeth *his Wife,* viz

	Born	Dyed
Ann	5 Aug. 81	21 Feb. 82
Anne	2 Ap. 82	1 June 84
William	11 Dec.	27 86
Humphry	6 Mar.	16 89
William	11 July 91	7 96
Robert	4 Mar. 92	6 Dec. 94
Francis	18 Aug. 94	27 Nov. 99
Mary	5 Nov. 96	3 Dec. 96

Elizabeth their Mother dyed 20 *May* 1700.

Not lost but gone before

I am fond of my two octavo volumes of *New View*; (Vol. I, pp. 1–352; Vol. II, pp. 353–824); they are remarkably light to handle and, read in bed, soothingly soporific.

The publication of Strype's *Survey* in 1720 inspired a number of writers to try their hand at writing a History of London.

In 1739 the Scotch antiquary William Maitland wrote *The History of London from its Foundation to the Present Time*, which was published serially in shilling numbers by 'T. Osborne and J. Shipton in Grays-Inn; And J. Hodges, near London Bridge'. An enlarged Second Edition of the *History* was published in 1756—a year before the author's death; the title page gives the credit for this edition to 'William Maitland, F.R.S. and Others'. It contains a mass of curious facts and figures and a number of maps, including one of the villages and the country within a circumference of ten miles of London. The title page proudly boasts 120 copper plates, 'by the best hands, and on so large a scale, that each Plate could not be sold separately for less than one shilling', but at the end of Volume Two there is a list of 147 plates and, in his dedication (of the Second Edition), to the Lord Mayor, Aldermen, Sheriffs and Common Councillors, Maitland claimed 'that there is no Act of Parliament, no Charter, nor Municipal Claim granted and enjoyed by the Citizens, but may be found in this History; nor any Monument of public Utility, that is not described in this Survey.'

The antiquary Richard Gough (1735–1809) recorded that Maitland 'was self-conceited and credulous, knew little and wrote worse'. But in considering this harsh criticism it is well to bear in mind that Gough was also a topographer; I am not, so I don't have to agree with him.

There is also a good index and a list of subscribers to the work, numbering some 1,100, but without their addresses, and without (the significance of this appears later) any excuse for the list of subscribers not being a larger one.

John Noorthouck, whose *History of London* is referred to in this chapter, wrote (in 1773) in his preface that Maitland was the last 'considerable improver' of Stow since Strype, but he complained that he and 'his continuator' (was he referring to the 'and Others' of the Second Edition, or the Rev. John Entick, the schoolmaster who, in 1775, brought Maitland's *History* up to 1772?) 'extended their details with abundance of frivolous particulars; and have destroyed the connexion and unity of the whole, by labouring at what proves at last to be a perplexed arrangement.' Whilst this may have been valid criticism in 1773 by an author justifiably anxious to publicize his own work it will not deter readers desirous of escaping from the present into the past.

If Maitland's First Edition of 1739 is to be considered as another edition of Stow it would, ranking after the Fifth Edition (by Strype in 1720), count as the Sixth. The 1754–5 Strype would be the Seventh, the 1756 Maitland the Eighth, and, presumably, the 1775 Maitland (edited by the Rev. John Entick) the Ninth.

Whether or not Maitland did or did not continue the series of Stow's editions, and I have not heard anyone else suggest it—it is not too much to say that had there been no book by Stow and, consequently, none by Strype there would have been none by Maitland! At least, not in its present form, for, in addition to using much of Stow's original text without any acknowledgement, he cites Stow, Strype, Hatton and others as his authority for various statements in other parts of his work.

Several of Maitland's plates had already appeared in Strype's work. The print of Bow Church, for instance, here reproduced from Strype, appears again 'W. H. Toms sculp'—but Kip had something which Toms seemed to lack.

Although the *Dictionary of National Biography* dismisses Maitland as 'of ephemeral reputation', his *History* is worth acquiring—at a reasonably low price. My copy (of the 1756 edition) has three separate prices marked in it; '21/-d', '£3. 15. 0. 1926' and '£4. 4. 0', and I bought it, with some thirty other London books, early in 1940, for three guineas—which was a guinea more than a dealer had offered the owner!

I recently came across a delapidated copy of the First Edition in Brighton marked three pounds ten shillings and rejected it; the bookseller offered to rebind it for thirty shillings—but I decided I could make better use of my five pounds.

The Rev. John Entick's own *A New and Accurate History and Survey of London, Westminster, Southwark, and Places Adjacent* in four octavo volumes appeared in 1766. I recently came across the books priced at half a sovereign, but as all the plates had been taken out I resisted, without difficulty, the temptation to buy. A former owner of the Greater London Council's copy of this work was more fortunate; a note in Volume One records: 'Bought in a lot of 15 books for which I paid 18s. at Ball's Sale at Sotheby's June 1886. Collated with Upcott and find perfect copy with all plates'. Lowndes says of this book 'In little estimation, no copy in Townley, Stonehead, Gosford, Hartley sales'.

A few years ago I came across *A New and Compleat Survey of London* 'In Ten Parts . . . in Two Volumes by a CITIZEN, and native of LONDON. Printed for S. Lyne, at the Globe in Newgate-street: and J. Ilive, in Aldersgate-street. MDCCLXII'.

In Part IV, entitled 'A Political Account of LONDON', is a section headed 'Of certain Parallels between London and divers other great Cities, both ancient and modern', in which is recorded, with inexplicable exactness, that Nineveh had 322,903, and Babylon 237,982 less inhabitants than London, that London contained about five times as many people as had lived in Jerusalem, 12,593 more than Alexandria, which had 300,000 Freemen, and the same number of Slaves, and 6,093 more inhabitants than Constantinople and Moscow put together.

We learn that London had three times as many markets and ovens as

Ancient Rome, which had nine or ten of the former and 321 of the latter, and that London contained three times as many houses as Peking. In comparing London with Paris we are told that 'the utmost Extent of the City of *Paris* is only three *English* miles, Seventy-seven Yards, Three Inches and a quarter; Whereas the City of *London* with its Suburbs, where shortest, is six Miles, Three quarters, Two hundred and Ninety-one Yards; which is Three Quarters of Mile, One hundred and Thirty-five Yards, Thirty-one Inches and a half more than double the Length of *Paris*. And *London*, where broadest, is Three Miles, One hundred and Seventy Yards and a Half; which is Ninety-two Yards and Thirty-four Inches broader than *Paris* is in length.'

Ilive writes entertainingly of the 'Divers Sorts of Provisions wherewith the City is supplied', all with great precision: for instance, he gives in detail the Clerk of the Market's Account for bulls, oxen and cows for the year 1725, which shows that on Monday, 3rd January, 713 animals were brought to market of which 708 were sold—and so on, throughout the year. Again, he notes that in the year 1727 the quantity of 'candle made' in the City and Suburbs amounted to 11,644,863 pounds.

Fascinating? Fascinating—for light reading.

In addition to such precision which in a survey of this description seems unduly ridiculous, Ilive was inclined to repeat himself, frequently finishing a paragraph with the same statement as that with which he had begun it.

But he was honest: he concludes this part of his work:

'Some Years ago I was of Opinion, that the excessive drinking of Tea would inhance the Price of Meat, for many Gentlemen and Farmers, who used to feed Beasts for the *London* Market, have converted their Meadows into Pasture Grounds, for feeding Cows, to make Butter for the Use of the Tea-Table, &c.

'But this enervated the Stomachs of the Populace, as to render them incapable of performing the Offices of Digestion; whereby the Appetite is so much deprav'd, that its Inclination to Food is much lessen'd, and the Consumption of Provisions greatly diminish'd; which has occasion'd Victuals, instead of rising, to fall in Price very considerably, to the no small loss of the Landed Interest.

'But the most surprising of all, is, that the Nobility and Gentry, in this City, seem to have conspir'd the Destruction of the Landed Interest, by the Ruin of their own Estates, in keeping their Servants (who are many Thousands in Number) at Board-wages, by which seemingly save they Money for the present; but their Domesticks, instead of a plentiful Table, as formerly, are reduced to take up with what they can get; and having fallen into drinking spiritous Liquors, require but little Food.

'This, tho' hitherto but little regarded, greatly contributes to the Reduction of the Consumption and Price of Victuals; and if Care be not taken to redress these growing Evils, the Estates of this Kingdom will soon be reduc'd both in their Rents and Value, to the great Loss of the Proprietors.'

I think this must be another of the books which John Noorthouck had in mind when he wrote in his preface: 'Maitland's Survey of London being thus rendered bulky, expensive, tediously prolix, though often obviously defective, some crude attempts have been made at giving meer abridgements of it with the titles of new performances; which have been executed both under real and under fictitious names.'

Although the book is in octavo, and consequently much easier to handle than the folios of Strype and Maitland, it is not one that can be read through—one can consult it—or keep it by the side of one's bed, to fall asleep at the end of a paragraph, without losing the thread of any particular story.

In the middle of this avalanche of London Histories, there appeared, in 1761, *London and its Environs Described*. 'CONTAINING An Account of whatever is most remarkable for GRANDEUR, ELEGANCE, CURIOSITY OR USE, In the CITY and in the COUNTRY Twenty Miles round it.' With 'a Plan of LONDON, a Map of the ENVIRONS, and several other useful CUTS.' The work was in six volumes, the author was anonymous and it was printed for R. and J. Dodsley in Pall Mall; it is odd that the publishers did not take the opportunity of reviewing this work in *The Annual Register* which was published by them.

The book is, in form, an alphabetical list of every place and object of interest, fully described; most of them have one of six signs designed to show whether the name was derived 'from the ground landlord, who built the street, lane, or alley, etc.' 'from signs', 'from neighbouring places, as churches, etc', 'from trees formerly growing there', 'from ridicule', or 'from their situation, as backwards, forwards, with respect to other streets'.

The anonymous author quotes from Stow, Strype, Maitland and others, but apart from the convenience of the alphabetical arrangement the work is not very inspiring, and the 'cuts' are by Samuel Wale. One does not look for light or enlightening reading in a dictionary, and although the work, says Lowndes, 'contains interesting matter not to be found elsewhere, and is valued for its account of the Duke of Devonshire's pictures at Chiswick' the books, which do not often appear on the bookseller's shelf, are only worth acquiring at a bargain price.

A New and Compleat History and Survey of the Cities of London and Westminster, the Borough of Southwark, and Parts Adjacent; . . . 'By a SOCIETY OF GENTLE-MEN, Revised, Corrected, and Improved, by HENRY CHAMBERLAIN of Hatton-Garden, Esq': was published by ('Printed for') J. Cooke, at Shakespear's Head. No. 17 Pater-noster-Row, in one folio volume. The dedication—to the Lord Mayor (of course!)—is dated, from Hatton-Garden, 2nd February 1771.

Although Chamberlain did not win a mention in the *Dictionary of*

National Biography I find his *History* very readable. The book starts off in a promising way—with a sprinkling of footnotes, quite often containing interesting facts which the author came across after he had written the book.

In one of these footnotes there is a reference to 'Montague's *History of England* . . . now publishing in weekly numbers', and the little number at the bottom left hand corner of every thirteenth (folio) page is an indication that Chamberlain's *History* also appeared in parts; John Cooke was indeed a successful publisher of works in weekly sixpenny parts.

The list of subscribers contained the names of 850 subscribers, of whom over 80 lived in Norwich. The address of most of the subscribers is given and we obtain glimpses of streets and places which have ceased to exist, such as Holbourn-hill and Holborn-bridge, Grub-street, Butchers-row, Clare-market, and names of a bygone age, such as Abraham Fivefoot and Thomas Puddifiant, although curiously enough neither of these gentlemen gave an address!

At the end of his list of subscribers there is a note which helps us to build up a picture of London 170 years ago: 'The publisher of this work hopes that no Subscriber will take it amiss, if he finds his name omitted in this list, as he has not been able to procure near one half of them, notwithstanding he gave a printed notice for that purpose, and delayed the publication several weeks entirely on that account. It is also hoped that no gentleman will be angry if he finds his name spelt wrong, as they are all printed exactly as they were delivered by the hawkers and others.'

Two of the subscribers are described—'The Rev. Matthew Taylor, D.D. and Author of England's Bloody Tribunal,' and 'The Rev. Thomas Cooke, A.B. Author of the Universal Letter Writer, and one of the Authors of the New Royal and Universal Dictionary of Arts and Sciences.' And here, not a digression, but an interjection: Not long after writing the previous sentence I bought a copy of the *Universal Letter Writer* to which is added *The Complete Petitioner* in a second hand-bookshop in Gloucester for two shillings.

And because it illustrates my point that one can pick up tit-bits about London and Londoners in unexpected places I reprint the following petition, one of the many, which may be read with pleasure and profit:

'From a Drayman, who had been taken riding on his Dray

to the Sitting Alderman.
To the Worshipful Sir W. B.
The humble petition of A. B.

Sheweth,

That your petitioner lately came from the country, and was employed as a drayman; that being used to ride in the country, he did not know, nor

GEORGE R.

GEORGE the THIRD, by the Grace of God, King of *Great Britain, France* and *Ireland,* Defender of the Faith, &c. To all to whom these Presents shall come, Greeting. Whereas Our Trusty and Well-beloved *John Cooke,* of Our City of *London,* Bookseller, hath, by his Petition, humbly presented unto Us, that he hath, for a long Time past, been at great Labour and Expence in collecting Books and ancient Manuscripts, and in employing divers learned and ingenious Men, to write and compile a valuable Work, entitled, " A new and compleat " HISTORY and SURVEY of our CITIES of LONDON and WESTMINSTER, the " BOROUGH of SOUTHWARK, and Parts adjacent ; from the earliest Accounts to the Year " 1770. Containing an Account of the original Foundation, ancient and modern state of those " Places, their Laws, Charters, Customs, Privileges, Immunities, Government, Trade, and Na-" vigation. A Description of the several Wards, Parishes, Liberties, Precincts, Churches, Palaces, " Noblemens Houses, Hospitals, and other public Buildings. An Account of the Curiosities of " the Tower of London, the Royal-Exchange, St. Paul's Cathedral, the British Museum, Westmin-" ster-Abbey, &c. with a general History of the memorable Actions of Our Citizens, and the Re-" volutions that have happened from the Invasion of *Julius Cæsar* to the present Time :" Which Work he most humbly apprehends will be of the utmost Use and Advantage to Our Subjects in general ; and to the Inhabitants of *London, Westminster* and *Southwark* in particular, as it treats of Matters in which they are peculiarly interested. And he humbly conceives that a Work in which the Rise, Progress, Increase and present State of the largest City in the Universe are faithfully deli-eated ; in which the many noble Actions of her Citizens are fairly recorded, and in which her superior Riches and Dignity, her amazing Commerce, and the Weight and Influence of her Power throughout every Part of the Globe are asserted and maintained, cannot fail of impressing the Minds of Our faithful Subjects the Citizens of *London, Westminster, &c.* with a true Sense of their own Importance, and of inspiring the rising Generation with a generous Ardor to imitate the Actions of their renowned Forefathers : Wherefore the Petitioner, desirous of reaping some advantage from his great Toil, Labour and Expence, most humbly follicits Our Royal Licence and Protection to himself, his Heirs, Executors and Assigns, for the sole Printing, Publishing and vending the said Work for the Term of Fourteen Years, so far as may be agreeable to the Statute in that Case made and provided. We being willing to give all due Encouragement to this Under-taking, are graciously pleased to condescend to his Request ; and We do therefore by these Presents, so far as may be agreeable to the Statute in that Case made and provided, grant unto him the said *John Cooke,* his Executors, Administrators and Assigns, Our Licence for the sole Printing and Pub-lishing of the said Work for the Term of Fourteen Years ; strictly forbidding all Our Subjects within our Kingdoms, or Dominions, to reprint or abridge the same, either in the like, or in any Size or Manner whatsoever, or to import, buy, vend, utter or distribute any Copies thereof reprinted beyond the Seas, during the aforesaid Term of Fourteen Years, without the Consent or Approbation of the said *John Cooke,* his Executors, Administrators and Assigns, under their Hands and Seals first had and obtained, as they will answer the contrary at their Peril ; Whereof the Commissioners and other Officers of Our Customs, the Master, Warden and Company of Stationers, are to take Notice, that due Obedience may be rendered to Our Pleasure herein declared.

Given at our Court at St. *James's.*

By his Majesty's Command,

ROCHFORD.

was ever told, that it was contrary to the law in London, and therefore was inadvertently guilty without any design of giving offence; that your petitioner is sincerely sorry for his fault, and promises never to offend in the like manner again, and therefore humbly prays, that your worship will be pleased to forgive this his first fault.

And your petitioner, as in duty bound, shall ever pray.'

To return from the interjection: not content with giving views to his readers Chamberlain inserted in his *History* some highly imaginary pictures, such as 'Blood and his Accomplices Escaping after stealing the Crown from the Tower', and 'The Ceremony of laying the first Stone of Black Friars Bridge by the Lord Mayor and Aldermen of the City of London.' These pictures, drawn by Samuel Wale, and engraved by Charles Grignion (the elder), are diverting, and not only for the costumes worn by the characters. Wale was one of the founding fellows, in 1765, of the Society of Artists of Great Britain, and three years later he was appointed the Professor of Perspective at the newly founded Royal Academy of Arts. Grignion was another of the founding fellows of the Society of Artists, and he executed plates for Horace Walpole's *Anecdotes of Painting in England*.

At the beginning of Chamberlain's book is a copy of the Licence granted by the King to John Cooke, who is described as a bookseller, for the sole printing and publishing of the book. I reproduce the Licence which recites Cooke's petition for the King's Royal Licence and Protection by reason of his 'great Labour and Expense in collecting Books and ancient Manuscripts, and in employing divers learned and ingenious Men, to write and compile' the work, and strictly forbids anyone else to reprint or abridge the book for the term of fourteen years.

Now, when one 'discovers' Walter Harrison's *A New and Universal History, Description and Survey of the Cities of London and Westminster, The Borough of Southwark, and their Adjacent Parts*, published in 1776—only five years after Chamberlain had obtained his licence for fourteen years, one is justified in wondering whether the latter took this lying down. Harrison would seem to have taken Chamberlain's *History* and made such verbal alterations in the text as he felt was necessary to protect himself from a charge of patent plagiarism.

When one examines the book one finds many chapters in which only one or two words in a paragraph were altered; in some paragraphs something new was added; sometimes the order of the paragraphs was changed, but one gets the impression that Harrison's labours consisted mainly in trying to disguise his 'pinch'.

Then one finds that many of Harrison's 'elegant copper-plate Engravings' (including for instance a copy of the one I have reproduced of Richard

S. Wale delin.   C. Grignion sculp.

RICHARD II Appeases the REBELS
on the Death of Wat Tyler in Smithfield

RICHARD II *appeases the* REBELS *on the* Death *of* Wat Tyler *in* Weſt Smithfield, LONDON.

Lodge

II appeasing the rebels on the death of Wat Tyler) are copies of those in Chamberlain's, and whilst some of them are signed by the artist, thus showing that they were, in effect, reproduced from Chamberlain, others are unsigned, and may have been re-engraved.

It would be interesting to make a collection of different artists' ideas on given subjects. To illustrate what I mean I reproduce here two more of Wale's prints depicting incidents in the Life—and Death—of Wat Tyler: the one from Walter Harrison's *History*, and the other from the 22nd Edition of *A New History of England*, 'By the Author of the Roman History by Question and Answer', published in 1790. Harrison's print also appeared in Russell's *History of England* (the twenty-second edition, published in 1790).

Wale might at least have been consistent in his architectural details! The building in the two prints 'Richard II appeases the rebels on the death of Wat Tyler in Smithfield', and 'Wat Tyler kill'd by the Lord Mayor in Smithfield' could be either St Bartholomew the Less which stood on the east side of Smithfield, or St Bartholomew the Great to the north-east of it.

The tree in the former print recalls the following passage in Stow:

'Then is Smithfield pond, which of olde time in Records was called Horse-poole, for that men watered horses there, and was a great water. In the sixt of *Henrie* the fift, a new building was made in this west part of Smithfield betwixt the said Poole and the River of the Wels, or Turnemill brooke, in a place then called the Elmes, for that there grew many Elme trees, and this had beene the place of execution for Offenders; since the which time the building there hath beene so encreased, that now remaineth not one tree growing.'

The gallows appear to have been removed to Tyburn about the reign of Henry IV.

Harrison's *History* was published by J. Cooke—who had published Chamberlain's *History* four years earlier. Lowndes's comment on Harrison's work is 'An inaccurate compilation, published in numbers'—there were ten folio pages to a number and the bound book 'enriched with upwards of One Hundred elegant copper-plate Engravings', cost fifteen shillings. We are entitled to ask why the book was not produced as a Second Edition of Chamberlain. Perhaps the work was intended to deceive the innocent book buyer into the belief that he was buying a new work. If this was Cooke's intention it would not seem to have come off; none of the subscribers to Chamberlain's *History* appear in the list of the 560 subscribers to Harrison's; and of course the list was incomplete, as the usual notice confirms.

In 1785, Alex Hogg, at the King's Arms, No. 16, Pater-noster-Row, published serially—each number containing eight folio pages, and occasionally more: *The New Complete and Universal History, Description, and Survey of the Cities of London and Westminster, the Borough of Southwark, and Parts Adjacent.*

'Written and Compiled from Authentic Records and other genuine Information: By a SOCIETY OF GENTLEMEN, the Whole REVISED, CORRECTED,
and IMPROVED, by William Thornton, Esq., Assisted by GEORGE SMITH
LL.D. The Rev. ALEX TOWNSEND, M.A. And Other Gentlemen.'

Although Thornton, in his preface, so long (nearly a page and a half)
that he has to crowd into half a page his dedication, to the Lord Mayor,
Aldermen and Common Council of the City, alleged that the 'more antient
Histories and Surveys are written in a style so totally unfit to afford Entertainment to a Modern Reader that he cannot peruse them without disgust,'
and attacked, in particular, the 'Copper-Plates in other works of this Nature'
as 'more a Disgrace than real Embellishments, being wretched Copies of old
and imperfect Publications, long obnoxious to a discerning Public'. He did
not scruple to insert many of Chamberlain's prints—transposed, and it is
amusing to compare the reproduction of a folio page from his *History* with
one of the same size from Chamberlain. Both prints of Richard II are from a
painting by Wale, engraved by Grignion for Chamberlain, and for Thornton
by Lodge, presumably John Lodge, the geographer and engraver of Charlotte
Street, Bloomsbury, who was working from about 1754 to 1794.

A legitimate question is whether Richard II gesticulated with his right
hand or his left.

Jack Cade's activity in Cannon Street and London Stone have been
immortalized by Shakespeare in *Henry VI* (Part 2, Act IV, sc. 6), and it is
curious that London Stone is not shown in Thornton's map of Walbrook
Ward. In Strype's map, by the way, it is shown on the south side of the street.
It is now on the north side, embedded in the wall of St Swithin's Church
(shown in Wale's picture), which was destroyed in the fire of 1666, and
rebuilt by Sir Christopher Wren.

Thornton certainly added a number of new engravings, and inserted
maps of the Parishes, but his 'New & Corrected Map of the Countries
upwards of Twenty Miles Round London: Drawn from Modern Surveys &
Engrav'd for Thornton's History of London etc.' is a copy in black and white
of Chamberlain's coloured 'New and Correct Map of the Countries Twenty
Miles Round London. by Thos. Bowen.'

Alex Hogg was no novice at building upon other people's foundations;
in the July of that year he had published the first monthly number of *The
New London Magazine* ... 'under the immediate Direction of a Society of
Literary Gentlemen, of London', and which was intended to cash in on the
popularity of other existing magazines.

A comparison of Chamberlain and Thornton Histories leave no doubt
that whatever William Thornton and his assistants may have been, they were
no gentlemen. Evidence to support this allegation is forthcoming as soon as
the first paragraph of each book is compared. Chamberlain's introduction

WAT TYLER *kill'd by the*
Lord Mayor in Smithfield.

S. Wale inv.t

S. Wale delin.   W. Walker sculp.

The Burning of St. John's Monastery,
near Smithfield, by Wat Tyler's Rabble.

begins: 'The great dignity, and antiquity, riches and splendor of the cities of London and Westminster, and the Borough of Southwark, may well demand the pen of the historian, to hand down their fame to future ages', whilst Thornton's preface opens: 'The *Antiquity*, *Dignity* and *Splendor* of the CITY of LONDON, the Glory of Great Britain, and the Envy of all Europe, have drawn forth the Pens of Historians to record its Fame to future ages.'

And such examples can be multiplied over and over again. A lot can be learnt about London by browsing through these two books—side by side— reading the one to learn, and the other to laugh—and tracing down, on the maps, the addresses of the subscribers to both works. Because, of course, Thornton had to insert 'A List of Subscribers to This Work, Being an uni-versally esteemed Undertaking, which has been uniformly carried on from the Beginning, and the LATTER NUMBERS of which (agreeable to our Promise in the Proposals) are delivered to the Subscribers as good in every Respect as the FIRST.'

Thornton was less reticent than Chamberlain in identifying a number of his subscribers. Thus, he includes 'Rev. George Brown, Author of the New and Complete English Letter-Writer, and the New Young Man's Companion'—possibly a rival to Chamberlain's Rev. Thomas Cooke. 'Mr. Clayton *one of Mr Towles' Twenty-Six Accomplices in the Persecution of the New Spiritual Magazine*', 'Dr Hunter, another of *Mr Towle's Accomplices* in the *Persecution* of the *New Spiritual Magazine*'; 'Mr Wills, another of the *Advertising Parsons*, who *lent Mr Towle* their *Names* to his *scandalous Advertisement* against the *New Spiritual Magazine*'; and I should not omit to mention, because he too figures in the list: 'Mr Towle, who had *distinguished himself* by being the *celebrated Persecutor* of the *New Spiritual Magazine*'—which is an odd way of showing gratitude to his subscribers, who number about 500—unless of course Thornton was interested in the success of *The New Spiritual Magazine*!

Naturally Thornton had an excuse for being able to show only such a short list of subscribers—and which is reminiscent of Chamberlain's, his footnote reading:

'The *Publishers* of this *Work* returns his most respectful Acknowledge-ments to the *numerous Subscribers* for their *great Encouragement*, and humbly solicits a *Continuance* of their *Favours* with respect to some of his other *New Publications*, (a list of which may be seen on some of the Wrappers of this Publication, etc.) assuring them, that nothing shall be wanting to render all the Periodical Works in which he shall be engaged, deserving the Public Patronage, in preference to any other performances of the kind hitherto published, or now publishing. Notwithstanding printed Notices given for the Purpose, four or five Weeks ago, and other necessary Steps taken for collecting the Whole, we have not been able to procure the Names of a tenth part of our obliging Subscribers. Those whose Names are not in the List, will therefore, of course, excuse the Omission; and such as find any Error in Spelling, will please to observe, that the Fault is not chargeable on the Publisher, as he has ordered the Names, Places of Abode, etc., to be literally transcribed from the Notes, as delivered in by the various Booksellers, Stationers, Newsmen, etc. etc.'

The persistence of these notices, and their similarity to each other reminds me of the stock note which one finds at the beginning of so many novels, announcing, in effect, that 'The characters in this book are inventions of the Author, and that any resemblance to living persons is purely coincidental.'

A study of subscribers' lists—the first appeared in John Minshew's *Guide Into Tongues* in 1617—might prove interesting. In the meantime one notes that Anthony Wood headed his list in *Athenae Oxoniensis* 'A Catalogue of part of the Subscribers to this Book: But Above one Third are omitted for want of Returning their names by the Booksellers that Subscribed for them.' Then follow 332 names, which invites the thought as to how many copies were printed, and how many had to be sold before the publisher recouped the cost of the book. One of the subscribers for the *Athenae Oxoniensis* in 1692 was 'Mr Awnsham Churchill Bookseller', one of the booksellers who, so Kingsford conjectures, had contemplated reprinting Stow's *Survey* in 1694.

Another of the eighteenth-century books to which I would like to refer is *A New History of London, Including Westminster and Southwark*; 'to which is added a general survey of the whole, describing the public buildings, late improvements, etc. illustrated with copper plates' written by that John Noorthouck, from whose preface I quoted when I was writing of Maitland.

The preface is dated from Barnard's Inn, Holborn, 28th March 1773, and after outlining the plan of his work—first the history of London, and then the survey of the several wards, and the suburbs, and referring to his authorities—Noorthouck goes on:

'As the writer was born a citizen of London, and has spent the greatest part of his life in the metropolis, it may be supposed his description of places and things are drawn from actual knowledge; and this is materially true in most instances, though it cannot extend to all cases. No faithful accounts of the same objects can substantially vary; and though, for his own ease in so multifarious an undertaking, he has frequently availed himself of delineations drawn up, and remarks made, by other hands, which in the most material instances are acknowledged, (as he wishes not to decorate himself with borrowed plumes) yet the frequent correction and addition they required, have in truth given him an exclusive property in almost whatever descriptive articles he has adopted. His acknowledgements are moreover due to several gentlemen for hints of private information, as well as to some whose names he is not at liberty to mention, as to those whose favours have been authenticated in the notes.'

I wish we could have been told the names of the gentlemen who so obligingly supplied Noorthouck with those hints of private information.

How true it is that history repeats itself; and how topical some of London's old history is. For instance, Noorthouck tells us of the 'motions of the French indicating an intention of invading England', in November 1755, and he goes on—'Under these apprehensions the forming of a national militia began to be agitated for the internal strength of the kingdom against any foreign attempts to disturb us. Every nation that pretends to freedom ought to hold their arms in their own hands, and under due regulation parochial musters far from being a burdensome care, might be rendered an agreeable and laudable amusement every Sunday before or after divine worship';—and here an asterisk refers us to a query at the foot of the page: 'What can so naturally coincide with the religious duties of the day, as a due attention to the protection of our country, and the safeguard of our persons and property?'

There is an appendix 'containing several charters of the city of London, with acts of parliament, and of common council, etc. relating to its government', and an addenda, in which is reprinted 'The Order of the Hospitalls of K. Henry the VIIIth and K. Edward the VIth, viz St Bartholomew's, Christ's, Bridewell, St Thomas's. By the Maior, Cominaltie, and Citizens of London, Governours of the Possessions; Revenues and goods of the said Hospitalls, 1557'.

There are over forty 'plates', and a map of the 'country, from thirty to forty miles round London.'

Noorthouck's book, with its 902 pages, is heavy and unwieldy, but I like it; it is well authenticated and easy to read. I paid five shillings and sixpence for my copy; it was one of my best buys.

4

John Luffman, Thomas Pennant, John Weever and James Peller Malcolm

In Farnham some years ago I paid four shillings (marked down from five!) for an old octavo book labelled on the spine 'Magazines &cc'. I had noted the title page—'THE HISTORY of LONDON and its ENVIRONS; From the earliest, well authenticated Accounts, to the close of the year 1794. By John Luffman,—Citizen and Goldsmith of London. Vol. I. London: Printed for T. Evans, No. 46, Pater-noster-Row; 1793.' I thought to compare a year's prophecy with what actually happened! But when, on arriving home, I looked into the book I found that it contained only forty pages of the *History*; the rest of the book consisted of a miscellaneous collection: several pages from William Beckford's *History of France* (in four volumes)—with some illustrations—and some hundreds of pages from *The General Magazine* for January and February 1793, *The Gentleman's Magazine* for May and July 1793, and March 1797, and from *The Universal Magazine* for July 1793. There was also a miscellany of illustrations, including one from Luffman's *History* and eleven from Bellamy's edition of Shakespeare's plays, published in 1791.

I certainly did not complain, but I should have preferred Luffman entire; particularly as his *History* is not mentioned in the G.L.C. Catalogue, although his *The Charters of London Complete, 1793* is. Lowndes lists *The Charters*, and another, *Elements of History and Chronology from the creation of the World to the Close of the Year 1804*, which was published in 1806.

But on examining the book more closely I found that at the end of the list of contents of *The General Magazine* it announced: 'and Twenty-Four pages of a NEW and COMPLETE HISTORY of LONDON, and its ENVIRONS, by John Luffman', etc. in the words of the title page.

The February number announced another twenty-four pages of Luffman and as there is no copy in the British Museum Library it is not unreasonable to suppose that it never was published separately.

The last paragraph on page 40, however, contains the answers to a question I am often asked: 'In 1191, in the Mayoralty of Henry Fitz-Alwin, an act or order was made by the Mayor and Alderman, that all houses in future to be built in the city of London and liberties thereof, should be of stone, with party walls of the same and covered with tiles or slates, the houses of this city at that period, being erected chiefly of wood, and covered with straw and reeds'.

And now for a popular work: different booksellers seem to have their own, often original, ideas of the value of *Some Account of London* by Thomas Pennant, LL.D. Dr Charles Burney (1726–1814) criticized his style as laconic; and Isaac Disraeli (1766–1848) criticized: 'on the whole, this is a superficial performance, as it regards manners, characters and events. That antiquary skimmed everything and grasped scarcely anything; he wanted the patience of research, and the keen spirit which revivifies the past.' With trepidation I disagree. I think he is underrated, and consequently undervalued. Much, of course, depends upon the condition of the book, and in a lesser degree upon the edition. Unless the aspiring tyro has ample time for reading and comparing he should aim at buying the *latest* edition of any particular book. He wants the most accurate information, with additions and corrections, and the latest edition should contain it.

A few words about Pennant: he was born in 1726, and had made his name as a traveller and naturalist before his *Some Account of London* was published in 1790. He tells us in his 'Advertisement' that the 'work is composed from the observations of perhaps half' his life—and this 'Advertisement' reveals a simple man who loved London.

The book was printed for Robt. Faulder, No. 42 New Bond Street. I bought a copy of the First (quarto) Edition (with loose sides) a couple of years ago for seven shillings, which I will insist was not too much to pay, particularly as its twelve prints are correctly inserted according to the 'Instructions to the Book-Binder', and are in mint condition. Six of them, Pennant tells us, were drawn and etched by Mr John Carter, presumably the architect who was writing in *The Gentleman's Magazine* at the end of the eighteenth century, and 'than whom', Allen, writing in 1828, tells us, 'no man has done more towards the elucidation of the beauties and perfection of English architecture.'

Lowndes writes that 'this work, though not quite accurate in some particulars, is one of the most pleasing topographical performances that has ever appeared'.

A Second Edition of the work, with additions and corrections, was published in 1791 and a third in 1793. I have a large octavo copy of the work (for which I paid ten shillings in Worthing) and which was described as being the third edition, printed for John Archer, and published—I suspect piratically—in Dublin in 1791.

T. Gainsborough pinx.ᵗ   Pub.ᵈ by ... Simpkin Street   J. Rowney sculp.ᵗ

Tho Pennant

THOMAS PENNANT, ESQ.ᴿ

It contains a list of the subscribers (571 copies were sold before publication), amongst whom was 'Mr Boswell' (who held a higher opinion of Pennant than did Johnson) 'Mr Joshua Carter' (maybe a relation of Mr John Carter, the architect) and 'Mr Henry Brocas, Engraver', who, for this edition, etched the prints which had been drawn for the First Edition by Mr John Carter.

In addition to two new prints a map of 'London and Westminster in the Reign of Queen Elizabeth Anno Dom: 1563' (reproduced here on pages 16 and 17) was added. As Shakespeare was not born until the following year the placing of 'Shakesperes Play House', on the south side of the Thames, was a splendid example of intelligent anticipation!

The Fourth (quarto) Edition 'with considerable additions' was published in 1805. I have two copies of this edition as issued, as well as three Grangerised copies, as they are called—after the Rev. James Granger who, during his short life (1721–1766) collected 14,000 engraved portraits and 'invented' the method of extra-illustrating the texts of biographical and topographical publications.

I paid five pounds many years ago in Bristol for the first of my Grangerised copies. It contains 388 extra illustrations, they are of all shapes and sizes, from good prints to pictures snipped out of journals, and they include many which I have not yet been able to identify.

I paid three pounds ten shillings for the second of my Grangerised Fourth Edition copies. Included in the price was *A Copious Index to Pennant's Account of London* compiled, from the Fourth Edition, by Thomas Downes, and published in 1814; From the 'Advertisement' to this *Index* it would appear to have been prepared specially for the 'Grangeriser'. Bound up in my copy of the book are the portrait of Pennant (here reproduced), another engraving of him, a title page of the Third Edition, and two (different) title pages of the Fourth Edition; fourteen pages in manuscript of 'Notes to Pennant' (I reproduce the last of them) and the title page of John Thomas Smith's *Antiquities of London and its Environs*, nearly one hundred views of 'Houses, Monuments, Statues, and other curious remains of Antiquity; engraved from the original subjects and Original Drawings, Communicated by several Members of the Society of Antiquaries: With Remarks & references to the Historical Works of Pennant, Lysons, Stow, Weaver, Camden, Maitland, etc.' which was published in 1791 by T. Sewell, Cornhill, R. Faulder, New Bond Street, T. Simes, Great Queen Street, T. Manson, Dukes Court, St Martin's Lane, Messrs. Molteno and Colnaghi, Pall Mall, J. T. Smith, Engraver, Edmonton, & Nath. Smith, Antient Printseller, No. 18 Great May Buildings, St. Martin's Lane.' Naturally, many of the prints in Pennant's book are from J. T. Smith's work.

My third Grangerised Fourth Edition is one of twelve copies 'Printed for the Illustrator'. I paid five pounds for the two volumes in imperial folio over thirty years ago, in an old shop at Mortlake, which has long since disappeared. It has 258 magnificent plates in mint condition, including a number by Wenceslas Hollar and is, from an artistic point of view, the highlight of my London collection.

Amongst the prints is one published by N. Smith on the 26th June 1799 of 'Cleveland House, by St James's', with a 'plan which exhibits Berkshire House on part of the site on which Cleveland House is built copied from a curious print inserted in the illustrated Pennant belonging to Thomas Thompson Esq, M.P. the richest collection of its kind, perhaps, that is now extant.'

In *Notes and Queries*, during the year 1945, I enquired as to the whereabouts of this book, but had no reply. At the same time I asked to be informed of any other Grangerised Histories accessible for inspection in London, as a result of which the Librarian of the London Library very courteously produced a Grangerised copy of the Fourth Edition, bound up in six volumes, 'Presented in Memory of Mrs Fraser Baddeley', and containing no less than 976 prints, and with notes of some missing ones, including a reference to some 'valuable Hollars', removed for Granger, which indicates that the collection was begun before 1766, the year in which Granger died. The volumes, however, could not have been bound up in the eighteenth century because they contain a number of Ackermann's coloured prints published in 1808–9, and a print of the Globe Theatre, Bankside, Southwark, published on the 8th May 1812 by Robert Wilkinson, No. 58 Cornhill, London, 'From a Drawing in the celebrated copy In Fourteen Volumes large folio, of Pennant's *London* Bequeathed by the late John Charles Crowle Esq. to the British Museum'.

Another print in my Grangerised copy is of Clarendon House (published on 10th August 1798) by N. Smith which includes a 'section' showing the site of the House, taken 'from a map of London (supposed to be unique) in the possession of John Charles Crowle, Esq., whose philanthropy is not exceeded by the splendor of the Illustrated Clarendon's History in which he has inserted it'.

Who was this John Charles Crowle, and how was he able to form the magnificent collection referred to? Both the *Dictionary of National Biography* and *Men and Women of the Time* ignore him; in *The Gentleman's Magazine*, 'Obituary; with anecdotes of remarkable persons' for March 1811 is the lone entry 'In Curzon-street, May-fair, Charles John Crowle, esq.'

The collection which he left to the nation consists of over five thousand items, and he valued it more than a century and a half ago—at £5,000.

I paid half-a-crown in the Charing Cross Road for a copy of the Fifth (octavo) Edition which was published in 1813, and was 'Printed by S. Hamilton of Weybridge' for 'J. Faulkner; White, Cochrane and Co; Long-

to Protestanism he died of the Plague at Leicester
Burleigh House — Here resided the Earl of Shaftesbury when
Chancellor in great state — The officers of the Court, Judges, Kings
Sergeants at Law, King's Attorney, and Solicitor General going be-
fore him to Westminster

An Account of the expences of 50 new Churches built in London by Sir **Christopher Wren.**

Church	Cost	Church	Cost
St Pauls Cathedral	736,752, 2, 5	St Michaels Proyal	7455.17.9
Allhallows the great	5541, 9, 9	St Michaels Crooked Lane	4541.5.10
Allhallows Broad Street	3342, 7, 2	St Martins Ludgate	5370.9.7
Allhallows Lombard Street	0050.15.6	St Matthews Friday Street	2391.8.1
St Albans Wood Street	3165, 0, 0	St Michaels Corn Hill	4604.10.0
St Anns and St Agnes	2440, 3, 10	St Margarets Lothbury	5340.8.1
St Andrews Wardrobe	9000, 6, 0	St Margarets Pattens	4906.10.4
St Antholines	5605, 5, 0, 7	St Mary Abchurch	4922.2.4
St Austins	3145, 3, 1	St Mary Magdalen	4291.12.9
St Bennets Gracechurch	3503, 9, 5	St Mary Somerset	6579.18.1
St Bennets Pauls Wharf	3320.10, 10	St Mary at Hill	3980. 12. 3
St Bennets Fink	4129, 16, 0	St Mary's Aldermanbury	5237.3.6
St Brides	11430.5.11	St Mary le bone	0071.18.1
St Bartholomews	5077, 1, 1	The Steeple too	7300.8.7
Christ Church	11770, 9, 6	St Nicholas Cole Abbey	5042.16.11
St Clements East Cheap	4,365, 3, 4	St Olives Jewry	5500.4.10
St Clements Danes	0706.17.2	St Peters Cornhill	5647.4.6
St Dionisius Back Church	5737.10.0	St Swithins Cannon Street	4674.6
St Edmonds the King	5207.11.0	St Stephens Walbrook	5652.13.0
St Georges Botolph Lane	4,509, 4, 10	St Stephens Coleman Street	4,020.16.6
St James Garlick Hythe	5357.12,10	St Michaels Broad Street	3705.13.6
St James Westminster	0500, 0, 0	St Michaels London Bridge	9579.4.6
St Lawrence Jury	11007, 1, 9	St Vedust Foster Lane	1053.15.6
St Michaels Bassishaw	2822.17.1	St Mildreds Poultry	4654.9.7
St Michaels East Hythe	4354.3, 6	Monument Fish Street Hill	0056.8.0
St Michaels Wood Street	2554.2.11		

man, Hurst, Reese, Orme & Brown; Cadell & Davies; J. Walker; J. Nunn; J. Booth; T. Maurman; R. Baldwin; Wilkie & Robinson; J. Richardson; J. & A. Arch; F. C. & J. Rivington; B. & R. Crosby & Co.' (a second title page puts them in a different order).

Fourteen publishers—including the original one! And an interesting hark-back to the custom of a hundred years earlier when a number of book-sellers published books co-operatively. Such an association was called a 'Conger'. I turn to a book published in 1811 entitled *Lexicon Balatronicum*, 'A dictionary of Buckish Slang, University Wit and Pickpocket Eloquence. ... By a Member of the Whip Club. Assisted by Hell-Fire Dick, and James Gordon, Esqrs. of Cambridge; and William Soames, Esq. of the Hon. Society of Newman's Hotel', James Gordon was an eccentric solicitor who made a living in London by waiting at coach houses. (Written in pencil in my copy is 'Pass word to our Crib in Temple Bar "Hold up your jemmy and show a Cove the trap" '). In this book conger is thus defined 'To conger; the agreement of a set or knot of booksellers of London, that, whosoever of them shall buy a good copy, the rest shall take off such a particular number, in quires, at a stated price; also booksellers joining to buy either a consider-able or dangerous copy'.

Such co-operative publishing was one method of protecting copyright against literary piracy, but the Copyright Acts made Congers unnecessary, and they faded out in the middle of the eighteenth century.

My fourth Grangerised Pennant is a copy of this Fifth Edition; it is well bound with nearly 100 extra, but not very exciting, illustrations—including the Kings of England. It also contains a portrait of Lord Bacon which, because it makes Bacon look as if he had two right arms, reminds me of Martin Droeshout's portrait of Shakespeare in the 1623 Folio which, Bacon-ians allege, is cunningly composed of two left arms and a mask.

Grangerised Pennants occasionally find their way on to the second-hand booksellers' shelves. Unless the copy has been meanly illustrated, and if the illustrations are in good condition, the book should certainly not depreciate in value. I have a note that in the Special Catalogue No. 3. of Books on London issued by Messrs. F. & C. Stoneham in 1926 an Extra Illustrated copy of the 1814 edition of Pennant, with an Appendix and the Index by T. Downes (mentioned above), enlarged to four volumes by the insertion of plates, from the Library of Edward Huth with his Bookplate was offered at £12. 0. 0. It was still being advertised, at the same price in Catalogue No. 6 issued in April 1928, but had disappeared in December 1929 Catalogue No. 7.

I have a curious little sextodecimo book published in 1806 entitled *London*, 'in its Ancient and Modern State, Described by Mr Pennant, with a correct colour Plan. To which is added, A Tour through the Universities of

Oxford and Cambridge, and to the Watering Places,' and which was 'Printed for Vernor, Hood, and Sharpe, 31, Poultry: and J. Harris, Corner of St Paul's Church-yard. At the Union Printing-office, St John's Square, by W. Wilson.'

The 'Advertisement', which is dated 1800, describes the book as a supplement to a work entitled *British Tourists*, but it is really Pennant's *London* bowdlerized; the Tours being written by the editor of the book.

I have recently purchased a book published in 1810 entitled *London*: 'being a Complete Guide to the BRITISH CAPITAL; . . . . Faithfully abridged from Mr Pennant's London, and brought down to the present year. Third Edition by John Wallis.'

The first forty-six pages of this book are innocuous, with brief histories of Ancient London, London in the Middle Ages and Modern London, and then the author seems to have decided to strike a new note, and the running headline of the remaining 238 pages is 'Pennant's London improved'. What Wallis did was to isolate each of the several places mentioned by Pennant and give them a heading, which turned the account of London into a guide book. This may be just what was wanted in what the author calls 'a portable description of the antiquities of London,' but I prefer my Pennant plain.

There are several interesting facts to be dug out of *The London Adviser and Guide* by the indefatigable Rev. D. Trusler. I have a copy of the Second (enlarged) Edition which was published in 1790; the First Edition was published four years earlier.

The author claimed the book to be 'useful and necessary to PERSONS LIVING IN LONDON AND COMING TO RESIDE THERE,' and its 215 (octavo) pages were cheap at three shillings and six pence.

It is not possible to say how many people were saved from a lifetime of misery by reading that 'Counterfeiting the superscription of any letters to evade the postage, is transportation for seven years'.

And in the eighteenth century it was certainly important to know that 'Drivers of hackney-coaches are to give way to gentlemen's carriages, under the penalty of 10s.'

And the gentlemen referred to were advised not to 'allow your coach-man the old wheels' because if you do he will 'often injure the wheels, if they are likely to last too long.'

Sundays were not always peaceful in the good old days: 'Milk and mackrell are allowed to be cried about the streets on Sundays, before nine in the morning and after four in the afternoon, but at no other time of the day, on pain of forfeiting the things so cried.'

But such annoyances were to be borne in silence, because: 'If any person shall curse or swear, and be convicted on the oath of one witness, before one justice, within eight days of the offence, he shall forfeit as follows: Every day-labourer, common soldier, or seaman, 1s; every other person under the degree of a gentleman, 2s. and every gentleman 5s. for the first offence, to the poor, and all charges; double the sums for the second, after conviction, or be committed to hard labour for ten days. Soldiers and seamen, instead of being committed, shall be set in the stocks one hour for a single offence, and two hours for more offences than one.'

Among the 'Entertainments *and* Exhibitions *in Town*' is Vauxhall:

'A public garden, illuminated in the evening, with a concert of vocal and instrumental music; open all summer. Admission 1s. each. All kinds of refreshments are here sold; and the company seldom leave the place, in fine weather, till two in the morning. This is two miles from town, but the road guarded'.

But if *The London Adviser* is to be believed, whilst life may have been hard, it was not dear, as witness the following extract from its pages:

An ESTIMATE of the Expences attending a Family consisting of a Man, his Wife, four Children and two Maid Servants, who conduct their domestic Arrangement with economy.

	Weekly.		
	l.	s.	d.
Bread for eight persons, 8d. per week each, (supposing the quartern-loaf at 6d.) – – – – –	0	5	4
Butter, 7 lb. on an average, at 9d. per lb.– – –	0	5	3
Cheese, 3 lb. and a half, at 5d. per lb. – – –	0	1	5½
Roots, herbs, spices, and the decorament of the table,–	0	3	6
Meat, or fish, or fowl, 1 lb. each, at 6d. per pound, on an average, – – – – – – –	1	8	0
Milk and cream, one day with another, 2d. – –	0	1	2
Eggs, 4d. and flour, 1s. 2d. – – – – –	0	1	6
Small-beer, at 14s. a barrel, 12 gallons, – – –	0	1	6
Tea, 2s. and sugar, 3s. – – – – – – –	0	5	0
Candles, 4 lb. take the summer and winter together, at 9d. – – – – – – – –	0	3	0
Coals, two fires in winter, one only in summer; 3 bushels for parlour fire, for 8 months, 4 ditto for the kitchen all the year, about 8 chaldrons and a half, at 34s. – – – – – – – –	0	5	6
Soap, starch, blue, and washing at home and abroad,	0	5	0
Thread, needles, pins, tapes, and all sorts of haberdashery, – – – – – – –	0	1	9
Sands, fullers earth, whitening, scowering paper, brick-dust, small coal, &c. – – – –	0	0	4

Repairs of furniture, table-linen, sheets, and all other utensils,– — — — — — — —	0	2	0
	3	13	5½
L. 3: 13: 5 halfpenny per week, is per annum,	189	18	8
Clothes for the master and mistress, and hairdressing	40	0	0
Clothes for the children, 6l. each, — — — —	24	0	0
Lying-in expences, 12l. suppose once in two years, —	6	0	0
Pocket expences for the master, including letters, 4s. per week, — — — — — — — —	10	8	0
Ditto for the mistress and children — — — —	5	4	0
Physic, and occasional illness,– — — — —	5	0	0
Schooling for the children, on an average, — —	8	0	0
Wages of two maid-servants and taxes, — — —	14	10	0
Standing rent 50l. taxes 16l. — — — — —	66	0	0
Entertainments for friends, — — — — —	20	0	0
Sundries for wine, pleasure, &c. suppose, for even money, – — — — — — — —	10	19	4
	400	0	0

And there are so many more sidelights on life in London at that time which could be quoted if space permitted.

Before passing on to Histories which were written in the nineteenth century, a note about two works which contain much information about the parish churches, and their graveyards—and which may be read together, because the one was written, lyrically, before the Great Fire of 1666 and the other, prosaically, well after it.

The first is *Ancient Funerall Monuments within the United Monarchie of Great Britaine*. ... 'Composed by the Studie and Travels of John Weever,' (to whom I referred in Chapter One) 'Printed by Thomas Harper, 1631. And are sold by Laurence Sadler at the signe of the Golden Lion in Little Britaine.'

Weever (1576–1632) was a contemporary of Shakespeare and Stow, and was himself a Poet and an Antiquary. His *Funerall Monuments* is described by the *Dictionary of National Biography* as:

'faulty, but valuable through subsequent destruction of originals', but Weever had already, in his introductory 'Epistle to the Reader', admitted 'Many are the errataes, I am afraid, which will be found in the printing;' and he recorded a couple of dozen. He made no apology, however, for his fulsome dedication 'To the sacred and Imperiall Majestie ... Charles. ...

The Patterne of True Pietie, and justice, and The President of all Princely Vertues. ... His Highnesse Most lowly, and most loyall subject John Weever, in all humility, consecrateth These his Labours: Though farre unworthy the view of so resplendent a Greatnesse.'

And as Weever penned those words 'From my house in Clerkenwell Close this 28. of May 1631', Charles had been governing for over two years without a Parliament, and was resorting to every artifice to fill his Exchequer at the expense of his people.

But it is the book, not the dedication, which interests me. It contains 871 pages, of which 366 deal exclusively with the Diocese of London, and will well repay a leisurely perusal.

Dip into the pages and read a contemporary's opinion of the author, 'not long since deceased', of the *History of Henry VIII*, 'Wherein hee is delineated to the life, by the matchlesse and never enough admired penne of that famous, learned and eloquent Knight, Sir Francis Bacon'.

I dip again and the following lines, the first four of an inscription on the Wall of Saint Michael's, Wood Street, catch my eye:

> John Casy of this Parish whose dwelling was
> In the North corner house as to Lad-lane you pass
> For better knowledge, the name it hath now
> Is called and knowne by the name of the Plow.

And so on to speak of his benefaction to the poor, and at once I am back in that old London in which, since very few of the people could read, a name over a shopfront meant nothing and signboards were the natural way in which tradesmen announced their existence to customers. These signboards were removed by legislation in the reign of George III after a proliferation of hanging and creaking signs had become a danger and a nuisance to the City.

And here at random, are some early instances—can they be the first? —of some up-to-date idioms. Thus, when Sir Thomas More's books and papers were taken away from him during his imprisonment, he shut the windows of his room, saying 'When the wares are gone, and the tooles taken away, we must shutt up shop!' Again in the reference to the Church (at Charing in Kent) destroyed in 1590 by fire—'which fire it caught from a peece discharged at a Pigeon then upon the Church . . . now in the hands of workmen to bee repaired.'

Then I particularly like Weever's reference to the epitaph 'Upon John Dunstable an Astrologian, a Mathematician, a Musician, and what not.'

But this is a digression, and in excusing myself let me quote finally from Weever, after he had wandered somewhat from his text—'For I am sure that this discourse is impertinent, and quite from the subject to which I have tied my selfe to treat of, Yet I hope these lines will not seeme much

JOHN WEEVER.

The Antiquary – Died 1632.

Published as the Act directs 1819.

unpleasing for my Reader to peruse, when his minde is overcharged with dull, heavie, and uncomfortable Epitaphs.' Weever was unnecessarily modest— and his book is full of interesting digressions.

By way of a postscript to Weever here are the verses in Anthony Munday's Fourth (1633) Edition of Stow's *Survey*, written presumably by him and which were followed by Weever's epitaph upon himself. Note Munday's spelling of Weever's name.

Upon my very worthy Friend, Master
John Weaver, *a learned*
Antiquary

> *Weaver*, who laboured
>   in a learned straine,
> To make men long since dead
>   to live againe,
> And with expence of Oyle,
>   and Inke, did watch,
> From the Wormes mouth
>   the sleeping Course to snatch,
> Hath by his industry
>   begot a way,
> Death (who insidiates
>   all things) to betray,
> Redeeming freely
>   by his care and cost,
> Many a sad Herse, which time
>   long since gave lost;
> And to forgotten dust
>   such spirit did give,
> To make it in our
>   memories to live.
> Where Death destroy'd
>   when he had power to save,
> In that he did not seeke
>   to rob the Grave,
> For where so e're
>   a ruin'd Tombe he found,
> His Pen hath built it
>   new out of the ground.
> 'Twixt Earth and Him
>   this interchange we finde,

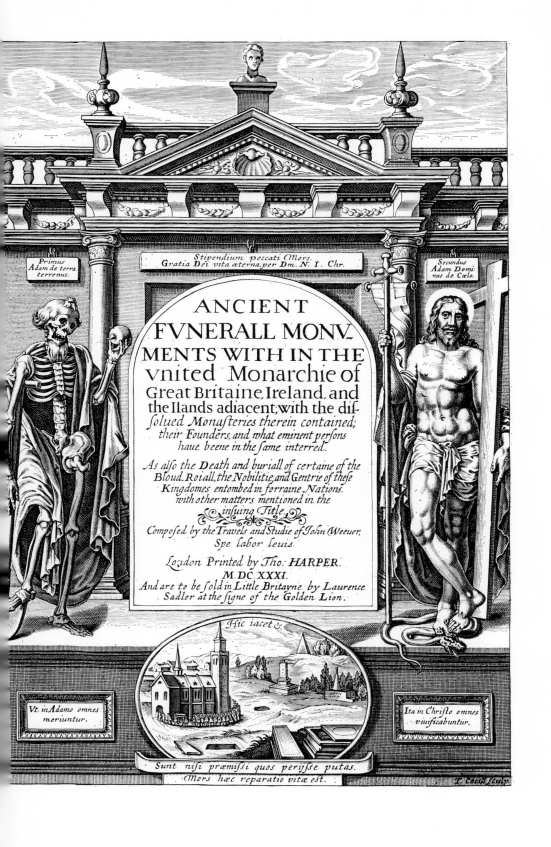

Primus
Adam de terra
terrenus.

Stipendium peccati Mors.
Gratia Dei vita æterna, per Dm. N. I. Chr.

Secundus
Adam Domi:
nus de Cælo.

ANCIENT FVNERALL MONV̄MENTS WITH IN THE vnited Monarchie of Great Britaine, Ireland, and the Ilands adiacent; with the dissolued Monasteries therein contained; their Founders, and what eminent persons haue beene in the same interred.

As also the Death and buriall of certaine of the Bloud. Roiall, the Nobilitie, and Gentrie of these Kingdomes entombed in forraine Nations. with other matters mentioned in the insuing Title.

Composed by the Travels and Studie of John Weeuer. Spe labor leuis.

London Printed by Tho: HARPER.
M.DC.XXXI.
And are to be sold in Little Britayne by Laurence Sadler at the signe of the Golden Lion.

Hic iacet &c.

Vt in Adamo omnes
moriuntur.

Ita in Christo omnes
viuificabuntur.

Sunt nisi præmissi quos periisse putas.
Mors hæc reparatio vitæ est.

Shee hath to him,
he bin to her like kinde,
Shee was his Mother,
he (a grateful Child)
Made her his Theme,
in a large worke compil'd
Of Funerall Reliques,
and brave Structures rear'd,
On such as seem'd unto her
most indear'd.
Alternately a Grave
to him she lent,
O're which his Booke
remaines a Monument.

Master *Weaver* upon himselfe.

Lankashire gave me breath,
And *Cambridge* education,
Middlesex gave me death,
And this Church my humation,
And Christ to me hath given
A place with him in Heaven.

Obiit Anno Ætat. suae 56.

The other work—the one written well after the Great Fire—is the four-volume *Londinium Redivivum; or an Ancient History and Modern Description of London* by James Peller Malcolm, F.S.A. 'Printed by John Nichols & Son, Red Lion Passage, Fleet Street, Sold by Longman, Rees, Hurst & Orme. Paternoster Row', 1802 and 1807, at two guineas.

Each of the volumes opens with an 'Advertisement', most of which is devoted to thanking, by name, the numerous authorities to whom Malcolm was indebted for the loan of manuscripts. He has to report 'A few solitary instances have occurred where denial was accompanied by rudeness and insult. Perhaps those are noticed, in the proper places, with rather too much asperity; but I trust it will be excused when the reader reflects, how severely imputations of sinister motives must gall a mind tinctured with the smallest portion of honesty.'

But, as he says: 'The reader will keep in his mind that mine is an *original* History of London, and that manuscript records are not to be obtained *but by favour*. Public Libraries afford *printed books*: with those I have nothing to do.'

Malcolm was born in Philadelphia in 1767. With typical American

FINSBURY-FIELDS.
NORTH

The Scale of scores & half scores.

Carington
Black boy

The
Purlues

Piller of powles
Pond
Stake by Stile
Place
Fields fell
Robinsons leg
Davis da
Cat & fiddle
Jones his ioy

Stone
Lion
Sapling by lio
Wells good will
Rainebow
Rosebrach
Whitbrooke

Pigion
Martinsmonkie
Happe
Perins
past gap
Hodgets hart holydaye
Brothers
Gravelie Lamb Baines
Wale noodle
Swans stake
Cornish chough
Longmeg
Parkins stone
Camell
Wards stake
Beehive
Turke stake
hare
Sheaf of arr
Cate
Parkes his pleasure
Humfrey iames
Thurloes rose
Maiors marygold
Kingstonb
Sta my pla
Bakers boy
Cawdries coffer
Binoist
Robinsons
Carters whip
Basing hall
Bores head
Brands boy
St George
Mabb
Bar
low
Whithorne
Will poste
Iron
Cucc
Lyon
Canale
Aspine
Ape
Hodges pie
Bibush
Cranes
Horselose
Flynt
Mercers maid
Stone by the pond
Swan
Wilcox
St
Andrew
Teuels timber
Townes end
Hand & rose
Spurringsport
Youngpewe
Maydenblush
Aredale
Swanharnestman
Brownes bak
Short starre
Gote by Har
Julius Cæsar
Queenes stake
Greenes sta
Egipc
Griphon
Watson
Harrisons fol
Out pitt
H of honestey
Snowhall
Cowslip
Martins maist
Kempton
Pyper
Pinder
Diall
Nelson
Gose son
Boxes lg
Kingsmace
B Nan
Lurchingstake
Lanterne st
Beartygoodman
Amias back
Begrphani
Stile
Besuyck st
Alloway
Theefe in hedge
Fuller St St Martines
Mils his back
Come
Rogers sta
St Rowland
Marshes St D Deed
Ston
Durkinsbey
H of Lancal
Bankes his st
Lees Lion
Fown sonne
Dick Marigold
Stone in plaine
Nonngere
Deues stak
Hawes
Saunders
Weepingcrosse
Loddyhoure
Morringsm
Redcross
Cooper
VHynde
H Clebb
Alhallowes
Red dog
Walkers Drag
Lure
Hurst
Spindle
Yeomanson
Long ston
Dent ston
Cowps Worms
Sct Leonards
Coxes content
Puttock
Nuns head
Curriers shaue
St Giles
Richard
St Batu
Waterbearer
Perelous pond

To his
affect frends MR
Baker & MR Sharpe
and all other louers of
Archerie frequent-
ing Finsbury fields

witt Hole

Princes stake
Wrilock
Sampit
Speed st
Dame Annis le cleere
Tinckers bud
Caleb
Brickelaier
Pewdeere
Friertuck
Sonday hill
Mouth Greatstone
Ralfes stones

TOVT MONDE
Bunhill

thoroughness, he painstakingly worked through the London parishes and unearthed a mass of interesting material.

The work contains forty-seven illustrations. I reproduce one of the most curious, traced from an old print in the Bodleian Library, and said by Malcolm to have been inserted in a work on archery by William Hole, showing the 'singular appearance' of Finsbury Fields from 1498, when 'all the gardens which had continued time of mind without Moorgate, to wit, about and beyond the township of Finsbury, were destroyed, and of them was made a plain field for archers to shoot in', till about the reign of Charles II; 'each butt may be distinguished by the targets on the tops'; and the number— there were 164 of them—is evidence of the popularity of this form of valiant exercise.

The print invites some curious queries: At the bottom of the print is *Bunhill*, but Bunhill is north-west of Finsbury Fields, not south. The three windmills to the north of 'Finsburie Fyeld' shown on the map reproduced on page 91, were erected in the reign of Queen Elizabeth on a deposit made in Finsbury Fields of 'more than one thousand cartloads of bones' (hence the name Bonehill or Bunhill), which had been removed in 1549 from the charnel house of Old St Paul's by order of the Protector Somerset. Stow relates that on these bones 'the soilage of the city' was laid, and three windmills 'in short space after raised'. Ralph Agas's map of London, which was prepared about 1560, also depicts these windmills, with the figures of a few archers shooting in the fields.

But to return to the print: *Dame Annis le cleere* and *Perelous pond* were also north of the Fields—in fact one might suggest that north should read south, but for the fact that Perelous pond was east of *Dame Annis le cleere* and if one turns the print upside down, as it were, Perelous pond would be on the east which would apparently be wrong, for Stow places it on the west, and records that it was so called because 'diverse youthes swimming therein have been drowned'. The site of Perelous pond is in Baldwin Street, City Road.

The Spring called Dame Annis le Cleere was named after a rich London widow, who 'matching herself with a riotous courtier in the time of Edward I, who vainly consumed all her wealth, and leaving her in much povertie, there she drowned herself, being then but a shallow ditch of running water'.

Many years later, in 1743, Perelous pond was converted into what we should now call a swimming pool, and adjacent to it was 'The Cold Bath', faced with marble and paved with stone by the bricklayer who rose in the world, was chosen to serve as Sheriff in 1796–97, knighted and, as Sir William Staines, was elected Lord Mayor of London in 1801.

Its site was near Paul Street, Finsbury, and nearby is St Agnes Terrace.

The print is also interesting for the names of the butts—such as 'Rohood' and 'Friertuck'. Some names would indicate that they were associated with the customers of Inns. 'Hand & Rose', for instance; then, 'Swan-harnestman' is a curious name, whilst 'Cat & Fiddle' is a reminder that in the earliest form of the story Dick Whittington is said to have heard Bow Bells from Bunhill instead of Highgate—but as Dick had died in 1423 that cannot be correct.

An intriguing name is 'Lond:ɛton' (note that the 's' is misprinted back to front). A favourite theory is that London Stone in Cannon Street was set up by the Romans in the centre of the City, and that all distances were measured from it. Walter Bell, a bold and imaginative London historian was, however, of the opinion that it was an honoured fragment of a house built of stone, when stone houses were rare, by Henry Fitz Alwin, London's first Mayor; he points out that it would have been a significant thing among London's poor wooden hovels. I think of London Stone as something different—as the very heart of the City, and as such to be defended to the last, at all cost—by its own bodyguard—a picked band of archers, whose practice butt was the 'Lond:ɛton' in Finsbury Fields. This idea of 'local' bands or clubs of archers is supported by the names of other butts, such as 'Piller of powles,' 'Allhallowes' and 'Basinghall.'

But no one is obliged to accept my theory any more than I am obliged to accept Walter Bell's. The important thing is to think such things out for oneself. Some years ago a writer, discussing the connection between certain London names, ended his article by giving it as his opinion that it was 'unimportant whichever way it was decided'. Such an attitude is incomprehensible to me. The advantage of antiquarian research of this description is surely that when it comes to guessing, the enthusiastic amateur stands as good as, if not a better chance of guessing correctly than the learned professor. The latter must argue logically, whilst the amateur can afford to put forward the most improbable and impudent solutions which, life being a succession of improbable and impudent events, are as likely as not to be right—and even if they are not the learned professor cannot *prove* them to be wrong!

And here is a curious fact to prove my point: In his 'Advertisement' Malcolm specifically thanked 'Mr Ellis of the British Museum', who had 'greatly obliged' him by 'presenting his accurate tracing of the antient plan of Finsbury-fields.'

Now, anxious to know more about this print, and hoping to clear up some of the points I have raised, I wrote to the Librarian of the Bodleian enquiring the date of publication of William Hole's work on archery, and learned that no trace of such a work can be found in the Short Title Catalogue, or British Museum Catalogue, and that it is most unlikely that William Hole ever published a book on archery. So Malcolm's statement was erroneous

View of an Ancient Shooting-match between the

CITIZENS of LONDON.

Representation of a grand SHOOTING MATCH by the London-Archers in the Year 1583.

OLD SADLER'S WELLS. SKETCH AND INSCRIPTION ON THE BACK

and there is a pencil note to that effect in the copy of his work in the Library's Gough collection.

Some time ago I came across a reference to a book called *The Bowman's Glory or Archery Reviewed* by William Wood, published in 1682, and wondered whether this may not have been the book to which Malcolm was intending to refer. A reference to the book would, of course, decide the question, and I applied to Mr J. Swift, the former ever-obliging Librarian of Holborn Library, but drew a blank; he had to report that the book is not in the library of the Royal Toxophilite Society which suffered badly during the war. Unhappily the British Museum collection of books on archery was also blitzed—almost out of existence—so this query must for the time being remain unanswered.

Thomas Edlyne Tomlins, to whose projected but unpublished edition of Stow's *Survey* I referred in Chapter Two, dealt fully with the archers' butts in Finsbury Fields in *Yseldon, a Perambulation of Islington*, which was published in 1858, and the first part of which had already been published in 1844.

My copy has the author's crest pasted in the cover, and is inscribed 'W. J. Lee with his uncle Tomlins best love in remembrance of the Author and of this day Nov. 6th 75'. I wonder what happened on that day?

The Tomlins would appear to have been an interesting couple; he, the nephew of the distinguished legal writer of the same name, Sir Thomas

Edlyne Tomlins, was himself a legal writer; whilst his wife had artistic leanings, as appears by a little sketch of Sadler's Wells lying loose (with a few other scraps—including three copies of their book-plate!) in the (1858) *Yseldon* when I bought it for five shillings in Earls Court Road some twenty years ago. I reproduce the sketch, and also the inscription on the back. The reference to 'Universal Harmony' is a reminder that one may come across references to, and pictures of London in unexpected places.

In his *Yseldon* Tomlins recorded that the print which Malcolm reproduced had been published in *The Gentleman's Magazine* (Vol. CII., P. 1. p. 209), and indeed there are articles on archery in the issues for May, June and July (1832) in which also appears an account of archery in England, and of William Wood, the archer.

It would seem that Malcolm was misinformed, and that William Hole was not the author of a work on archery, but that the print was dedicated by him 'To his affect. friends Mr R. Baker and Mr R. Sharp, and all other lovers of Archery frequenting Finsbury-fields'.

I reproduce, without comment, the view of an ancient Shooting Match taken from Chamberlain's History (1770), and the Representation of the same match taken (even more *le mot juste*) by—and from—Harrison's (1777).

A unique book, which I am pleased to possess, contains thirty-eight eighteenth-century 'Views Near London', which were presumably collected and stuck in the book by 'Thomas Edlyne and Elizabeth Tomlins. 1830', whose crest pasted inside the cover takes the place of a book-plate.

Many of the pictures were the work of John Baptist Claude Philippe, a draughtsman and engraver (1710–1771), who lived in Chelsea, was, says the *Dictionary of National Biography*, 'of improvident habits', and, in the name of Chatelaine, 'engraved chiefly landscapes'.

Amongst the thirty-eight prints is 'A View of St Mary's Church Islington', which was reproduced in Tomlins's *Yseldon* entitled 'South-west View of *old* St Mary's Church, Islington, 1750'.

A View of St Mary's Church Islington.

Printed for Rob.t Sayer Printseller in Fleet Street.

98

5

Some Other London Histories

I have an interesting little pocket book—140 pages of small print (including a two-page index) entitled *A View of London; or, the Stranger's Guide through the British Metropolis*. The frontispiece is headed 'Crosby's View of London' and it was 'Printed for B. Crosby & Co. Stationers' Court, Paternoster-row. By Lewis and Co. Paternoster-row'.

Benjamin Crosby will ever be remembered for having, in 1803, purchased the manuscript of *Northanger Abbey* from Jane Austen for £10. Lacking the confidence to publish it he sold it back to her for the same sum three years later.

'Crosby's View' contains many interesting facts; for instance: 'The Thames is about a quarter of a mile broad, and is continually agitated by a brisk current, or a rapid tide. It is not in general more than twelve feet in depth; but, at spring tides, it sometimes rises fourteen feet above its level.'

Then we are given the following abstract taken from the population returns which had been made under 'An Act for taking an Account of the Population of Great Britain, and of the Increase or Diminution thereof', which had been passed on 31st December 1800.

	In 1700	In 1750	In 1801
1. City of *London* within the walls	139,300	87,000	78,000
2. City of London without the walls (including the Inns of Court)	169,000	156,000	155,000
3. City and Liberties of Westminster	130,000	152,000	165,000
4. Out-parishes, within the bills	226,900	258,900	379,000
5. Parishes, not within the bills	9,150	22,350	123,000
Total of the metropolis	674,350	676,750	900,000

Then, in 'A Sketch of the State of Society and Manners in the English Metropolis', we are told:

'When our country gentlemen first visit *London*, they undergo a complete metamorphosis. The transition from the cool breezes that ventilate their

99

rural retreat to the warm atmosphere of the metropolis, affects those rustics with a malady which may be termed a brain fever; under its influence they become delirious, and madly rush into the vortex of fashionable dissipation. The facility with which the Squire adopts the modish dress, phraseology, effeminacy, and vices, of the townbred rake, is almost incredible.'

London; Being an Accurate History and Description of the British Metropolis and its Neighbourhood to Thirty Miles Extent, From an Actual Perambulation, by David Hughson LL.D., (whose real name was Ed. Pugh) was published in six small octavo volumes between 1805 and 1809, at the price of two pounds. The work is dedicated to George III, with fervent wishes that he and his 'illustrious Successors, and the British Nation, be long preserved a bright example of the joint Confidence, Esteem, and Gratulation of a beloved Monarchy, and a happy Country. . . . May such Happiness consolidate that Fabric which Discord cannot separate, nor Arrogance, with Impunity, invade.' The dedication ends: 'Every Briton, possessing a Constitution replete with such united Blessings must adopt in his prayers—"ESTO PERPETUA!"'

Volume One (562 pages) gives a 'brief' history of London to the end of the year 1800, with full details of various affairs. For instance, there is a detailed 'Account of the Royal Coronation of their most excellent Majesties King George III. and Queen Charlotte, on 22 September, 1761', commencing with the 'Order of the Procession', by 'The King's Herb Woman, with her six Maids, strewing the Way with Herbs.' Then we read 'The Manner of disposing, seating, and placing the several Persons who came in the Grand Procession, after their Entrance into the Church. . . .', The Recognition, the First Oblation, The Litany, The Sermon, The Oath, The Anointing, The Investing, The Crowning, The Investiture per Annulum et Bacculum, The Second Oblation and Benediction, The Inthroning and Homage, and the Anointing, Crowning and Inthroning of the Queen, all given in detail.

The account concludes:

'The celebrated Mr Bonnel Thornton, wrote an entertaining and familiar detail of the particular circumstances attending the Coronation, in a letter to his friend in the country; which, on account of its peculiar merit, is submitted as a close to our description of that magnificent spectacle:

Dear Sir,

Though I regret leaving you so soon, especially as the weather has since proved so fine, that it makes me long to be with you in the country, yet I honestly confess, that I am heartily glad I came to town as I did. As I have seen it, I declare I would not have missed the sight upon any consideration. The friendship of Mr. Rolles, who procured me a pass-ticket, as they call it, enabled me to be present both in the Hall and the

Abbey; and as to the pro-cession out of doors, I had a fine view of it from a one-pair of stairs room, which your neighbour, Sir Edward, had hired at the small price of one hundred guineas, on purpose to oblige his aquaintance. I wish you had been with me; but as you have been deprived of a sight, which probably very few that were present will ever see again, I will endeavour to describe it to you as minutely as I can, while the circumstances are fresh in my memory, though my description must fall very short of the reality. First, then, conceive to yourself the fronts of the houses, in all the streets that could command the least point of view, lined with scaffolding, like so many galleries or boxes raised one above another to the very roofs. These were covered with carpets and cloths of different colours, which presented a pleasing variety to the eye; and if you consider the brilliant appearance of the spectators who were seated in them (many being richly dressed) you will easily imagine this was no indifferent part of the show. The mob underneath made a pretty contrast to the rest of the company. Add to this, though we had nothing but wet and cloudy weather for some time before, the day cleared up, and the sun shone auspiciously, as it were in compliment to the grand festival. The platform, on account of the uncertainty of the weather, had a shelving roof, which was covered with a kind of sail-cloth; but near the place where I was, an honest Jack Tar climbed up to the top and stripped off the covering; which gave us not only a more extensive view, but let the light in upon every part of the procession. I should tell you, that a rank of foot soldiers was placed on each side within the platform; and it was not a little surprising to see the officers familiarly conversing and walking arm in arm with many of them, till we were let into the secret, that they were gentlemen who had put on the dresses of common soldiers, for what purpose I need not mention. On the outside were stationed, at proper distances, several parties of horseguards, whose horses, indeed, somewhat incommoded the people, that pressed incessantly upon them, by their prancing and capering; though luckily, I do not hear of any great mischief being done. I must confess, it gave me much pain, to see the soldiers, both horse and foot, most unmercifully belabouring the heads of the mob with their broadswords, bayonets, and muskets; but it was not unpleasant to observe several tipping the horse soldiers slily from time to time (some with halfpence, and some with silver, as they could muster up the cash) to let them pass between the horses to get nearer the platform; after which these unconscionable gentry drove them back again. As soon as it was day-break (for I chose to go to my place overnight) we were diverted with seeing the coaches and chairs of the nobility and gentry passing along with much ado; and several persons very richly dressed, were obliged to quit their equipages, and be escorted by the soldiers through the mob to their respective places. Several carriages, I am told, received great damage: Mr. Jennings, whom you know, had his chariot broke to pieces; but providentially neither he not Mrs. Jennings, who were in it, received any hurt.

Their majesties (to the shame of those be it spoken who were not so punctual) came in their chairs from St. James's through the Park to Westminster about nine o'clock. The king went into a room which they call the Court of Wards, and the queen into that belonging to the gentleman-usher of the Black-rod. The nobility and others, who were to walk in procession, were mustered and ranged by the officers of arms in the Court of Requests, Painted Chamber, and House of Lords, from whence the cavalcade was conducted into Westminster Hall. As you know all the avenues and places about the Hall, you will not be at a loss to understand me. My pass-ticket would have been of no service, if I had not prevailed on one of the guards, by the irresistible argument of half-a-crown, to make way for me through the mob to the Hall-gate, where I got admittance just as their majesties were seated at the upper end, under magnificent canopies. Her majesty's chair was on the left hand of his majesty; and they were attended by the great chamberlain, lord high constable, earl marshal, and other great officers. Four swords, I observed, and as many spurs, were presented in form, and then placed upon a table before the king.

There was a neglect, it seems somewhere, in not sending for the dean and prebendaries of Westminster, &c. who, not finding themselves summoned, came of their own accord, preceded by the choristers, singers, &c. among whom was your favourite, as indeed he is of everyone, Mr. Beard. The Hall-gate was now thrown open to admit this lesser procession from the Abbey, when the bishop of Rochester (that is, the dean) and his attendants brought the Bible and the following regalia of the king, *viz* St Edward's crown, rested on a cushion of gold cloth, the orb with the cross, a sceptre with the dove on the top, another tipt with a cross, and what they call St Edward's staff. The queen's regalia were brought at the same time, *viz.* her crown upon a cushion, a sceptre with a cross, and a rod of ivory with a dove. These were severally laid before their majesties, and afterwards delivered to the respective officers who were to bear them in procession.

Considering the length of the cavalcade, and the numbers that were to walk, it is no wonder that there should be much confusion in marshalling the ranks. At last, however, everything was regularly adjusted, and the procession began to quit the Hall between eleven and twelve. The platform leading to the west door of the Abbey was covered with blue baize for the train to walk on; but there seemed to me a defect in not covering the upright posts that supported the awning, as it was called, (for they looked mean and naked) with that or some other coloured cloth. As I carry you along, I shall wave mentioning the minute particulars of the procession, and only observe that the nobility walked two by two. Being willing to see the procession pass along the platform through the streets,

I hastened from the Hall, and by the assistance of a soldier made my way to my former station at the corner of Bridge Street, where the windows commanded a double view at the turning. I shall not attempt to describe the splendor and magnificence of the whole; and words must fall short of that innate joy and satisfaction which the spectators felt and expressed, especially as their majesties passed by; on whose countenance a dignity suited to their station, tempered with the most amiable complacency, was sensibly impressed. It was observable that as their majesties and the nobility passed the corner which commanded a prospect of Westminster Bridge, they stopped short, and turned back to look at the people, whose appearance, as they all had their hats off, and were thick planted on the ground, which rose gradually, I can compare to nothing but a pavement of heads and faces.

I had the misfortune not to be able to get to the Abbey time enough to see all that passed there; nor, indeed, when I got in, could I have so distinct a view as I could have wished. But our friend Harry Whitaker had the luck to be stationed in the first row of the gallery behind the seats allotted for the nobility, close to the square platform which was erected by the altar, with an ascent of three steps, for their majesties to be crowned on. You are obliged to him, therefore, for several particulars which I could not otherwise have informed you of. He tells me, as soon as their majesties entered the church, the choir struck up with an anthem; and, after they were seated, and the usual recognition and oblations were made, the litany was chanted by the bishops of Chester and Chichester, and the responses made by the whole choir, accompanied by the whole band of music. Then the first part of the communion-service was read; after which a sermon was preached by the bishop of Salisbury, now archbishop of York. I was not near enough to hear it, nor, perhaps you will say, did I much desire it; but, by my watch, it lasted only fifteen minutes. This done, Harry says he saw very distinctly his majesty subscribe the declaration, and take the coronation oath, the solemnity of which struck him with an unspeakable awe and reverence; and he could not help reflecting on the glorious privilege which the English enjoy, of binding their kings by the most sacred ties of conscience and religion. The king was then anointed by his grace of Canterbury on the crown of his head, his breast, and the palms of his hands; after which he was presented with the spurs, and girt with the sword, and was then invested with the coronation robes, the armills, as they are called, and the imperial pall. The orb with the cross was also presented, and the ring was put upon the fourth finger of his majesty's right hand by the archbishop, who then delivered the sceptre with the cross, and the other with the dove; and being assisted by several bishops, he lastly placed the crown reverently upon his majesty's head. A profound awful silence had reigned till this moment, when, at the very instant the crown was let fall on the king's head, a person having been placed on the top of the Abbey dome, from whence he could look down into the chancel, with a flag which he dropt as a signal; the Park and Tower guns began to fire, the trumpets sounded, and the Abbey echoed with the repeated shouts and acclamations of the people. The peers, who before this time had their coronets in their hands, now put them on, as the bishops did their caps, and the representatives of the dukes of Aquitaine and Normandy their hats. The knights of the Bath in particular made a most splendid figure, when they put on their caps, which were adorned with large plumes of white feathers. It is to be observed, that there were no commoners knights of the Garter; consequently, instead of caps and vestments peculiar to their order, they being all peers, wore their robes and coronets of their respective ranks. I should mention, that the kings of arms also put on coronets.

Silence again assumed her reign, and the shouts ceasing, the archbishop proceeded with the rest of the divine service; and after he had presented the Bible to his majesty, and solemnly read the benedictions, his majesty kissed the archbishops and bishops one after another as they knelt before him. The *Te Deum* was now performed, and this being ended, his majesty was elevated on a superb throne, which all the peers approached in their order, and did their homages.

The coronation of the queen was performed in nearly the same manner with that of his majesty; the archbishop anointed her with the holy oil on the head and the breast, and after he had put the crown upon her head, it was a signal for Princess Augusta and the peeresses to put on their coronets. Her majesty received the sceptre with the cross, and the ivory rod with the dove, and was conducted to a magnificent throne on the left hand of his majesty.

I cannot but lament that I was not near enough to observe their majesties going through the most serious and solemn acts of devotion; but I am told, that the reverent attention which both paid, when (after having made their second oblations) the next ceremony was, their receiving the holy communion, it brought to the mind of every one near them, a proper recollection of the consecrated place in which they were. Prayers being over, the king and queen retired into St Edward's Chapel, just behind the altar. You must remember it—it is where the superstition of the Roman Catholics has robbed the tomb of that royal confessor of some of its precious ornaments: here their majesties received each of them a crown of state, as it is called, and a procession was made in the same manner as before, except in some trifling instances, back again to Westminster Hall, all wearing their coronets, caps, &c. You know I have often said, that if one loses an hour in the morning, one may ride after it the whole day without being able to overtake it. This was the case in the present instance for, to whatever causes it might be owning, the procession most assuredly set off too late: besides, according to what Harry observed, there were such long pauses between some of the ceremonies in the Abbey, as plainly shewed all the actors were not perfect in their parts. However it be, it is impossible to conceive the chagrin and disappointment which the late return of the procession occasioned; it being so late indeed, that the spectators, even in the open air, had but a very dim and gloomy view of it, while to those who had sat patiently in Westminster Hall, waiting its return for six hours, scarce a glimpse of it appeared, as the branches were not lighted till just upon his majesty's entrance. I had flattered myself that a new scene of splendid grandeur would have been presented to us in the return of the procession, from the reflection of the lights, &c. and had therefore posted back to the Hall with all possible expedition; but not even the brilliancy of the ladies jewels, or the greater lustre of their eyes, had the power to render our *darkness visible;* the whole was confusion, irregularity, and disorder.

However, we were afterwards amply recompensed for this partial eclipse by the bright picture which the lighting of the chandeliers presented to us. Your unlucky law-suit has made you too well acquainted with Westminster Hall for me to think of describing it to you; but I assure you the face of it was greatly altered from what it was when you attended to hear the verdict given against you. Instead of the inclosures for the courts of Chancery and King's Bench at the upper end, which were both removed, a platform was raised with several ascent of steps, where their majesties in their chairs of state, and the royal family, sat at table. On each side, down the whole length of the Hall, the rest of the company were seated at long tables, in the middle of which were placed, on elevations painted to represent marble, the desserts, &c. Conceive to yourself, if you can conceive, what I own I am at a loss to describe, so magnificent a building as that of Westminster Hall, lighted up with near three thousand wax-candles in most splendid branches; our crowned heads, and almost the whole nobility, with the prime of our gentry, most superbly arrayed and adorned with a profusion of the most brilliant jewels; the galleries on every side crowded with company for the most part elegantly dressed: but to conceive it in all its lustre, I am conscious that it is absolutely necessary one must have been present. To proceed in my narration—Their majesties table was served with three courses, at the first of which Earl Talbot, as steward of his majesty's household, rode up from the Hall gate to the steps leading to where their majesties sat; and on his returning the spectators were presented with an unexpected sight, in his lordship's backing his horse, that he might keep his face still towards the king. A loud clapping and huzzaing consequently ensued from the people present. The ceremony of the champion, you may remember we laughed at, at its representation last winter; but I assure you it had a very serious effect on those ladies who were near him (though his horse was very gentle) as he came up, accompanied by Lord Effingham as earl-marshal, and the Duke of Bedford as lord high-constable, likewise on horseback: it is needless to repeat what passed on this occasion. I am told, that the horse which the champion rode was the same that his late majesty was mounted on at the glorious and memorable battle of Dettingen. The beast, as well as the rider, had his head adorned with a plume of white, red, and blue feathers.

You cannot expect that I should give you a bill of fare, or enumerate the number of dishes that were provided and sent from the temporary kitchens erected in Cotton Garden for this purpose. No less than sixty haunches of venison, with a surprizing quantity of all sorts of game, were laid in for this grand feast: but that which chiefly attracted our eyes, was their majesties dessert, in which the confectioner had lavished all his ingenuity in rock-work and emblematical figures. The other desserts were no less admirable for their expressive devices. But I must not forget to tell you, that when the company came to be seated, the poor knights of the Bath had been overlooked, and no table provided for them; an airy apology, however, was served up to them instead of a substantial dinner; but the two junior knights, in order to preserve their rank of precedency to their successors, were placed at the head of the judges table, above all the learned brethren of the coif. The peers were placed on the outermost side of the tables, and the peeresses within, nearest to the walls. You cannot suppose that there was the greatest order imaginable observed during the dinner, but must conclude, that some of the company were as eager and impatient to satisfy the craving of their appetite as any of your country squires at a race or assize ordinary.

It was pleasant to see the various stratagems made use of by the company in the galleries to come in for a snack of the good things below. The ladies clubbed their handkerchiefs to be tied together to draw up a chicken or a bottle of wine; nay, even garters (I will not say of a different sex) were united for the same purpose. Some had been so provident as to bring baskets with them, which were let down, like the prisoners boxes at Ludgate or the Gate House, with a *Pray, remember the poor.*

You will think it high time that I should bring this long letter to a conclusion. Let it suffice then to acquaint you, that their majesties returned to St. James's a little after ten o'clock at night; but they were pleased to give time for the peeresses to go first, that they might not be incommoded by the pressure of the mob to see their majesties. After the nobility were departed, the illustrious *mobility* were (according to custom) admitted into the Hall, which they presently cleared of all the moveables, such as the victuals, cloths, plates, dishes, &c. and, in short, every thing that could stick to their fingers.

I need not tell you that several coronation medals, in silver, were thrown among the populace at the return of the procession. One of them was pitched into Mrs. Dixon's lap, as she sat upon a scaffold in Palace Yard. Some, it is said were also thrown among the peeresses in the Abbey just after the king was crowned; but they thought it below their dignity to stoop to pick them up.

My wife desires her compliments to you: she was *hugeously* pleased with the sight. All friends are well, except that little Nancy Green has got a swelled face, by being up all night; and Tom Moffat has his leg laid upon a stool, on account of a broken shin, which he got by a kick from a trooper's horse, as a reward for his mobbing it. I shall say nothing of the illuminations at night: the newspapers must have told you of them, and that the Admiralty in particular was remarkably lighted up. I expect to have from you an account of the rejoicings at your little town; and desire to know whether you was able to get a slice of the ox which was roasted whole on this occasion.

Since my writing the above, I have been informed for certain, that the sword of state, by some mistake, being left behind at St. James's, the lord mayor's sword was carried before the king by the Earl of Hunting-don, in its stead; but when the procession came into the Abbey the sword of state was found placed upon the altar.

Our friend Harry, who was upon the scaffold, at the return of the procession closed in with the rear; at the expence of half-a-guinea was admitted into the Hall; got brim-full of his majesty's claret; and, in the universal plunder, brought off the glass her majesty drank in, which is placed in the beaufait as a valuable curiosity.'

In Volume Two the Administration of London is described, and the reader is conducted round the wards east of the Royal Exchange in four of those 'perambulations' of which the old historians were so fond. There are a few illuminating anecdotes as, for instance, one which relates how when Mar-shal La Condamine first saw the pavement of the City he fell upon his knees and exclaimed—'God be praised! This is a country in which *foot-passengers* pass for something!'

Volume Two includes an old ballad entitled London Lyckpeny (or Lackpenny), written by John Lydgate, a Benedictine monk of Bury St Edmunds some 500 years ago. It is worth quoting in full, since it gives a humorous description of London in the time of Henry V, by a poor country-man who, having lost his hood in Westminster Hall, saw it hung up for sale in Cornhill, which at that time was inhabited by fripperers or upholders, who sold old clothes and household furniture. This ballad is full of topographical allusions, and contains the earliest mention of London street cries.

LONDON LYCKPENY.

A Ballade compyled by Dan John Lydgate Monke of Berry, about — yeres agoe, and now newly oversene and amended.

> To London once my stepps I bent,
> Where trouth in no wyse should be faynt;

To Westmynster ward I forthwith went
To a man of law to make complaynt:
I sayd, fore Mary's love, that holy saynt,
Pity the poore that would proceede;
But fore lack of mony I cold not spede.

And as I thrust the prese amonge,
By froward chaunce my hood was gone,
Yet for all that I stayd not longe
Tyll at the kynge bench I was come:
Before the judge I kneled anon
And prayd him for God's sake to take hede;
But fore lack of Money I myght not spede.

Beneth them sat clarkes a great rout,
Which fast dyd wryte by one assent;
There stoode up one and cryed about
Rychard, Robert, and John of Kent:
I wist not well what this man ment,
He cryed thycke there indede;
But he that lackt mony myght not spede.

Unto the common place I yode thoo,
Where sat one with a sylken hoode;
I dyd hym reverence for I ought to do so,
And told my case as well as I coud,
How my goods were defrauded me by falshood;
I gat not a man of his mouth for my meed,
And for lack of mony I myght not spede.

Unto the Rolls I gat me from thence,
Before the clarkes of the chauncerye;
Where many I found earnyng of pence,
But none at all regarded mee;
I gave them my playnt uppon my knee,
They lyked it well, when they had it reade;
But lacking mony I could not be sped.

In Westmynster-hall I found out one
Which went in a long gown of raye,
I crouched and kneled before hym anon,
For Mary's love of help I hym praye;
'I wot not what thou meanest' gan he say;
To get me thence he dyd me bede,
For lack of money, I cold not spede.

Within this hall neithere ryche nor yett poor
Wold do for me ought although I shold dye;
Which seeing I gat me out of th' doore,
Where Flemynge began on me for to cry,
'Master, what will you copen or by;
'Fyne felt hatts or spectacles to reede
'Lay down your sylver, and here you may spede.'

Then to Westmynster gate I presently went,
When the sunn was at hyghe pryme;
Cokes to me they tooke good entent
And profered me bread with ale and wyne;
Rybbs of befe both fat and ful fyne,
A fayre cloth they gan for to sprede
But wantyng mony I might not be speede.

Then unto London I dyd me hye,
Of all the land it beareth the pryse;
Hot pescods one began to crye
Strabery rype and cherryes in the ryste:
One bad me come nere and by some spyce
Peper and sayforne they gan me bede
But fore lacke of mony I myght not spede.

Then to the Chepe I began me drawne,
Where mutch people I sawe for to stande;
One ofred me velvet, sylke, and lawne,
And othere he taketh me by the haunde,
'Here is Paris thred the finest in the launde',
I never was used to such things in dede
And wanting mony I myght not spede.

Then went I forth by London Stone
Throughout all Canwyke street
Drapers mutch cloth me ofred anone
Then comes me one, cryd 'hot shepes feete';
One cryde mackerell ryster greene, other gan greete,
One bad me by a hood to cover my head,
But for want of mony I might not be sped.

Then I hyed me into Estchepe,
One cryes rybbs of befe and many a pye;
Pewter potts they clattered on a heape,
There was harpe, pype, and mynstrelsye;

'Yea by cock,' 'nay by cock' some began crye;
Some sang of Jenken and Julyan fore there mede,
But fore lack of mony I myght not spede.

Then into Cornhyll anon I yode,
Where was much stolen gere amonge;
I saw where honge myne own hoode,
That I had lost amonge the thronge:
To by my own hood I thought it wronge,
I knew it well as I dyd my crede,
But for lack of mony I could not spede.

The Taverner took me by the sleve,
'Sir,' sayth he, 'wyll you our wyne assay';
I answered, 'That can not mutch me greve,
A penny can do no more than it may':
I dranke a pynt and for it dyd pay,
Yet sore a hungered from thence I yede.
And wanting my mony I cold not spede.

Then hyed I me to Belynges Gate,
And one cryed "Hoo, go we hence:'
I prayd a barge man for God's sake,
That he would spare me my expence;
'Thou stepst not here,' quo' he, 'under ij pence,'
I lyst not yet bestow my almes dede;
Thus lacking mony I could not spede.

Then I conveyed me into Kent;
For of the law wold I meddle no more,
Because no man to me took entent,
I dyght me to do as I dyd before:
Now Jesus that in Bethlem was bore
Save London, and send trew lawyers there mede
For who so wants mony with them shall not spede.

Explicit London Lyckpenny.

In Volume Three we are taken on five perambulations westward of the
Royal Exchange. The history of the Bank of England is particularly entertaining; and there is an interesting paper 'which was printed and circulated by
some friend' of the Bank of England on the 13th March 1797 to convince and
reassure 'that part of the public not immediately concerned or connected with
commercial affairs' who 'were cautious in receiving Bank notes'. The final

paragraph is worth quoting: 'Under these circumstances, nothing short of a collusion or confederacy (which is inconceivable) between the government and the Bank, can furnish a doubt of the solidity and ultimate security of Bank notes', after which it is pleasant to read that in November 1797 '*After paying every demand upon them*' the Bank of England 'possessed, upon the national faith, a clear balance in their favour of FIFTEEN MILLIONS, FIVE HUNDRED AND THIRTEEN THOUSAND, SIX HUNDRED AND NINETY POUNDS STERLING'!

Volume Four concludes the history of London and includes Westminster, Southwark and the Suburbs in Surrey with an appendix containing 'Remarks on the Costume of the Court and Citizens of London, from the Norman Conquest To the present Period'.

This appendix is lightly written and amusing. It gives such information as that in the time of George III 'Every modish gentleman seemed by the length of his *skirts*, to be dutch wasted; they hung so low, that on a wet day a wag called out '*pray, dear sir, pin up your petticoats!*'

Volumes Five and Six describe the environs of London from such suburbs as Paddington and Kensington out to Hemel Hempstead and Dagenham, and the volume closes with a list of subscribers with their addresses. Each of the volumes is indexed and has a number of maps and illustrations scattered throughout.

A more formal work appeared in 1806. This was *The History and Survey of London and its Environs from the Earliest Period to the Present Time* in four volumes by B. Lambert, 'Editor of Berthollet's Chemical Statics; Michaux's Travels in America; Villiers' Essay on the Reformation; and Various other Works'.

In his search for novelty Lambert added 'Biographical Sketches of Eminent Men, Born in or connected with London and its Environs,' and in his 'Advertisement' he claims that this 'department . . . may be considered a new feature in a history of London.'

I have no great liking for this work; and find it heavy—in places dull, and the fifty-four prints and two maps are uninspiring. But I could not resist the temptation to buy the set which came from the collection formed by Sir Thomas Phillips Bt. (1792–1872). There are five prints missing, but several extra ones, mostly from Malcolm, have been added, whilst the books are beautifully bound—and a delight to handle.

The work does not often appear on the shelves of the second-hand bookseller; the last time I saw it one of the volumes was missing—and the price was a guinea.

The first volume of *London and Middlesex; or an Historical, Commercial & Descriptive Survey of the Metropolis of Great-Britain: Including Sketches of its Environs and a Topographical Account of the Most Remarkable Places in the Above County*, 'Illustrated with Engravings. In two Volumes by Edward Wedlake Brayley', was published in 1810 'Printed by W. Wilson, St John's Square, for Vernor, Hood, and Sharpe; Longman, Hurst, Rees, Orme, and Brown; J. Cuthell; J. Harris; J. Cundee; B. Crosby and Co.; and J. and J. Richardson'.

The volume is dedicated to the Lord Mayor and the Aldermen, and the common Councillors, while the 'Advertisement', dated from Newman Street, 1st Sept 1810, explains how it was found 'impossible to confine the *Survey of Middlesex* to the limits originally proposed,' that it was therefore intended to devote two volumes to that survey, and to sell them separately from the rest of the work. Consequently a 'distinct Title page' was being prepared 'for the conveniency of those' who wished to purchase the *London and Middlesex*. The 'Advertisement' goes on: 'continued illness of the Author, an Illness of several successive years, and from which, till the present summer, recovery had long seemed hopeless to him, has occasioned great Delay and irregularity in the Publication of the different numbers of this Volume.'

This explains why the second volume was not published until 1814, and in the meantime the publishers had become 'J. Harris; Longman & Co; J. Walker; R. Baldwin; Sherwood and Co; J. and J. Cundee; B. and R. Crosby and Co; J. Cuthell; J. and J. Richardson; Cadell and Davies; C. and J. Rivington; and Cowie and Co.' The 'Advertisement' explains that the 'Volume, as far as page 720', (there are only 803 pages in the volume) 'is the composition of Mr Brayley; but, for several reasons not requisite to be stated in this place, it became necessary to engage another Editor to finish it: accordingly Mr Nightingale undertook to conclude Mr Brayley's very interesting History and Description of the East India Company and House, in Leadenhall Street, and with that account, and the usual Indexes etc, etc, to the end of the volume.'

Mr Joseph Nightingale excused himself with the reader for any defects in his work, explaining how difficult it was 'to continue the narrative with that spirit and uniformity of manner and character in which it had been begun', and that 'the train of Mr Brayley's authorities was not easily discovered'.

He added that he had not had an opportunity of conferring with Mr Brayley, which would seem to indicate friction, because Brayley was by no means 'done for'; indeed, in 1828 he produced his *Londiniana*; four octavo volumes of disconnected stories, well illustrated and priced at two guineas. He was the Librarian and Secretary of Russell Institution, Great Coram Street, from 1825 until his death in 1854.

The work was continued: a third volume, containing over 750 pages, was published in 1815. In his 'Advertisement' to this volume Nightingale remarked that 'The candid reader will have observed the difficulty under which it has been executed, arising chiefly from a deficiency of information respecting the precise plan intended to have been adopted by my predecessor, had he completed it.'

A fourth volume, containing Volume Three—Part II, was also published in 1815. It was dedicated to the Rt. Hon. Charles Abbott, M.P., speaker of the House of Commons, with the explanation that 'the condescending politeness which you have shown in permitting both myself and Mr. J. P. Neale, our Artist, to enrich and embellish the Work with views and descriptions of your own House, and of such other places as are immediately under your care and government, have heightened that hope into an assurance, that your wonted liberality will be exercised in excusing whatever imperfections may appear to your cultivated taste.'

J. Norris Brewer edited a fifth volume, containing Volume Four, which was published in 1816. His dedication is worth quoting:

TO THE

MOST NOBLE AND PUISSANT PRINCE,

DUKE AND EARL OF NORTHUMBERLAND, HIS GRACE, HUGH,

Earl Percy; Lord Percy, Lucy, Poynings, Fitz-Payne,
Bryan, and Latimer; Baron Warkworth, of
Warkworth Castle, K. G. &c. &c.

MY LORD,

With sentiments of profound Respect, and feelings of the most lively Gratitude, I take advantage of the permission so condescendingly allowed, and presume to dedicate to your Grace the following Delineations in the County of Middlesex. I shall ever consider the hour in which I was honoured with this Permission, to be the most flattering, and the most truly pleasing, in my literary life.

Emboldened by the benign condescension of your Grace, I venture, thus publickly, to return heartfelt thanks for the notice with which I was favoured during my investigations of SYON HOUSE, the noblest residence, independent of the Royal Palaces, which ornaments the County that I have been engaged in describing.

A gracious readiness of communication, when the interests of Literature would appear to be implicated, might be expected from a Nobleman so anxious to uphold in every particular the true dignity of his country;—but the manner in which your Grace was pleased to communicate to me information, has rendered your condescension of indelible value to me as an individual, and is calculated to impress fresh Respect for the dignified rank of which your Grace, by Birth, by Talents, and by Virtues, is one of the most conspicuous members.

Pardon me, my Lord, if I trespass on your indulgence by the freedom of my Expressions. They proceed from the zeal of veneration creat-
ed by your kindness.

> I have the Honour to be,
> My Lord,
> Your Grace's
> Devoted, and Most Obedient, Servant,
>
> J. NORRIS BREWER.

Kennington, Surrey.
January 7th, 1816.

In his prefatory remarks Mr Brewer explained the difficulties encounter-
ed by Mr Brayley, Mr Nightingale and himself who each executed his part
'without a previous inspection by either party of the portion contributed by
the other.'

Various persons are thanked for help received—with a special mention
of the clergy of Middlesex, who 'almost invariably endeavoured to facilitate
my object by introducing me to sources which promised other novelty of
intelligence.' An asterisk after the word 'invariably' refers the reader to the
following footnote: 'If the Vicar of Hillingdon appeared to treat me, and the
subject of my investigations, with indifference, it undoubtedly arose from his
want of inclination for topographical pursuits, owing, possibly, to an exclusive attachment to more serious studies.'

Another, and even more cutting footnote records: 'Although an unpleasing duty it is equally imperative on the writer to state unkindness as to
acknowledge favours. Mr. Middleton, who drew up for the consideration of
the Board of Agriculture "A General View of the Agriculture of Middlesex",
declined to communicate to me such intelligence as he might chance to
possess, owing to a "distaste for the County of Middlesex". The intelligence
thus witheld was, probably, of little consequence to the work in which I was
engaged.'

Then, after a reference to the Manor House at Cranford in Middlesex is
the footnote: 'The Countess of Berkeley refused us permission to view the
interior of Cranford Lodge, but we are informed that in addition to family
pictures, there are original portraits of Fuller, the historian; Dr Harvey;
Dean Swift; Sir William Temple; and several other persons of public
interest.

'It may not be obtrusive to observe in this place, the residence of Lady
Berkeley is the only mansion appertaining to nobility in the County of Middlesex, to which we have been denied admission for the purpose of making
such remarks as might assist in rendering our topographical undertaking
satisfactory to the public.'

He records that there was one other 'seat in the County' which was not 'politely opened to my inspection'; it was 'the residence of—Calvert, Esq. at Whitton'.

This is an entertaining volume, and the whole set is well worth acquiring. Authorities are given for statements made, and while it is not possible to quote from each of the volumes, as a postscript to the account in Hughson's *History of the Coronation of George III* the following extract from Volume III of Brayley's (or Nightingale's) *History* details some of the Jubilee celebrations on 25th October 1809 when George III entered into the fiftieth year of his reign: 'The illuminations of the public buildings and offices were unusually tasteful and splendid on the occasion; to heighten the public joy, a proclamation was also issued for pardoning all deserters from the Fleet, whether they returned to their duty or not. Another proclamation announced the pardon of all deserters from the land forces, provided they surrendered in two months. The Lords of the Admiralty ordered an extra allowance of four pounds of beef; three quarters of flour, and a pound of raisins to every eight men in his Majesty's ships in port, or half a pint of rum each man. Eleven Crown debtors were also on this occasion discharged from prison by the Society for the relief of persons confined for Small Debts.'

At the end of the first volume is a 'List of the Principal Books, Maps, Plans and Prints that have been published in Illustration of the Antiquities, History, Topography, and other Subjects treated of in this Volume.' The list is prefaced with the words 'Middlesex and London', and it is followed by a short section headed 'Maps, Plans and Prints.' The fourth volume contains a similar list of books dealing with the County of Middlesex.

There is an intriguing reference in the list in volume four to a projected work by the Rev. Joseph Nightingale—'After a labour of many years, the Editor of the present Volume of the History of London and Westminster, has nearly completed '*The Dictionary of London*; or, A complete Guide to every Place, Office, Object or Matter of Public Importance in the Cities of London and Westminster; the Borough of Southwark and the Suburbs in general; giving plain and easy Directions concerning the Place, Time, Terms, and best Methods of Transacting Business at all the government offices, India Warehouses, Houses of Chartered Companies, Societies, Institutions, Establishments, and places of Public resort, whether commercial, literary, scientific, political, ecclesiastical, or recreative.'—A truly noble 'prospectus', which was followed by a second, and even longer paragraph describing the three parts into which it was proposed to divide the work, and which concluded 'To be continued annually'.

The Dictionary of London is not referred to in Lowndes, and I have never come across a copy. It is not to be confused with Henry A. Harben's *A Dictionary of London* to which I have already referred.

The five books were published at six guineas; I bought my copies in Bedford some years ago for fifteen shillings.

In 1811, nine years after the author's death, *The History of London, Containing an Account of the Origin of the City*, by the late Rev. Henry Hunter, D.D. and other Gentlemen, appeared. It was printed for John Stockdale, Piccadilly, by S. Gosnell, Little Queen Street, Holborn. It had been published in parts, the first of which appeared in 1776, and a second volume containing an account of all the towns, villages and country within twenty-five miles of London was published at the same time. I have a copy of the first volume only. The preface, which is dated 20th February, 1811, explains: 'In a work of this magnitude, a considerable time must necessarily elapse from its commencement to its completion; but it will be admitted, that, in the execution of the volumes now offered to the public, a much longer space has been employed than could have been anticipated. To readers in general, it would be uninteresting to detail the causes of this delay. They have been such that the proprietor could neither foresee, nor prevent.' 'Magnitude' was the right word—the first volume contained 924 pages in elephant quarto, and the second 811.

After a short description of the growth of London's docks and the canals which lead into and out of London, the author tells us that he has 'reason to believe, that, by the introduction of canal navigation into some of the inland counties, more than 15,000 horses have been dispensed with, as unnecessary to the purposes for which they formerly had been used', and that land previously cultivated to feed these horses will be 'applied to the production of food for man', that wheat will be grown instead of oats with the grand result that 'we shall hereafter become much less dependent on our neighbours for bread, the great support of life.'

The list of subscribers, without addresses, and numbering nearly 500, included Thomas Pennant, one Bernard Shaw, and Lord Braybrooke, who many years later was to edit the fourth edition of Pepys' *Diary*. The Grand Junction Canal Company also subscribed for a copy, perhaps as some return for being mentioned in the preface! Another prepublication purchaser was Dr J. C. Lettsom, 1744–1815, the doctor who insisted upon signing his prescriptions with the old-fashioned initial 'I', and who has been immortalized in the following rhyme:

> If any folk applies to I,
> I blisters, bleeds and sweats 'em;
> If after that they please to die,
> Well, what cares I? I Lettsom.'

We are told about a project for a tunnel under the Thames and another

VIEW of TEMPLE-BAR.

Published Feb.y 23.d 1799, by I.Stockdale, Piccadilly.

one through Highgate Hill—'A cold, wet, and noisome cavern, about a mile and a quarter long'. The House of Commons rejected it. 'Other projects of the day' included bridges across the Thames—'one at Vauxhall; a second to open into the Strand, opposite Catherine Street; and a third from the bottom of Queen Street, Cheapside', and all of which it was presumed 'must demand very heavy tolls'.

I reproduce one of the volume's fourteen prints—a View of Temple Bar Looking Eastward—it shows Stockdale's Advertisement for the History: on a placard are the words 'Stockdale's History of London'. On the left of the clock of St Dunstan's in the west, is the famous old bulk shop. The last of its kind, it was removed in 1846. Upon its face was inscribed 'Short and Son, late Creed, Fishmonger, established in the reign of King Henry VIII'.

The title page of *Memorials of Temple Bar* by T. C. Noble does not give the date of publication, but both the dedication (to the Lord Mayor, of course!) and the preface are dated 6th November 1869. The book, which the author claims is the first one to be devoted to the history of Temple Bar, contains, one would imagine, everything that can possibly be said on the subject, and the statements are well documented. Noble, however, entertained hopes of writing an even 'more worthy work' on the subject, and asked that information for such a book might be sent to him care of Messrs. C. & G. Noble, Booksellers, 312 Strand.

I only paid half a crown for my copy which contains a hand-written *Errata* slip (with only two items) signed by the author from '79 Great Dover Street, London'.

The stones and other material of Temple Bar were numbered and carted away to vacant ground in Farringdon Road in January 1878. There were suggestions for re-erecting the old bar in the grounds of Mr Gurney at Stratford, and on the Thames Embankment. However, on 3rd December 1888 it was re-erected at the entrance to Sir Henry Meux's private grounds at Theobalds, Waltham Cross. And there it still stands.

I also paid only half a crown for a small octavo book published in 1821, entitled *A History of London, from the Earliest Period to the Present Time*, 'with some account of the present state of its most important public buildings; compiled from the best authorities. By John William Abbott, Esq.'. I bought it because it contained as frontispiece a portrait of 'Mr Alderman Wood, M.P. Twice Lord Mayor of London.'

It was to the house of Alderman Wood in South Audley Street that the unhappy Queen Caroline, Consort of George IV, went on 6th June 1820 on returning from the Continent to assert her rights on the death of King George III. In 1837—sixteen years after the book was published—Queen Victoria, at the Guildhall, bestowed her first title—a baronetcy on Sir Matthew Wood.

The History and Antiquities of London, Westminster, Southwark and Parts

Wivell delt.

Cooper sculpt.

Mr. ALDERMAN WOOD, M.P.

Twice Lord Mayor of London.

London, Printed for Thos. Kelly, 17, Paternoster Row, July 1,1820.

119

Adjacent by Thomas Allen 'with engravings', was published in four octavo volumes in 1827–8.

In his preface the author recorded that 'his sole ambition was to be correct and impartial: his first object, to ascertain what was true; his second, to relate those truths in a plain unvarnished manner.'

The result is a soundly documented history of London and its wards through the ages, not so anecdotal or easy to read as Hughson, but preferable to Brayley.

I enjoy browsing through these volumes, whilst the engravings, by the author, (some of them were dedicated to different people), have an unusual interest, by reason of the author's dual personality as writer and artist.

Allen reproduced many interesting documents. For example, the second volume includes the seventeen regulations, imposed in 1586 when England was threatened by the Spanish Armada, under the title of 'The Manner of ordering the Citizens of London, to the Safekeeping and defence of Her Majesty's City, against the traitorous and sudden Attempts of all Conspirators and Traitors whatsoever'. One or two of them may be accepted as evidence that history repeats itself, for the dangers of the present were also the dangers of the past. For instance, no. 9: 'For quenchings of sudden fiers, yt will be necessarie to have a thowsand trustie persons to carry leather bucketts and ladders; and that to them of the graver cittyzens, there be appoynted leaders, to lead them as nede may be, by hundred and fifties, for to be ready to releve anye fiered place. And that likewise under like leading, there be appointed five-hundred pyoners, with mattockes and shovels, ready to make tranches and rampyers at all occasions.'

Then no. 16: 'That such recusants as have greate houses and lodgings within the liberties of the Citties; and likewise all dangerous and suspicious persons to the state, may by her majestie's authority be removed from lodging within the walles of the cittie (or suburbs yf that may be), for those houses are like to harbour and cover dangerous persons, to be nearer and readyer to make suddeyn invasion upon the cittie'—nothing was said as to where this 'Fifth Column' was to be removed.

There is also reprinted, in the same volume, 'on account of its extreme scarcity and curiosity' a small tract published by John Day, 'containing the customs and orders for meeting on particular days, and for wearing the habits' prescribed by 'the court of lord mayor and aldermen' in 1562, 'for fixing the days whereon their several coloured robes should be worn'. There were thirty-two such days, and the tract shows when scarlet gowns are to be worn, and when violet with or without cloaks, with or without furs—and with or without horses. Such days range from attendances *On St Bartholomew's even, for the fair in Smithfield* (violet gowns lined, without cloaks, with horses), *On St Bartholomew's day for wrestling* (scarlet gowns lined—and horses to be

brought to them after dinner), to *Good Friday* when 'My Lord and the aldermen' were to meet at St Paul's-cross, at one of the clock, to hear the sermon,
in their pewk gowns, and without their chains and tippets.'

Many changes having occurred during the succeeding 200 years, Allen
thoughtfully brought the information up to date, by reference to another
pamphlet published in 1789, entitled 'The names and addresses of the several
officers of the city of London, the dates of their appointments, and an abstract
of their respective duties; and also a state of the customs on elections, and
other public occasions, prepared by the direction of the court of common
council'.

In the fourth volume of his *History*, when referring to Westminster Abbey
and the coronations performed there, Allen excuses himself—'want of space
prevents the notice of many curious customs now disused in that imposing
ceremony, but it would be improper to pass over the *Coronation of his most
excellent majesty King George IV, on Thursday the 19th day of July, 1821.*' This is
even fuller than Hughson's account of the Coronation of George III. It
commences with the 'Arrangement for the assembling of the peers and
officers . . . from the official programme, printed by order of lord Howard of
Effingham, acting for the earl marshal of England'.

Following the accounts of the two ceremonies through one can note little
differences, both in the procedure and the description of it. For instance,
whilst Hughson expanded himself on the grouping round King George III
during the sermon which was preached by the Bishop of Salisbury (nominated
to the See of York), Allen tells us that the sermon preached by the Archbishop of York before George IV, was on the text 'He that ruleth over men
must be just' (II Samuel 23.3 & 4.), and lasted from twelve fifteen to about
a quarter to one.

At the end of this volume is 'A List of the Principal Books, etc. that have
been published in Illustration of the Antiquities, History, Topography, and
other subjects treated of in this Work', most of which had already been
listed by Brayley, Nightingale and Brewer.

The work is well worth acquiring; I paid twelve shillings and sixpence
for Volumes I, II and III, thirty years ago, and sixpence for Volume IV
(lacking a list of the contents and an index) twenty years later.

Then recently I was lucky enough to find the second edition: the first
volume was published in 1830, and the second, third and fourth, 'continued
to the present time, by Thomas Wright, Esq. of Trin. Coll. Cambridge,
Author of '*History of Essex* etc.' in 1839. A fifth volume, for which Thomas
Wright was also responsible, and which includes the suburbs, was published
in 1837—five years after Allen's death, at the age of thirty.

In 1828, *The Wards of London* was published; 'comprising a Historical and
Topographical Description of every object of importance within the Boun-

daries of the City with an account of all the Companies, Institutions, Buildings, Ancient Remains, etc. etc. and Biographical Sketches of all Eminent Persons concerned therewith', in two octavo volumes by Henry Thomas. Despite the poor illustrations I do not regret having paid twelve shillings and sixpence for the two volumes.

In the issue of *The Gentleman's Magazine* for June 1832 the following paragraph appeared:

'A new *History of London and Westminster* is commenced in monthly numbers, price 1s. It is expected to consist of 32 parts, or four volumes. This work is intended for what are now called, *par excellence*, "the useful classes of society". Compilations, termed "Histories of London", have of late been frequently published, but every work relative to this great metropolis is sure of a ready support. We heartily wish some spirited publisher would undertake a complete History of London and Westminster, founded on the last edition of Stow's Survey, and brought down to the present time. Such a valuable work is much wanted.' Unfortunately there is no clue as to the author of the History.

Peter Cunningham's *Hand-Book of London, Past and Present*, was published in 1849. The preface which is dated from 'Victoria Road, Kensington 1st June, 1849' is interesting because it details the wide research the author made over a period of seven years to enable him to write the book.

Cunningham tells us that he had made considerable progress with the book, on the basis of a progressive narrative, before scrapping what he had written in favour of giving the results of his researches, and the substance of all the passages relating to the several streets or buildings 'the *ipsissima verba* of every writer in the manner of a dictionary maker', contenting himself, as he says 'with receiving the character which Dr Johnson assigns to a dictionary maker, of being at the best a harmless drudge', and he explains the advantages of the dictionary form—'for the visitor who finds himself in a certain street, or near a certain building, and wishes to read on the spot whatever is known about them, has, where the alphabetical order is followed out, only one reference to make—he goes direct to the article itself.'

I quote another paragraph from the preface because it clears up doubts and difficulties which must perplex many people as they read some of the earlier histories of London:

'The materials from which this work has been composed are of a varied, and not unfrequently, of an original character. I have not contented myself with mere references to the best books about London; I claim the merit, such as it is, of being the first writer on the subject who has not confounded Stow with his continuators, with Munday and with Strype. The student who turns to the following pages will not find Stow, who died in the reign of James I., describing streets and buildings not laid out or erected till thirty,

or more frequently full a hundred, years after his death. Nor have I confounded Strype with *his* continuators; the 1720 edition of Strype's Stow is
here kept apart from the edition of 1754, published seventeen years after his
death, with the additions to which he had nothing to do. As little have I confounded Maitland with *his* continuator, Entick; for Maitland was in no new
way connected with what is called the best edition of Maitland's London; he
was dead long before it was published, and his own edition, that in one
volume folio, 1739, is very unlike the two thick volumes folio of 1775. Stow's
own text is only to be read in its integrity in the editions of 1598 and 1603,
and in the careful reprint of 1842, superintended by Mr Thoms. Strype's
own text (the text for which he is responsible) is only to be found in the
edition of 1720; and Maitland's own text in the folio volume of 1739. These
I have been especially careful to consult on all occasions, and nowhere to
confound with editions which bear the original authors' names, but are not
theirs.'

I paid four shillings for 'A New Edition corrected and enlarged', which
was published in one volume in 1850: The preface (dated from Victoria
Road, Kensington, 8th April, 1850) listed the several authorities (who were
not named in the first edition), who had assisted the author, both in the
writing of the work, as well as in its revision and expansion, and it serves as a
reminder that it would not be so simple to compile a similar list of *popular*
writers on London history and topography today.

The book contains 'A Chronology of London Occurrences', Cunningham
claimed it as 'the first of the kind', and anyone with a good memory who is
prepared to spend time studying it should soon be able to pose as an authority
on the history of London!

Hatton, with an alphabetical list of streets etc, in his *New View of London*
in 1708, laid the bare foundations for the dictionary method of a history of
London, whilst the anonymous author of the six volumes, published by R.
and J. Dodsley in 1761, erected a capital building on those foundations.
Cunningham's *Hand-Book* is to Dodsley what a modern block of flats is to such
a building erected a hundred years ago.

Cunningham must have had an unhappy life: in 1842, when he was
twenty-six and working as a clerk in the Audit Office in Somerset House, he
edited a book for the Shakespeare Society, entitled *Extracts from the accounts of
the revels at court in the reign of Queen Elizabeth and King James I, from the account
books of the Masters and Yeoman*. Two of the little account books which Cunningham republished excited great interest. They contained four pages, on
three of which were records of the performances in 1604–5 'by his majesties
plaiers' of nine of Shakespeare's plays, with a marginal note that they were
written by Shaxberd which, of course, was accepted as a reference to Shakespeare, and as evidence of the date of the production of the plays referred to.

But in 1858 an elderly, broken-down man appeared at the British Museum and offered for sale a manuscript which he claimed contained records of much value about the early English drama, and which, he had been told, was worth sixty guineas. The volume was retained for examination before purchase, and proved to be the 'Revels Accounts' containing the three sheets referring to Shaxberd's plays. Being public property it was of course held. It was then discovered that the sheets were not genuine—and there could be no question but that it was Cunningham himself who had forged them.

Cunningham lived on until 1869. His story shows the extraordinary lengths to which enthusiasm in research will lead a man.

Henry B. Wheatley based his excellent *London Past and Present* (three volumes published in 1891) on Cunningham's work, and, like everything which Wheatley wrote, it is a mine of information.

Old and New London: A Narrative of its History, its People and its Places is a work which can be found in almost any secondhand book shop. It was published by Cassell, Petter, Galpin and Co. between the years 1873 and 1878 (according to the British Museum Index of Books), appearing in parts of twelve pages each. When finished, each of its six volumes contained forty-eight parts—that is 576 pages and a sixty-page index in five parts completed the work.

An exact date is difficult to specify, but in addition to my undated First Edition, I have a set—'A New Edition, carefully revised and corrected',—in Volume I of which there is a note by a previous owner that the first part was published in 1877. Volume II, which is the only other volume in the set with a date, is dated 1881.

I recently saw a 'Popular Edition', of which Volume VI was dated 1897; none of the other volumes were dated.

Some clue is given by the fact that Volumes I and II were edited by Walter Thornbury, who died in 1876, while the remaining volumes were by Edward Walford. (He incidentally edited two additional volumes, entitled *Greater London* which also appeared in twelve-page parts.)

For light bedside reading these books are admirable; they were obviously produced for the beginner who did not want his text cluttered with learned references! There are over 1,600 illustrations in the eight volumes, and maps were published with Parts 67, 68, and 69—the first a reproduction of 'Civitas Londinum A^{no} D^M Circiter MDLX', the second a copy of 'A Plan of the City's of London, Westminster and Borough of Southwark with the new Additional Buildings: Anno, 1720' and the third an undated 'New Map of London'.

Whilst the books are plentiful the maps are not; the 'Popular Edition' to which I have referred was plainly bound, and with the maps (in a slip case) was priced at three guineas.

Another justly popular work is W. J. Loftie's *History of London*, published in 1883 in two volumes with maps and illustrations.

Loftie's preface opens: 'In the multiplicity of books on London it is strange that for more than forty years no history has appeared. Thomas Allen's five volumes reached a second edition in 1839, being continued, but unfortunately not corrected by Thomas Wright. Since that time no serious attempt has been made to tell the story of our great City's origin and growth, although the materials have gradually accumulated in abundance; and many chronicles, diaries, and collections of records have been printed.'

Loftie tackled the problem of compression in a different way from his predecessors; he went to authorities, either unknown or ignored by them, and, in the Volume I, after a topographical account of the site and a description of the effects on London of the Roman and Saxon invasions, he wove the history of the City, as told by chroniclers, into a continuous narrative; writing of the Guilds, the Wards, the Churches, the Monasteries and the City Companies in mediaeval times, and explaining that he had practically ignored the later periods because of the previous works by Maitland, Malcolm, Lysons and others.

Volume II contains a detailed account of each of the suburbs, prefaced by a sketch of the History of Middlesex.

The introduction to the London volume of the *Victoria County History* series tells us that Loftie 'brought together an immense amount of information and, although his conclusions do not always meet with universal approval, students of history owe him much for his effort to give an account of London drawn largely from original sources'.

Amongst the persons thanked for assistance received is 'Mr C. Trice Martin of the Record Office', and of the two volumes which I bought in Chiswick a few years ago for four shillings the Volume I is inscribed—'With the Author's Compliments, 5th June 1883', and signed 'C. Martin P.R.O.' while Volume II has 'C. T. Martin from the Author.' Both volumes contain his—cryptic—book-plate.

A supplement to the First Edition, published in 1884, contains 'Addition and Corrections' as well as additional maps, including those of the Grosvenor and Portman estates, which have a special interest for us today. I paid half a crown for my copy.

Loftie's *Kensington Picturesque and Historical*, 'with upwards of three hundred illustrations (some in colour) by WILLIAM LUKER JUN.' was published in 1888 at three guineas. It is a charming book which every resident in the Royal Borough should read. Not unnaturally it leans on Faulkner's *History of Kensington* published sixty-nine years earlier, and indeed it contains a list of the subscribers to that work, concerning which Loftie wrote: 'It may be of interest to the descendants of those who subscribed to Faulkner's HISTORY

OF KENSINGTON in 1820 to see their names appended to the following list of subscribers who have honoured my book upon trust with their kind notice', and Loftie refers specifically to 'Mr John Merriman, Young Street' who subscribed in 1820, and he conjectures that the 1820 subscriber is the 'John J. Merriman, 45 Kensington Square' (which was the same house) who subscribed for his book.

Three years later Loftie's *London City* was published; 'A most interesting and superbly illustrated quarto' (said the advertisements), W. Luker, jr. was again the artist. But the paramount interest which the book holds for me lies in the fact that the list of subscribers contains the names and address of my mother and my father, which may be some indication that my interest in old London dates from the tender age of six months, for in the book is the prepublication receipt for £2 5. 0 issued to my father on 25th July 1890, for 'one large paper copy' of the book 'to be delivered when published'.

6

'The Suburbes without the Walles'

Stow had calculated that the man who walked round Old London Wall covered 'two English miles and more, by 608 feet'. If a man left the City he stepped, as he passed through one of the gates, into 'the Suburbes without the Walles'.

One hundred and fifty years after Stow had made his calculation, the Rev. Dr Thomas Birch—in 1749—had a mind to undertake something similar, and in the 1787 edition of his life of Dr Samuel Johnson, Sir John Hawkins wrote concerning Dr Birch's feat:

'I heard him once relate that he had the curiosity to measure the circuit of London, by a perambulation thereof. The account he gave was to this effect: He set out from his house in the Strand towards Chelsea, and having reached the bridge beyond the waterworks (Battersea Bridge), he directed his course to Marylebone, from whence, pursuing an eastern direction, he skirted the town, and crossed the Islington road at the Angel. There was at that time (circ. 1749) no City Road, but passing through Hoxton he got to Shoreditch, thence to Bethnal Green and from thence to Stepney, where he recruited his spirits with a glass of brandy. From Stepney he passed on to Limehouse, and took into his route the adjacent hamlet of Poplar, when he became sensible that, to complete his design, he must take in Southwark. This put him to a stand; but he soon determined on his course for taking a boat he landed at the Red House at Deptford, and made his way to Sayes' Court, where the great wet-dock is, and, keeping the houses along Rotherhithe to the right, he got to Bermondsey, thence by the south end of Kent Street to Newington, and over St. George's Fields to Lambeth, and, crossing over at Millbank, continued his way to Charing Cross and along the Strand to Norfolk Street, from whence he had set out. The whole of this excursion took him up from nine in the morning to three in the afternoon, and, according to his rate of walking, he computed the circuit of London at above twenty miles. With the buildings erected since (1787) it may be supposed to have increased five miles.'

And one hundred years ago the limit of London, as defined by Act of Parliament for Parliamentary purposes, was 'the circumference of a circle, the radius of which is of the length of 3 miles from the general Post Office.'

Stow's *Survey* did not carry him very far from the walls of the old City. *Fitzstephen* 'hath these words', he wrote:

'Upwards on the West is the Kings Palace, which is an incomparable building, rising with a Vawmure and Bulwarke aloft upon the River, two miles from the Wall of the City, but yet conjoyned with a continuall Suburbe. On all sides, without the houses of the Suburbs, are the Citizens Gardens and Orchards, planted with Trees, both large, slightly, and adjoyning together. On the North side are Pastures, and plaine Medowes, with brooks running thorow them, turning Watermils, with a pleasant noise. Not farre off, is a great Forrest, a well woodded Chase, having good covert for Harts, Buckes, Does, Bores, and Wild Bulls. The Corne fields are not of a hungry sandy mould, but as the fruitful fields of Asia, yeelding plentifull increase, and filling the Barnes with Corne. There are neere London, on the North side, especiall Wells in the Suburbs, sweete, wholesome and cleare. Amongst which, Holywell, Clerkenwell, and Saint Clements well, are most famous, and most frequented by Schollers and Youths of the City in Summer evenings, when they walke forth to take the ayre', and Stow concludes: 'Thus farre out of *Fitz Stephen*, for the Suburbes of that time.' Stow then writes about Wapping in the 'Woze' (corrected in the Second Edition to 'East'):

'The usuall place of execution for hanging of Pirates and sea-Rovers, at the low water marke, there to remaine, till three tides had overflowed them, was never a house standing within these forty yeares: but since (the gallowes being after removed farther off) a continuall streete, or filthy straight passage, with Alleyes of small tenements or Cottages is builded, inhabited by Saylors and victuallers, along by the river of Thames, almost to *Radcliff*, a good mile from the Tower.'

Stow has another note about Pirates a few lines further on:

'I reade that in the yeare 1440 in the lent season, certaine persons with 6 ships brought from beyond the seas fish to victuaile the city of London, which fish when they had delivered, and were returning homeward, a number of sea theeves, in a barge, in the night came upon them, when they were asleep in their vessels, riding at anker on the river Thames, and slew them, cut their throates, cast them over boord, tooke their money, and drowned their ships for that no man should espie or accuse them. Two of these theeves were after taken, and hanged in chaynes upon a gallowes set upon a raysed hill, for that purpose made, in the field beyond East Smithfield, so that they might be seene farre into the river Thames.'

Another work of general appeal is *The Environs of London*: 'being an Historical Account of the Towns, Villages, and Hamlets, Within twelve

Miles of that Capital; Interspersed with Biographical Anecdotes. By the
Rev. Daniel Lysons, A.M., F.A.S. Chaplain to the Right Hon. The Earl of
Orford,' to whom the work is dedicated.

The work is more suitable for the study than the bedside table. It is in
four volumes: the First, 'Printed by Strahan, for T. Cadell in the Strand',
dealing with the County of Surrey, was published in 1792; the Second and
Third, 'printed for T. Cadell, Jun. and W. Davies (Successors to Mr Cadell)
in the Strand', deal with the County of Middlesex and were published in
1795, and the Fourth, dealing with the Counties of Herts, Essex and Kent
was published by the same firm in the following year.

The work is a storehouse of well documented and indexed facts, useless
as well as useful. It contains pleasant plates: the one reproduced of Richmond
Palace was engraved by Vandergutch, probably from a drawing of Hollar,
early in the seventeenth century. Note the derrick or winch on the extreme
left of the print, and the three horsemen watering their horses: the dress of
the courtiers in the foreground is in strong contrast with that of the sailors.

As one browses through these books one comes across a number of
interesting little stories: I have not the space to quote at length, but note,
for instance, in the First Volume how in 1675, Sir Samuel Morland obtained
a lease of Vauxhall-house, Lambeth, and employed his talents as 'a mechanic'
in every part of the house; 'the side-table in the dining-room was supplied
with a large fountain, and the glasses stood under little streams of water.
His coach had a moveable kitchen, with clock-work machinery, with which
he could make soup, broil stakes, or roast a joint of meat. When he travelled
he was his own cook.'

I enjoyed reading what is described as the 'whimsical' inscription on the
tomb, in the churchyard in Carshalton, of a corpulent barber, who was a
famous dancer:

> Tom Humphreys lies here, by death beguil'd,
> Who never did harm to man, woman, or child;
> And since without foe no men e'er was known,
> Poor Tom was nobody's foe but his own;
> Lay light on him earth, for none would than he
> (Though heavy his bulk) trip it lighter on thee.
>
> Died Sept. 4. 1742, aged 44 years.

I read, in the Second Volume, that in 1558 a man was fined at Edgware
'for selling ale at an exhorbitant price, viz. a pint and a half for a penny.'

And in the Third Volume Lysons singles out from amongst the names
extracted from the Parish Registers of Bethnal Green that of 'Roger Crab,
Gent. of Bethnal Green, buried Sep. 14, 1680,' and goes on to relate:
'This man was one of the eccentric characters of the last century. The

RICHMOND

most that we know of him is from a pamphlet (now very rare) written principally by himself, and entitled "The English Hermit, or the Wonder of the Age." It appears from this publication that he had served seven years in the parliamentary army, and had his skull cloven to the brain in their service; for which he was so ill requited that he was once sentenced to death by the lord protector, and afterwards suffered two years imprisonment. When he had obtained his release, he set up a shop at Chesham, as a haberdasher of hats. He had long been settled there before he began to imbibe a strange notion, that it was a sin against his body and soul to eat any sort of flesh, fish, or living creature, or to drink wine, ale, or beer. Thinking himself at the same time obliged to follow literally the injunction given to the young man in the Gospel, he quitted business, and disposing of his property gave it among the poor, reserving to himself only a small cottage at Ickenham where he resided, and a rood of land for a garden, on the produce of which he subsisted at the expense of three farthings a week, his food being bran, herbs, roots, dock-leaves, mallows, and grass; his drink, water. How such an extraordinary change of diet agreed with his constitution the following passage from his pamphlet will shew, and give at the same time a specimen of the work:"Instead of strong drinks and wines, I give the old man a cup of water; and instead of rost mutton and rabbets, and other dainty dishes, I give him broth thickened with bran, and pudding made with bran, and turnep-leaves chopt together, and grass; at which the old man (meaning my body), being moved, would know what he had done that I used him so hardly, then I showed him his transgression: so the warres began; the law of the old man in my fleshly members rebelled against the law of my mind, and had a shrewd skirmish; but the mind, being well enlightened, held it so that the old man grew sick and weak with the flux, like to fall to the dust; but the wonderful love of God, well pleased with the battle, raised him up again, and filled him full of love, peace, and content of mind, and is now become more humble; for now he will eat dock-leaves, mallows, or grasse." '

The pamphlet was published in 1655. Prefixed to it is a portrait of the author cut in wood; which, from its rarity, bears a very high price. Over the print are these lines:

> Roger Crab that feeds on herbs and roots is here;
> But I believe Diogenes had better cheer.

> *Rara avis in terris.*

'I know nothing of this man's future history, or whether he continued his diet of herbs. A passage in his epitaph seems to intimate that he never resumed the use of animal food. It is not one of the least extraordinary parts of his history that he should so long have subsisted on a diet which, by his own account, had reduced him almost to a skeleton in 1655. It appears that he resided at Bethnal-green at the time of his decease. A very handsome tomb was erected to his memory in the church-yard at this place; which being decayed, the ledger-stone was placed in the pathway leading across the church-yard to Whitehorse-street, where it still remains, but the inscription is almost defaced. It is given beneath from Strype; who adds, "this Crab, they say, was a Philadelphian, or sweet singer." '

Strype had recorded the following on the south side of the church-yard of St Dunstan's Stepney—not Bethnal Green:

> Tread gently, Reader, near the Dust,
> Cometh to this Tomb-Stone's trust.
> For while 'twas flesh, it held a guest,
> With universal love possest.
> A Soul that stemm'd Opinion's Tyde,
> Did over Sects in Triumph ride.
> Yet separate from the giddy crowd,
> And Paths Tradition had allowed.
> Through good and ill Reports he past;
> Oft censur'd yet approv'd at last.
> Wouldest thou his Religion know?
> If brief 'twas this: To all to do
> Just as he would be done unto
> So in kind Nature's law he stood,
> A Temple undefil'd with blood:
> A Friend to everything that's good.
> The rest Angels alone fitly can tell:
> Haste, then, to Them and Him; and so farewell.

This Crab, they say, was a Philadelphian, or Sweet Singer.

The *Oxford Dictionary of Quotations* gives the origin of 'Do as you would be done by . . .' to Philip Dormer Stanhope, Earl of Chesterfield, in a letter to his son, dated 16th October 1747—sixty-seven years after Crab's death, and twenty-seven years after the publication of his epitaph by Strype.

Strype had also recorded that in Bunhill Fields was buried 'Humphrey Beane of London, Esq. Jan 17. *Anno Salvationis Mundi* 1679. *Aetat Suae* 66' with these verses:

> Who after he had liv'd to see
> In two worlds much vanity;
> But in the Third he is at Rest
> With the Eternal, and there blest.
> A God he did believe to be
> Triune in one and Veritie.

> His form is ceast, his life cant dy,
> But's gon from Time into Eternity,
> So that blest Soul hath tane his Flight
> From earthly Body into Heaven's Light.
> Where he in glory now's at Liberty
> To praise the Lord to all Eternity

and Strype added: '(This Beane fined for Alderman, and was of the Sect. of the *Sweet Singers*; and some of that Society, I suppose, made these Verses for him)'.

As Lysons records, Roger Crab was a Sweet Singer or a Philadelphian, and the members of that Society appear to have been known indiscriminately by either name.

The Philadelphians were founded in London in 1652 by Jane Leade and Dr John Pordage to expound the philosophy (of contradictions) of the German Jacob Boehme or Behmen, who was born in 1575 and died in 1624. To quote from *A Register and Chronicle Ecclesiastical and Civil*. . . . taken 'from the Restauration of King Charles II. Faithfully taken from the Manuscript Collections of the Lord Bishop of Peterborough—1728: 'The Great Plot for Restoring Popery' (published 1663) 'exposed' the number of Sects and parties 'spawned by the Jesuits' and the Sequestrations and Subdivisions amongst them, and included amongst the 'Hiders of several Sorts'—'1. The Vanists, whose game was first plaid openly in New-England, where God gave in his testimony against them from Heaven upon their two Prophetesses, Mrs Hutchinson and Mrs Dyer. 2. The next sort of Hiders are the Paracelsians, Weigelians, and Behmenists, who go the same Way in the main with the former, and are indeed the same party, but think meet to take another name, and fetch their Vizor from Jacob Behmen.'

But if the Behmenists were Jesuits and there was any connection between them and the Philadelphians or Sweet Singers it is curious that Humphrey Beane—a Jesuit—should have been 'fined for Alderman'.

Another extract from the Parish Registers reproduced in Lysons *Environs* reads—'The Rev. Mr John Entinck, buried May 28. 1773' (in the Index the name is correctly spelt 'Entick'), and in the same volume is the following biographical note: 'Mr Entinck who was by profession a school master, was engaged during the greater part of his life in writing for the booksellers, who kept him in constant employ. He was for a considerable length of time a writer in an anti-ministerial paper, called the Monitor; this occasioned his being taken up under a general warrant, for which he afterwards recovered damages. About the year 1738, he proposed publishing an edition of Chaucer, which never took effect. And of his voluminous works, the principal are; A Naval History, in folio; a History of the late War in five volumes, 8vo; a present state of the British Empire, in four volumes 8vo; an improved edition of Maitland's History of London; a Spelling Dictionary, and a Latin and English Dictionary, of both which 20,000 copies have been printed at a time; an Edition of Phaedrus, &c.'

Lysons is very readable, despite its unwieldy format—I could quote endlessly . . . but to round off the Third Volume I noted with interest that he lists seventeen 'instances of three children at a Birth' in Stepney but unhappily has to record that most of them died within a few weeks.

In the Fourth Volume amongst many interesting records there is a section entitled 'General View of the former and present state of MARKET GARDENS, and of the Quantity of Land now occupied for that Purpose within Twelve Miles of LONDON,' which amplifies some observations in the First Volume 'relating to the first introduction of the culture of vegetables for sale in this kingdom'—and which appears to have dated from about 1590.

There were, in 1796, nearly 10,000 acres (in the twelve-mile radius) cultivated by market gardeners for the supply of garden vegetables, and in particular asparagus, fruit of various kinds and potatoes, as well as food for cattle, principally cows, by persons who were called 'farming gardeners'.

Discussing prices, Lysons records: 'A singular instance of fluctuation of prices occurred a few years ago in the article of Caroline raspberries, which when they were first introduced, sold at 2s. 6d. or 3s. a pottle. They were very prolific, an acre yielding about 3,000 pottles. The gardeners, tempted by the high price, overstocked their plantations, the market became glutted, and at last they fell to two pence a pottle, which was not sufficient to pay the gathering and carriage'.

Shortly after the Second World War I paid three shillings and sixpence for a copy of 'The Third Edition improved and enlarged', of the *Ambulator; or, the Strangers Companion in a Tour Round London, within the Circuit of Twenty-five Miles,* 'Printed for J. Bew in Pater-Noster-Row, 1787,' There are 257 octavo pages in the book though in my copy the 'New Map' is missing.

The *Ambulator* must have filled a need, for the Second Edition was published in 1782; following the First Edition, *Collected by a Gentleman for his private Amusement,* which had been published in 1774, at half a crown.

The *Ambulator* described, alphabetically, 'whatever is remarkable either for grandeur, Elegancy, Use, or Curiosity, within the circuit of twenty-five miles'.

It is a highly entertaining little guide; one can open the book anywhere, and be sure of finding something of interest. For instance, we learn why Poplar Marsh was called the Isle of Dogs, and that 'it is reckoned one of the richest spots of ground in England; for it not only raises the largest cattle, but the grass it bears is esteemed a great restorative of all distempered cattle.'

And in the following item 'Portland Place' we learn that 'If Lord Foley's house could be taken down, and the design continued to Oxford Road, Portland Place would be the most magnificent street in the world for spaciousness, extent, and regularity.' The Langham Hotel, now occupied by the British Broadcasting Corporation, was built on the site of Lord Foley's house.

Or we may read that in the Musick-Room of the Keeper's Lodge in Windsor Great Park (at that time the seat of the 'ranger', Henry Frederick, Duke of Cumberland) were pictures of 'several of the late Duke's breeding mares, and over the chimney is Marshall Saxe', a curious juxtaposition.

There is an interesting list of the paintings in the pavilions in Vauxhall Gardens—including such intriguing subjects, as 'Two Mahometans gazing in astonishment at the many beauties of the place,' and 'New-river-head, at Islington with a family going a walking, a cow milking, and the horns archly fixed over the husband's head'.

Then we are given 'an account of the provisions and wines as they are sold in the gardens'; bottles were cheap in those days: they included:

Maderia	4.	9.
Sherry	3.	3.
Mountain	2.	9.
Red Port	2.	3.
Lisbon	2.	3.

whilst a quart of 'arrach' cost 8.0.; a slice of bread cost a penny, but a pat of butter, and a slice of cheese cost two pence each. The compiler added a note: 'To the honour of the proprietors, it must be observed that they were the first that reduced the price of the wines marked in Italic (being those of the growth of Spain and Portugal), in consequence of our late commercial treaty with France. And we understand, that as soon as they can take the benefit of all the regulations consequent to this treaty, a still further reduction is intended.'

The preface to the Tenth Edition is dated from 'Islington Nov. 27, 1806'.

I paid ten shillings (in Worthing) for the Eleventh Edition 'with considerable Additions and Improvements', published in 1811. The Advertisement is dated from 'Chiswick, 4th Oct. 1810.' The book was then called *The Ambulator; or a Pocket Companion Etc.*; it is 'embellished with Fourteen Elegant Engravings, and a Correct Map'; and a charming—coloured—map it is too. My copy has two inscriptions in it: 'E. Lloyd Chemist Richmond 1842,' and 'H. Lloyd Chemist Richmond June 1885. A gift from His Friend Dr Duncan who purchased it at a Dealer's in Richmond.'

The book, by that time (1811) increased to 310 pages, is full of fun— and again I open—at random—to find: 'CLAPHAM RISE, is a continuation of houses from Stockwell Swan to the common, and very aptly so named, being *suited* to the *rapid rise* of some of its inhabitants.

> Here tailor's rich, who cabbag'd long in town,
> Raise *garden* cabbage, and their trade disown.
> The *pricking-needle* to the *dibble* yields,
> And geese *alive*, hiss round their *brick-burnt* fields;
>
> Thus parch'd and *over-roasted* when *alive*,
> These pondless commoners no longer thrive;
> In *dusty* solitude are sickly seen,
> And prove at table, any thing but green.
>
> A.'

And, of Stockwell: 'This village, like Cock Lane, has had its impostors, and much about the same period [1762]; it is however to be regretted that they were not detected and brought to punishment. This ghost did not pretend to tell about murders committed, but merely broke plates, dishes, glasses, &c. and tormented a pious old widow lady.'

Or, again at random—I find the following epitaph on John Spong, a carpenter, in the church-yard at Ockham, 'Surry'.

> Who many a sturdy oak had laid along,
> Fell'd by Death's surer hatchet, here lies Spong;
> Posts oft he made, yet ne'er a place could get,
> And liv'd by railing, though he was not wit,
> Old saws he had, although no antiquarian:
> And stiles corrected, yet was no grammarian.

The last—the Twelfth Edition of the *Ambulator* was published in 1820. Its full title reads: *London and its Environs, or, the General Ambulator, and Pocket Companion for the Tour of the Metropolis and its Vicinity.* I paid fourpence for my 'slightly mutilated' copy in Chiswick, many years ago. It contains the signature of a former owner, 'F. P. Murray. August 1826', and then: 'This Book was given to Sergt. John Clark by Mr Murray R.N. on board H.M. Ship Druid the 22 day of Jany. 1833'. The book is swollen out to 422 pages, of which the first 152 consist of 'An Account Historical and Descriptive of the Metropolis'.

This edition would seem at first sight to be written with a heavier hand than the others—and the jolly entries take more finding; but probably what reads like a heavy hand—compared to the other editions—is in reality the sure and expert touch of Edward Wedlake Brayley, who edited this edition— although there is nothing in the book to show it.

I also own tattered and battered copies of the Fourth, Eighth and Ninth Editions; I expect I shall find the missing volumes some time somewhere.

A more solemn work is the *Handbook to the Environs of London, Alphabetically Arranged*, by James Thorne F.S.A. published in 1876. The two parts into which it is divided are sometimes bound in separate volumes. I paid five shillings for my two volumes—and find it a useful and well documented reference book. Thorne refers, slightingly, to the various editions of the *Ambulator*, although I wonder whether Thorne's *Handbook* would have been written if the author had not had the benefit of the *Ambulator*. He refers, also slightingly, to other historians who have written about the Environs of London: Lambert's History is 'tedious' he says, and Hughson's is 'still more tedious'.

Many years ago I wrote to the librarian of each of London's twenty-eight boroughs, and asked for a bibliography of books dealing with his district. At that time not one of the boroughs possessed such a list; however, all the librarians with the exception of Stepney (which had been badly blitzed), sent me a list of books dealing with his locality, and I was surprised to find how many books of purely local interest have been written.

To me one of the most interesting of these is *Some Account of the Hospital and Parish of St Giles in the Fields, Middlesex*, 'by the late Mr John Parton, Vestry Clerk', which was published in 1822. The name of the publisher is not shown on the title page, but it was 'Printed by Luke Hansard and Sons, near Lincoln's Inn Fields.' Their address underneath the frontispiece is given as 'Great Turnstile Holborn'. I decided that it would be a pleasant duty to try and find out what was known about the author.

The Advertisement (which is dated December 1821) relates how Parton availed . . .

'himself of every opportunity afforded him by his official situation, during a number of years, to collect materials for a history of the district. These in time became considerable and being subsequently increased by the collections and communications of friends, who had engaged in the same pursuit, he at length thought proper to have the whole arranged and formed into a fair Manuscript'. Then referring to Parton it continues:

'Two-thirds of the work had been printed off, when death robbed it of the superintending care and abilities of that gentleman; fortunately the continuation of the volume being nearly ready for the press, the task of proceeding with it did not require much. That little has been executed with strict attention to Mr Parton's known wishes on the subject, by a literary friend, whose intimacy with Mr Parton and similarity of taste for such researches, not only led him to take a peculiar interest in the work from its commencement, but enabled him to afford material aid in its progress, and conducting it to a close; and the work, as now produced, if wanting in some advantages

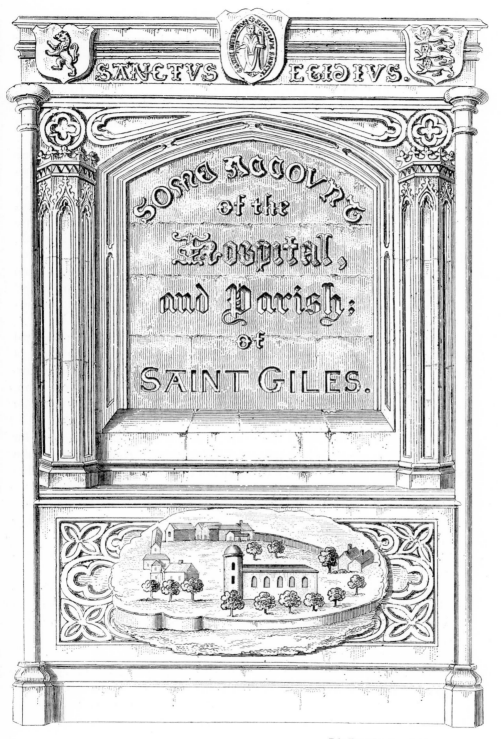

SANCTVS EGIDIVS.

Some Account
of the
Hospital,
and Parish;
of
SAINT GILES.

Luke Hansard & Sons, Printers,
Great Turnstile Holborn.

which Mr Parton's extensive knowledge of the local law and customs of the district might have given it, may at least be said to be finished in the true spirit of its intention.'

At the end of the sixth chapter of the account of the Parish (page 413), appears the following:

'P.S. Thus far the Author had prepared his copy before the illnesses which terminated his life . . .'

The reference in the Advertisement to the 'fair Manuscript' made me curious to see it, and I was pleasantly surprised to inspect it in the Borough Council Library, which had purchased it some twenty years previously from a local bookseller, for fifteen pounds, upon an undertaking not to seek to discover the identity of its former owner! The 'fair manuscript' is bound into four (fully indexed) volumes labelled respectively, 'Topographical', 'Hospital', 'Historical', and 'Biographical'.

And whereas the published Parton contains approximately 165,000 words on 428 large quarto pages with 15 illustrations, the 'fair manuscript' contains approximately 350,000 words on some 1,207 pages with 148 illustrations, many of them of unique interest.

But of John Parton, the author of the *Account*, little is known: on 23rd July 1801 he was, at the request of William Robertson, the Vestry Clerk of the United Parishes of St Giles in the Field and St George Bloomsbury, appointed to the office of Vestry Clerk in conjunction with William Robertson, and when the latter resigned, Parton continued as sole clerk of the Vestry, an office which he held until his death, after two years' illness, in 1821.

The Times does not record his death, and *The Gentleman's Magazine* for September 1821 contains the simple entry 'August 27. At Kentish Town, John Parton, Esq., Many years Vestry Clerk etc. of the Parishes of St Giles-in-the-Fields, and St George Bloomsbury.'

The 'etc.' is intriguing, but the only clue to what it can include is contained in a Minute of the Joint Vestries which Mr C. F. S. Chapple, former Town Clerk of Holborn, very kindly sent me. It reads:

'It was moved by Mr Luke Hansard and seconded by Sir John Silvester—that this Vestry entertains a just and high sense of the distinguished and exemplary manner in which Mr John Parton (late Vestry Clerk) uniformly discharged the duties of his Situation during a long series of years in the varied Concerns of these Parishes—which was agreed to unanimously, and ordered to be fairly transcribed on Vellum, framed and glazed and presented to his Son.'

I wonder whether the Vellum, 'framed and glazed' is still in existence.

Rowland Dobie refers to Parton in his *History of the United Parishes of St Giles in the Field and St George, Bloomsbury*, 1829: 'Mr Parton, the late clerk of the Vestry of the parishes, collected materials for a work of this description, which was published in an imperfect state after his decease. .... Mr Parton had exclusive advantages to aid him in such a work, having the custody of the parish records, to which he alone had free access—a privilege of the highest importance. ... Occupying a station both lucrative and influential, Mr Parton too frequently forgot the impartial province of the historian in his zeal for advocating the cause of the assumed Vestry under whom he held his appointment ...', but these remarks must be read in the knowledge that Dobie was a member of an association founded in 1828 in the United Parishes 'for the laudable purpose of investigating and correcting the abuses which had too long prevailed under government of a Select Vestry, possessing no claims to power but what were founded on assumption and usurpation.'

Parton's will, which is dated 1st August 1821, gives his address as Charlotte Street, Bloomsbury, and describes him as 'Gentleman'. It overflows with overgrown legal foliage, and in its six pages he does no more than express a desire to be buried 'in the burial ground of St Giles in the Fields at an expense not exceeding thirty pounds', and leaves everything (including his books and his prints) to his four children, Elizabeth, Jane, John and Mary Ann—with the appropriate trusts during the minority of John and Mary Ann.

His Executors were George Frederick Gordon of Haslemere, Charles Starbridge of Tavistock Street Bedford Square, gentleman, and Alfred Richard Corber of Nasham Street Westminster, gentleman, and the witnesses to the will were J. Ansell, 'clerk to the said John Parton,' G. N. Hamblett, another of his clerks and Barnd. C. Corker of Nassau Street, Soho.

There is, of course, nothing at Somerset House to indicate what his estate consisted of, nor which of his children took over his books and his prints.

And naturally there is nothing to show his ancestry.

The guess I like to think is the correct one is that our John Parton named his son John after his father, John Parton who died intestate, and to whose estate Letters of Administration were granted in January 1773.

Parton's *Account* was published at five guineas with twelve copies printed on large paper at ten guineas, but when we ask 'what did his contemporaries think of it?' we are compelled to admit that we cannot say.

In 1818 Boydell and Company of Cheapside published *London Before the Great Fire* 'or, a Series of Engravings (with Historical and Topographical Accounts) Illustrative of the Early State, Buildings, Monuments, and Antiquities of the Metropolis'.

No. 1. (at ten shillings and sixpence) had an account of the 'North-West Suburb, Including St Giles Parish', and the following footnote:

'This information, and whatever else may appear new in the above slight account of this neighbourhood, is inserted (per favour) from an extensive MS. history of St Giles's parish—a work compiled almost entirely from original

INFESSUS AGENDO

THOMAS FAULKNER.

records, at the sole expense of a liberal and public spirited gentleman of that parish—and the substance of which, may, perhaps, be shortly given to the public! Its contents are highly curious and valuable'.

But I have not succeeded in finding any contemporary notices of the *Account*.

There is an obvious reference to the 'literary friend' mentioned in the 'advertisement' in Bohn's new edition of Lowndes's *Bibliographer's Manual*, which concludes its mention of the work; 'The text said to be drawn up by J. Herbert'.

Who J. Herbert was remains to be answered.

A topographical writer of whom we know more was Thomas Faulkner, who was born in 1777 and died in 1855.

His *An Historical and Topographical Description of Chelsea and its Environs*, his native district, was published in 1810. He was himself a publisher, and Nichols & Son, Parliament Street, and Simpkin and Marshall, Stationers, Hall Court, were associated with him in the publication of this book.

Faulkner tells his story by taking his readers for walks round the district, and his book makes interesting reading. To quote at length is not practicable, but two items from his 'Extracts from the Parish Books' give a clue to what one may expect to find in them—and indeed in all parish books: 'Payd Mr Tuley for cureing Charles Matthew's toes of a mortification. £2. 5. 0', and 'Gave Stacey for shaveing a childs head 0. 6.' A greatly enlarged Second Edition, in two volumes—was published in 1829; I have a copy of Volume Two which I bought only because it contains a number of extra illustrations, and it only cost me two shillings!

Faulkner's *An Historical and Topographical Account of Fulham, Including the Hamlet of Hammersmith*, was published in 1813. His list of subscribers, over 150 of them, included 'Mr Faulkner of Walham Green'; 'Mr J. Faulkner of Jermyn Street'; 'Mr I. Faulkner of King's Road', and 'Mr W. Faulkner of Guernsey'; 'The Rev. Daniel Lysons, M.A., F.R.S. Rector of Rodmarton, Glous.', and his brother 'Samuel Lysons Esq., F.R.S. Keeper of His Majesty's Records in the Tower', and 'J. Nichols, Esq., F.S.A. Islington', the publisher.

The account of Fulham and Hammersmith is stretched to include Shepherds Bush and Brook Green, as well as the 'Two small rural Villages' of Stamford Brook Green and Gaggle Goose Green. There are twenty-three illustrations and a good index.

I think that Faulkner improved as a writer between 1810 and 1813, and that his *History and Antiquities of Kensington*, published in 1820 is even better than his former works. And he had gained in stature: he had dedicated his book on Chelsea to Captain the Hon. George Cadogan, and his book on Fulham to the Bishop of London; he dedicated this book to King George IV.

I reproduce the engraving of Faulkner which forms the frontispiece.

Kensington, looking West.

J. Scott Sculp.

I paid five shillings for my copy, over twenty years ago. Inside the front cover is the signature 'Geo. L. Craik', whom I like to think was George Lillie Craik, author of amongst other works, *The Pictorial History of England*. Born in 1798, he did not die until 1866, so it may well have been.

The list of subscribers—still under 200—included 'The Right Hon. George Canning M.P., Gloucester Lodge'; 'The Hon. Richard Henry Fox, Holland House'; 'The Hon. Miss Caroline Fox, Little Holland House'; 'Mr Faulkner, of Walham Green, Fulham'; 'Mr James Faulkner, of York Street, St James'; 'Mr J. Faulkner of Fulham'; and 'Mr W. Faulkner', who by this time had left Guernsey, and gone to Amsterdam; and 'Edward Orme Esq., Bayswater', a bookseller who carried on business in Bond Street, and after whom Orme Square was named. Samuel Lysons and Rev. D. Lysons again figure in the list, and so does John Nichols, F.A.S., now in Highbury.

The growth of Kensington can be measured by comparing the picture of 'Kensington looking West' from Faulkner with Chatelaine's print reproduced from the book to which I have referred at the end of chapter four. A careless printer has left the 'e' off his name under the print.

Faulkner also wrote *The History and Antiquities of the Parish of Hammersmith*, a much more matter-of-fact book published in 1839, and dedicated to the Queen. Finally, in 1845, he produced a history of Brentford, Chiswick and Ealing.

The nearer a suburb was to the walls of the old City, the closer would be its link with the history of old London. Thus it is that Islington's history is an old and interesting one, and there are many books which are more than the history of the locality.

One such is *The History, Topography, and Antiquities of the Parish of St Mary Islington*, by John Nelson, published in 1811, 'illustrated by 13 engravings'. My copy has a few marginal notes, which, I think makes a book so much more interesting: I feel that I can sense the previous owner's personality when I find that he has been sufficiently interested to stick in newspaper cuttings, and so on.

I have already (in chapter four) referred to Tomlins's *Yseldon*, and another 'local' book to be bought on sight is *The History of Clerkenwell* by William J. Pinks, published in 1865, five years after the death of its author.

The *History* was published in monthly parts, each part consisting of 24 pages of letter press; the first part was issued in January 1863, there was a double number in May 1865, and the conclusion, comprising five monthly parts, was published in August of that year. Publication of the complete volume was delayed for a couple of years owing to the necessity for alterations in the map, due to railway extensions in the parish.

The book contains 756 (large octavo) pages including an appendix and a supplement contributed by E. H. Wood, who edited the work after Pinks's

The South East View of Kensington Church.

The South View of Kensington.

Publish'd according to Act of Parliament.

death—and there is a fifty-page index. The style is discursive and anecdotal. Every district is dealt with in detail, with a lavish inclusion of illustrations, poems and extracts from old journals.

George Clinch is another reliable author. In 1890, and the two years that followed, he published histories of Marylebone and St Pancras, Bloomsbury and St Giles, Mayfair and Belgravia. These books are worth acquiring for the reproductions of the old prints in them. Local histories come and go, in all shapes and sizes; frequently the work of enthusiasts without pretensions to any literary style, they still make fascinating reading, and I buy them (mostly in the sixpenny or shilling boxes) whenever I see them—if only for the sake of their respective authors. 'A fellow-feeling makes us wond'rous kind'.

7

Old Londoners

Old books which conjure up the Londoners of the past often clothe the bare bones of topography. An observation of William FitzStephen, to whose twelfth-century *Description of London*, first published by Stow in 1698, I have already referred, suggests that the old London was not so very different from its modern counterpart.

In the section dealing with sports and pastimes, FitzStephen, explaining why he writes about children's sports, declares: 'seeing we all have beene children' (which is Stow's translation; I prefer Professor H. E. Butler's [1934] 'for we were all boys once') and, conveniently forgetting the references to fighting cocks and archery, FitzStephen conjures up a picture of present-day school playgrounds, with references to ball games, leaping and putting the stone.

The print of 'The New Hall Christ's Hospital', reproduced from T. Allen's *The Panorama of London or Visitors' Guide*, published in 1830, was no doubt produced to show off the building; but my interest is in the boys, who were possibly only added by the artist to give the picture life. Boys still play leapfrog and marbles; teams still engage in a tug-of-war; but it is many years since I saw a boy bowling a hoop or spinning a top. It is an interesting little book which may well be acquired for a few shillings; my copy was given me by a friend.

Two books which take us back to the Londoners of the thirteenth, fourteenth and fifteenth centuries are *Liber Albus: The White Book of the City of London*, and *Memorials of London and London Life*.

The former was published in 1861, and the latter seven years later. *Liber Albus* was compiled as a 'Repertory', by John Carpenter, Common Clerk and Richard Whittington, Mayor, from the records, in the Archives of the City of London, of 'transactions and events, social, political, ecclesiastical, legal, military, naval, local, and municipal, in which, closely or remotely, the City in its Corporate character has been interested.'

It was translated from the original Latin and Anglo-Norman by Henry Thomas Riley, who, explains in his Introduction that the larger portion of the

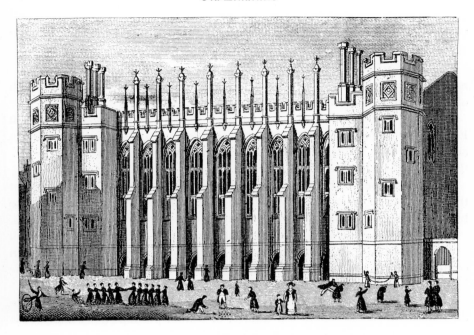

THE NEW HALL, CHRIST'S HOSPITAL.

work 'is extensively devoted to details which must of necessity interest those who care to know something more about their forefathers than the mere fact that they have existed'. Copies are not infrequently to be found in second-hand bookshops. My copy had been priced six shillings and sixpence, five shillings, and then three shillings, which is what I paid for it.

The *Memorials* are not so often met with. I searched for some months before I found a 'Presentation Copy', presented, that is, to one of the City Aldermen; it cost me seventeen shillings and sixpence. The book contains extracts, local, social, and political from the City archives, selected and translated by H. T. Riley who had worked on *Liber Albus*. There are interesting little facts in both books.

Thus, from *Liber Albus*, the provision: 'And that no barbers shall be so bold or so daring, as to put blood in their windows openly or in view of folks; but let them have it carried privily unto the Thames, under pain of paying two shillings unto the use of the Sheriffs.'

And here, from the *Memorials*, is a report of a meeting held on a Saturday in February, 1418, the fifth year of Henry V . . . 'present, the Mayor, R. Chichily, Walderne, Crowmere, Fauconer, Wottone, Sevenoke, Nortone, Cauntbrigge, Pervys, Whityngham.'

'On this day Alan Everard was dismissed from the Aldermanry of the Ward of Bredstrete, by reason of his dulness of hearing and other infirmities.' The deaf J.P. is obviously not a modern problem!

A good idea of what the young people of earlier generations were like may be obtained from books written for their instruction and guidance; such old books make entertaining reading.

I paid three shillings in an old junk shop in Worthing for the Fifth Edition of *A Present for an Apprentice*; 'or, a Sure GUIDE to gain both Esteem and Estate with Rules for his Conduct to his MASTER, and in the WORLD.' 'By a late Lord Mayor of *London*.'

This little octavo book of seventy-six pages was 'Printed for J. Hodges at the *Looking-Glass*, over against *St Magnus Church, London Bridge*: and sold also by M. Cooper, at the *Globe* in Pater-noster-Row, 1747 (Price One Shilling.)'

The book is dedicated to Sir John Barnard (1685–1764), who had himself been Lord Mayor in 1737, and across the page in my copy is written, in contemporary hand writing 'Vintners Hall 6th Sept. 1749 The Gift of the Worshl. Company of Vintners London.'

The work begins 'Dear Son,' who is told what to do—and what not to do—under thirty-six separate headings, of which, perhaps not unnaturally, the what-not-to-dos are of greater interest than the what-to-dos. The latter, as rules of conduct, have remained fairly static through the ages; it is the former which, by its prohibitions *should* prove that civilization has progressed.

I quote one example to explain what I mean—'Dear Son' is advised: 'never be prevail'd upon to set your Foot behind the Scenes at a Play-house; the Creatures, to be found there, being but so many Birds of Prey, that hover round you, only to devour you. Full of Fawning and Flattery, to win your Favour; and, insolently, ridiculing the Cit, the Moment your Back is turn'd.'

Then one may read with interest and amusement *Anecdotes of the Manners and Customs of London* by that J. P. Malcolm, whose *Londinium Redivivum* I have already mentioned. Malcolm's work is in two parts: the first (published in 1811) 'From the Roman Invasion to the year 1700, including . . . the Amusements of the Citizens . . . and various Particulars concerning Public and Private Libraries,' and the second (published in 1808) 'During the Eighteenth Century; including The Charities, Depravities, Dresses, and Amusements, of the Citizens . . . with a review of the state of Society in 1807', which is a collection of stories from contemporary books, newspapers and official documents. Both volumes contain plates drawn by the author himself.

I have already referred to the 'waspishness' displayed by Malcolm in his 'Advertisement' of *Londinium Redivivum*. In the preface to Part Two of the Second Edition of the *Anecdotes* he attacked the critic of the *Eclectic Review* who had incurred his displeasure because his commendation of the work was not one hundred per cent fulsome. Indeed, he attacked reviews in general, and quotes Dr Blair, writing to commiserate with 'Mr Bruce, the celebrated Abyssinian Traveller', who had apparently been scurvily treated by the *Monthly Review*: '. . . I entirely agree with Dr Douglas that the Reviews are beneath your notice. They are always guided by the interest of some booksellers . . .' In view of the success which his work had enjoyed—it had been published in March 1808, and a Second Edition had been called for in May 1809—Malcolm may have been justified in feeling a trifle hurt.

In 1829 appeared *Londiniana*; 'or Reminiscences of the British Metropolis: including characteristic Sketches, antiquarian, topographical, descriptive, and literary', by Edward Wedlake Brayley, who had been replaced by the Rev. J. Nightingale as editor of *London and Middlesex* nearly twenty years earlier. The work is in four volumes octavo, and contains a number of short articles, bounteously illustrated and well indexed.

For instance, entries from the books of St Giles's parish are given as illustrative of the many restrictions to which the people were subjected during the period of the civil wars:

		£	s	d
1641.	Recd. of the Vinter at the *Catt* in Queene Street, for p'mitting of tipling on the Lord's day – –	1	10	0
1644.	Recd. of three poore men, for drinking on the Sabbath daie at Tottenham Court – – –	0	4	0
——	Recd. of Mr Hooper that he had of defaulters in a suspected bawdie house, on the Fast day – –	0	12	0
——	Recd. of Mr Richard Bigg, for a fault done by his servant John Roberts – – – – –	0	1	0
1645.	Recd. of John Seagood, constable, which he had of a Frenchman, for swearing three oathes– –	0	3	0
——	Recd. of Mrs. *Thunder*, by the hands of Francis Potter, for her being drunk, and swearing seaven oathes – – – – – – – –	0	12	0
1646.	Recd. of Mr Hooker, for brewing on a Fast day	0	2	6
——	Pd. and given by Lyn and two watchmen, in consideration of their paines, and the breacking of ij halberts, in taking the two drunkards and swearers y^t p^d – – – – – –	1	4	0
1646.	Recd. of four men, travelling on the Fast day –	0	1	0
——	Recd. of Mr Wetherill, headboro', which he had of one for an oath – – – – – –	0	3	4
1648.	Recd. from the Citty marshall, sent by the Lord Mayor, for one that was drunke at the *Forts* in our parish – – – – – – – –	0	5	0

——	Recd. from Isabel Johnson, at ye Coleyard, for drinking on the Sabbath day – -- – –	0	4	0
1652.	Recd. of Mr Huxley and Mr Morris, who were riding out of town in sermon time on a Fast day	0	11	0
1654.	Recd. of William Glover, in Queen Street, and of Isaac Thomas, a Barber, in Holborn, for trimming of bearde on the Lorde's day. [The sum is not stated.]			
1655.	Recd. of a Mayd taken in Mrs Jackson's ale-house on the Sabbath day – – – – –	0	5	0
——	Recd. of a Scotchman drinking at Robert Owen's on the Sabbath – – – – – –	0	2	0
1656.	Recd. of Hen. Colewist in Maslyn Fields, for breach of ye Sabbath – – – – –	0	7	0
1658.	Recd. of Joseph Piers, for refusing to open his doores to have his house searched on the Lorde's daie – -- – – – – – –	0	10	0
1659.	An entry occurs of 'one Brooke's goods sold for breach of the Sabbath', but the produce is not set down.' – – – – – – – –			

And following a section dealing with the fines to be imposed upon aldermen who, not having been exempted, had refused to serve the office of Lord Mayor, we are treated to an account of how, 'in former times, even *Minstrels* and *Singing children* might be pressed into the service of the crown; and that parents were liable to have their offspring torn from their homes to become choristers in the royal chapels.'

We are told of an ordinance of the time of Henry the Sixth for 'pressing minstrels', and that in the year 1550 a *commission* was granted to Phillip Van Wilder, Gentleman of the privie chamber, 'to take to the king's use', in 'anie churches or chapells within England, such and so many singing children and choristers as he and his deputy thought good'.

Again, in the following year, the master of the king's chapel had licence 'to take up, from time to time, as many Children to serve the King's Chapel as he shall think fit'.

Thomas Tusser (1515–1580), the well known agricultural poet, mournfully complained:

> Then for my voyce
> I must (no choice)
> Away; of force
> Like posting-horse,

> For sundry men
> Had placards, then,
> > Such child to take
> (The better breaste,
> The lesser reste)
> To serve the queen;
> For time so spente
> I may repente,
> > And sorrowe make.

My four volumes were acquired on three separate occasions, and should encourage the collector not to ignore the odd volume. I bought Volume Two marked 'odd vol', but full of plates and interesting reading, before the war, for one shilling, at a bookshop in Cheltenham where my interest in London is well known. Early in the war I paid half a crown for Volume One in the Charing Cross Road, and eleven months later I bought Volume Three for two shillings and, in the same shop, Volume Four for one shilling—because the binding was not so good. It follows that the binding of each of my volumes is different—a fact which must shock the real bibliophiles, but which has never cost me a moment's sleeplessness.

Incidentally the work was advertised in the Twenty-Fourth Edition of *The Original Picture of London*, published early in 1826: 'Early in Spring will be Published, in Five Volumes, small 8vo Illustrated by 150 Engravings, a New Work, entitled LONDINIANA. ....' I wonder why publication was delayed for three years. The preface is dated from the Russell Institute, 20th November 1828. What happened to the Fifth Volume, and why were the 150 engravings reduced to 99?

Not to be confused with *Londiniana* is *Londoniana*, by Edward Walford M.A., which appeared in 1879 in two volumes, being a series of sketches which had already appeared in various periodicals, but whilst they are more concerned with London than with Londoners there are several interesting stories about people. For instance, Walford tells of two 'Eccentric Lord Mayors', one of whom was that same Sir John Barnard to whom *A Present For An Apprentice* was dedicated, and whose eccentricity appears to have lain in his sturdy independence and incorruptibility; even Sir Robert Walpole, who alleged that 'every man has his price' was unable to 'buy' him. Walford adds—somewhat unnecessarily—'Nor am I venturing to detract from his merits when I say that possibly one good reason for his spotless honesty may be found in the fact that he lived and died immensely rich'.

The other Lord Mayor described as 'eccentric' by Walford was Sir William Staines (1730–1807; Lord Mayor 1801), who 'began life as a paviour and stonemason, made a fortune honourably, and married his cook-maid'. And it is given as an example of his eccentric behaviour that 'at a City feast when Sheriff, sitting by General Tarleton, he thus addressed him, "Eat away at the pines, General, for we must pay all the same, eat or not eat" ', from which Walford deduces that the Sheriff 'had not studied carefully the motto of William of Wykeham, "Manners Makyeth Man" '.

Another 'standard' work frequently to be seen is *London*—six volumes, each containing twenty-five papers, written by Charles Knight and other authorities in their respective fields. This was published from 1841 to 1844.

Most of the Papers are stolidly written and are stiff with facts, and the development of the various arts, crafts and innumerable activities of the Londoners are entertainingly described.

We can read the history of the Lord Mayor's Show which originated in the procession from the City to Westminster to obtain the approval of the City's choice by the King or his judges, which was King John's stipulation when, in 1215, he granted a Mayor to the City. The Mayor's right to the prefix *Lord* was granted by Edward III in 1354, with the style of Right Honourable.

Until 1453 the Mayor rode on horseback, but in that year the Lord Mayor Sir John Norman elected to travel up the Thames, with a pageant— the first Lord Mayor's Show. And Robert Fabyan who died in 1513, and who wrote *The Concordaunce of Historyes*, mentions that the Watermen, no doubt delighted with this fillip to their trade, wrote a song in his praise—thereby unconsciously forestalling Handel!

The part which music played in the life of the City forms the subject of another article. Royalty lead the way and there is a charming story of Queen Elizabeth and the composer Christopher Tye, who, says Knight, 'was playing somewhat too scientifically' before the Queen. A verger was sent to complain that he was playing out of tune, to which the offended musician retorted 'Tell her her ears are out of tune'.

There is reading to suit all tastes in these six volumes. Charles Knight was a glutton for work, an enthusiastic purveyor of education for the masses— and his death in 1873, when well over eighty, brought to an end a lifetime of service in spreading knowledge.

A number of books combine the topographical with the historical, and conduct the reader round the various districts in London with a running commentary, as it were, of the different personalities who have made these districts famous—or infamous—as the case may be.

One of the best of this type of book is *The Town, Its Memorable Characters and Events* by Leigh Hunt, published in 1848. It dealt, appropriately, with the streets between St Paul's and St James's 'being that part of the great highway of London which may be said to have constituted "The Town", when that term was commonly used to designate the metropolis', as Leigh Hunt wrote in the 'Advertisement' to Volume One.

The work is, for the most part, a reprint of articles which had appeared thirteen years earlier in the monthly supplements to Leigh Hunt's *London Journal* under the title of 'The Streets of London', and the book is delightfully chatty and easy to read, full of documented information and quotations in prose and in poetry, illustrative of the text, with forty-five not so very good illustrations.

The *Spectator* said of the book when it first appeared: '*The Town* is a book for all places and all persons; for the study, when one is tired of labour; for the drawing-room, parlour, carriage, or steam-boat.'

Interesting are the numerous *aliases* of London which Leigh Hunt collected, principally from Camden, and enumerated in his book:

Troja Nova, Troynovant, or New Troy.
Tre-novant, or the New City, (a mixture of Latin and Cornish).
Din Belin, or the City of Diana.
Caer Ludd, or the City of Ludd.—These are the names given by the fabulous writers, chiefly Welsh.
Londinium.—*Tacitus, Ptolemy, Antoninus.*
Lundinium.—*Ammianus Marcellinus.*
Longidinium.
Lindonium, (Λινδόνιον).—*Stephanus* in his Dictionary.
Lundonia.—*Bede*
Augusta.—The complimentary title granted to it under Valentinian, as was customary with flourishing foreign establishments.
Lundenbyrig.
Lundenberig.
Lundenberk.
Lundenburg.
Lundenwic, or wye.
Lundenceastre (that is, London-*castrum* or camp.)
Lundunes.
Lundene, or Lundenne.
Lundone.—Saxon names. Lundenceastre is Alfred the Great's translation of the Lundonia of Bede.
Luddestun.
Ludstoune.—Saxon translations of the Caer Ludd of the Welsh.
Londres.—French.
Londra. Italian. The letter *r* in these words is curious. It seems to represent the *berig* or *burgh* of the Saxons; *quasi* Londrig, from London-berig, in which case *Londres* would mean London-borough.

Two or three years ago I paid half a crown (which happened to be the original price) for a copy of a New Edition, published in 1859, in one small octavo volume with 448 pages, but wanting as I afterwards discovered, four pages. It almost fits comfortably into my pocket. Perversely, not very long ago, I paid eighteen pence for the First Volume of the First Edition, in the firm belief that I had the Second Volume at home—waiting for its better half—but after searching for some hours I was forced to conclude that I had merely *seen* that Second Volume in a shop, and not bought it.

Inside the front-cover is the label '*T. Smith's Circulating Library*, 20 Brewer Street, Golden Square, near Regent Street', giving 'Terms of Subscription'. '£1. 1. 0 per year for Old Works', '£2. 2. 0 per year for all New Works, Magazines, Reviews, etc.' I believe that the New Edition in one volume was reprinted in 1893.

A Saunter Through the West End, another of Leigh Hunt's works, must not be ignored. It covers, as its title explains, the West End of London, in the same way as *The Town* deals with districts further east.

He begins his book with 'Readers for some years past have shown such a regard for this subject, and been so willing to hear any lover of it who had his mite of information to add, or his opinion to express, that the writer now before them will make no apology to his old acquaintances for entering upon it without further preface.'

Then, because it explains so well the scheme followed by the other books I have been writing about, I quote the concluding words of the same paragraph: '. . . it is proposed in the following work to go with the reader through the streets of the West End, as if the writer and he were actually so doing: that is to say, as if they were lovers of local associations walking along the pavement at their leisure, and noticing any topic of interest which presented itself, new or old.'

My copy of *A Saunter* cost me three shillings and fourpence, in the Charing Cross Road—the book has fourteen chapters—they are very cheap at less than threepence each!

Leigh Hunt cannot be criticized; he is eminently readable—and I quote the opinion of an admirer, unknown by name to me, who wrote, in the middle of the last century: 'Leigh Hunt has illumined the fog and smoke of London with a halo of glory, and peopled the streets and buildings with the life of past generations'.

Literary and Historical Memorials of London by J. Heneage Jesse was published in 1847, and followed, in 1850, by his *London and Its Celebrities*.

In the preface to *London; Its Celebrated Characters and Remarkable Places*, published in three octavo volumes in 1871, 'an amalgamation', as he calls it, of these two books, Jesse gives a brief glimpse at the difficulties with which writers of books, other than fiction, have to contend: he tells us that while preparing *London and its Celebrities,* the second of his earlier books, Charles Knight's periodical publication *London* appeared. Strype had spent some twenty years preparing his edition of Stow's *Survey,* yet here we have Jesse complaining about a periodical publication which began to appear in 1841 'cutting in on' a book of his which was not published till 1850. This is an indication of the time which it takes to write a book requiring research, as compared with a work of fiction which, as distinct perhaps from an historical novel, can be written as quickly as the man of imagination can think and type or dictate.

Jesse was justified in pointing out that Knight's work differed from his own; for Knight had dealt with objects—collectively—rather than persons. But Jesse's troubles were not, as he tells us, at an end. *London and its Celebrities* was already in the hands of his publisher when *The Town* appeared, to be followed by Peter Cunningham's *Hand-Book,* which Jesse describes as 'the most valuable work on London which has appeared since the time of Stow'. However, Jesse's work does differ from theirs, and he was able, after having re-written portions of it, to publish *London its Celebrated Characters and Remarkable Places.*

It is very readable and full of anecdotes, but not so fully documented as it might be. I picked up my three volumes, very nicely bound, a few years ago in Cheltenham for half a guinea, and certainly have no cause to regret my purchase.

Jesse could, with more reason, have complained about a book which had been published the previous year, entitled *The Streets of London, with Anecdotes of their More Celebrated Residents* by John Thomas Smith, who had been Keeper of the Prints and Drawings in the British Museum. Smith died before the publication of the book, which was edited and also three parts written—says his biographer Wilfred Whitten—by Charles Mackay, LL.D., author of *The Thames and its Tributaries: or Rambles Among the Rivers* which was published in 1840.

Although the title page does not so name it, the first chapter of J. T. Smith's book is headed 'A Ramble in the Streets of London,' and the pages throughout the book are so headed.

The book would appear to have been a popular one; I have two copies, one 'New Edition', published in 1854 (for which I paid three shillings), and the other, published in 1861, which was given me by a friend.

This book, like *The Town,* has no index and though the contents of each chapter are stated in full, the book is not so easy to refer to, as to read.

John Timbs is a name we continually come across on the second-hand booksellers' shelves. He was an indefatigable collector of facts—a 'scissors' if not also a 'paste' man. Born in 1801 he died in 1875, and he wrote— anecdotally—a great number of historical and topographical books. His

Curiosities of London 'exhibiting the Most Rare and Remarkable Objects of Interest in the Metropolis; with nearly Sixty Years Personal Recollections.' is an encyclopaedic work of magnitude, and valuable (almost invaluable) as a reference book. The First Edition was published in 1855, and I quote from the preface, which is dated from '88, Sloane-street, Chelsea, 16 Jan., 1855': 'Twenty seven years since (in 1828) I wrote in the parlour of the house No. 3. Charing Cross (then a publisher's), the title and plan of a volume to be called "Curiosities of London". . . .'

And I follow up this extract with one from the preface to the Second Edition—from 'Hornsey-road, Dec. 1867';

'*The Curiosities of London* originally appeared in the Spring of 1855, in a small octavo volume of 800 pages, when it was received by the Critical Press with almost unanimous approval; or, in some respects, an inclination to take the word for the deed, and in others to kindly regard the difficulties of the labour. In either case I am bound to be grateful. The edition, over 3,000 copies, was sold within a comparatively short period, considering the character of the work, then regarded as almost exclusively *antiquarian*, although the above reception induces the belief that "the Present has its Curiosities as well as the Past". The book remained for several years entirely out of print, and second-hand copies could only rarely be obtained by advertisement, I then resolved upon its revision, and its reproduction, enlarged and more perfect in its details than hitherto; and the present volume of library size, 880 pages is the result . . .'

I paid one shilling and sixpence for my First Edition (minus the title page) and I reproduce Timbs' portrait which forms the frontispiece to the book. It is from a painting exhibited at the Royal Academy in 1854, by Thomas John Gullick, when it was 'pronounced to be the work of an artist of great promise'. Gullick painted Timbs at least once more, for the frontispiece to the Second Edition is from another of his paintings.

There are many interesting names amongst the 192 subscribers (a few of them bought more than one copy) to the First Edition (my copy of the Second has no list). They include Harrison Ainsworth of Arundel Terrace, Kemp Town, Brighton; H. Blencowe Churchill of Raymond-buildings, Grays Inn; F. Crace of Vine Cottage, Blythe Lane, Hammersmith; Alfred Crowquill of Portland Place North, Clapham-road; Peter Cunningham F.S.A. of Victoria-road, Kensington; Edward and George Dalziel—the former at Camden-street North, and the latter at Albert-street, Mornington Crescent; F. W. Fairholt, F.S.A. of Montpellier-square, Brompton; Birket Foster of Clifton-road, St. John's Wood; there were two Gullicks, Thomas of Pall Mall and Thomas John of Sloane-street; J. O. Halliwell, F.R.S., F.S.A., of Avenue Lodge, Brixton-hill; Douglas Jerrold of Circus Road, St. John's Wood; J. M. Langford of Raymond-buildings, Grays Inn; Mark Lemon of

Engraved by W.H. Mote, from a Painting by T.J. Gullick.

*Yours faithfully,
John Timbs.*

London: Longman & Co. 1868.

Gordon Street, Gordon Square; Charles Mackay LL.D., F.S.A., of Camden-square; W. M. Smith of the Strand, who bought two copies; W. M. Thackeray of Young-street, Kensington; Martin Farquhar Tupper, D.C.L., F.R.S., Albury, Surrey; Joseph Tussaud, Baker-street, Portman-square; and John Tymbs, Worcester—a relation, maybe, and another way of spelling the author's name?

Then, I have a copy of his '*London and Westminster: City and Suburb. Strange events, characteristics, and changes of Metropolitan life.*' In two volumes published in 1868, which I bought some ten years ago for six shillings, contains the bookplate of the Right Honble Charles Lindley Viscount Halifax, with his motto 'I like my choice', a sentiment which finds an echo in my heart.

Books by John Timbs may be found almost anywhere, at any price and at any time—from eighteenpence upwards; I have several. One cannot fail to be interested in everything he wrote. It may be that one knows it already, but the chances are that one may learn more about London from Timbs than from any other of the books about which I am writing.

Two books by William Harvey, a surgeon who wrote under the name of 'Aleph', are worth acquiring—the first is *London Scenes and London People*, published in 1863, and the second *The Old City, and its Highways and Byways*, published two years later.

Both books contain reprinted articles from the *City Press* and both books follow the same lines in that, as the Publishers in the preface to the second of them record, they 'preserve in an elegant and permanent form a series of sketches which, for their literary and antiquarian excellence, merit some more lasting home than the columns of a newspaper.' They are (reasonably) well illustrated, and will repay the few shillings for which one should be able to buy them.

Inside the cover of my copy of *The Old City*, is an interesting label; about a third of it is taken up with a picture of 'Chichester Literary Society & Mechanics Institute', and underneath is the information 'This Book One of a collection of 347 Volumes, was bequeathed to the Institution by the late Mrs Margaret Phelps M.DCCC.LXXIV. In order to preserve the Donor's generous Bequest from damage, it is requested that Special Care be taken of this Book, and that any injury to it be at once noted to the Librarian. '10 Days allowed for Reading'. As the book contains 362 pages it could not have been easy for the Members of the Institute to read—and digest—it in ten days. Perhaps they did not try, which would account for the very good condition of my copy.

At the end of *London Scenes and London People* is an interesting list of some 900 subscribers and their addresses, amongst whom was George Cruikshank (who was then living at 48 Mornington-place). Messrs Ring and Brymer of

THE WATER GATE, 1860.

Cornhill subscribed for five copies; I wonder to whom these old established caterers to the City presented those copies. Francis Ravenscroft, son (or grandson) of Birkbeck, founder of Birkbeck College of 29, Southampton-buildings, later of the Birkbeck Bank, subscribed for a copy, as did John Timbs, F.S.A., who was then living in Grays Inn.

William Harvey died at Lonsdale Square, Islington, on the 18th March 1873, aged 77.

In the same category I class *Haunted London* by Walter Thornbury, published in 1865; I have a later edition edited by Edward Walford published in 1880. One should not be misled into thinking that this book has anything to do with ghosts; it is about 'this London of the present haunted by the memories of the past', and contains anecdotes of the districts, roughly comprising the Borough of Holborn and the City of Westminster.

There are a number of illustrations by F. W. Fairholt, the most interesting, perhaps, showing the Water Gate (which is now at the bottom of Buckingham Street) as it was in 1860, with the Thames actually lapping the steps; this was before the construction of the Victoria Embankment, in 1862, drove the Thames away from the Gate.

There is a work which will be found on every other secondhand book-seller's shelf—two fat octavo volumes, bound in shining black, entitled *Walks in London*, by Augustus J. C. Hare, an indefatigable writer who, born in Rome, in 1834, compiled many guide books to that city, and wrote several topographical and other books before he died in 1903. His *Walks in London* was published in 1878, some of the chapters having appeared in a condensed form in *Good Words* the previous year. It must have met with a considerable measure of success, for my copy of the Fifth Edition (revised) is dated 1883.

The First Volume is chiefly devoted to the City, and the Second to the West End and Westminster, and, whilst Hare realized the impossibility of being original, he could claim that, taking Charing Cross as a centre, he described all the objects of interest in London and the peoples connected with them, in a consecutive way.

There are some charming little illustrations, mostly from sketches by Hare himself, 'Carefully transferred to wood by the skill of Mr T. Sulman, and executed by Mr W. Quick', as the Author tells us in his preface.

I do little more than mention *The Hallowed Spots of Ancient London* 'Historical, Biographical, and Antiquarian Sketches, Illustrative of Places and Events as they appeared and occurred in the olden Time', by Eliza Meteyard. I only paid three shillings for a 'New Edition' published in 1870—a prize awarded at Midsummer 1873 to John E. Nicoll of Sandwich School, Kent 'for passing the Cambridge local Examinations Junior Division London Centre.'

The authoress, referring of course to London writes in her preface: '. . . for the first time perhaps, apart from special histories, I have brought together a vast number of curious facts relating to its churches and chapels, its halls and streets, its prisons and houses, as also the lives of those who hallowed them by potential services, of which the memory can never die, at least with those who know that such services effected for the advance of civil and religious freedom, for breadth of thought, and purity of moral life.'

The religious or patriotic tone of the preface need not put anybody off; nor the not very good engravings by C. W. Sheeres. Copies abound in secondhand bookshops, and the book is a safe buy.

Walter Besant is a name to conjure with in any discussion about London. His *London* published in 1892—with 124 illustrations, and in a cheaper edition without the illustrations the following year, is a 'must'. Copies of the book are not scarce—I bought my copy of the 1892 edition in Worthing, a few years ago, for two shillings.

Besant presented what he very happily called 'instantaneous photo-graphs, showing the streets, the buildings and the citizens at work and at play'.

Equally to be instantaneously recognized as a first class book is his

Westminster, with 130 illustrations, published a few years later. Besant's theme is that Westminster was a place of resort and traffic before London existed, and he goes on to postulate that the beginning of London was not, as is commonly believed, a port, but that the twin hillocks overhanging the river, on either side of the Walbrook, were covered with huts, in which lived the hunters and the fishermen who 'fed' Westminster. And in the book is a long chapter on 'The Streets and the People' which is both suggestive and helpful. Besant was probably the most prolific and the best of London's historians of the last hundred years. Any and all his books can safely be bought on sight. Many of them have splendid illustrations and maps, and the more serious the student of London lore the greater will grow his need for Besant's books.

Such a student will now be satisfied that the subject is not prescribed by narrow bounds, but is all embracing, and unlimited in the opportunities which it presents to read with a roving eye for the out-of-the-way facts and ideas.

Thus I spotted an interesting fact when I was reading a chapter in Walter George Bell's *Unknown London*, entitled 'Letters from London during the great Plague'. Bell describes a series of 190 letters written by John Allin, a parson and a medical student who was living in London in 1665, to two friends at Rye. Bell quotes passages written by Allin asking his friend to send him more specimens of a certain plant, and for 'the moss that grows on dead men's sculls and bones'—for his medical experiments. The quoted passages seem to indicate that Allin may have been on the track of penicillin, for mould can resemble moss.

Walter Bell asserted that the letters were still in existence, and in his subsequently published work on the Plague he stated that they are in private ownership. In May 1947 I enquired as to their whereabouts in *Notes and Queries*, but received no reply.

Walter Bell, who was born in 1868, only died a few years ago. His books are a little too modern for my collection—*Unknown London* was published in 1920—but they are certainly well worth acquiring, and make ideal bedside books.

Bell's *Unknown London* is not to be confused with a book of the same name by A. T. Camden Pratt, and which consists of 47 articles reprinted from *The Globe* and *St James's Gazette*. The date of publication is not given, but the articles were certainly written over half a century ago, and very interesting they are. I paid four shillings for my copy in Epsom over twenty years ago.

8

Londoners as Seen by Their Contemporaries

As distinct from the authors of the last century who wrote about the Londoners of the past, there were many who wrote about the Londoners they knew. Their works ranged from the eternally pessimistic, emphasising the seamy side of life, written by men apparently incapable of smiling, to the everlasting optimist, who must be held responsible for the continual belief in the 'good old days'.

There is no need to emphasize that the diaries of Samuel Pepys (1632–1703) and John Evelyn (1620–1706) are invaluable aids to the study of their period; less well known is the diary of their contemporary Anthony à Wood (1632–1695)—the 'à' was assumed by him—the author of the *Athenae Oxonienses*, extracts from whose fascinating Biography and Journal Notes have been published by the Oxford University Press. I quote from Llewelyn Powys's Introduction to the book: 'Anthony à Wood had nothing of the lovable personal aplomb of Pepys, nothing of the sober well-bred dignity of Evelyn. He was, however, *a character*, a splenetic character, who went about his dedicated business with tireless intention. It may well be that the narrowness of his mind, his signal lack of imagination, his signal lack of literary artifice, actually adds to the value of these miscellaneous and indiscreet jottings he left behind him. They are blunt, unaffected annotations upon events and upon persons, intimately revealed by the details of their daily lives.'

Wood wrote principally of the daily happenings in Oxford, but he made many references to Londoners. The following entry in his *Journal* for 10th December 1682 is typical: '. . . News also that some prentices standing in the pillory in Cornhill for breaking the King's and Lord Mayor's order about bonefiers and burning the pope, they were all the while fed with good things (they say custards and chees-cakes) by the presbyterians and after they were taken downe were hug'd—if others had stood, or if their fault had been for favouring popery, they would have been pelted to death'.

This is a splendid book for the bedside, and I strongly recommend it.

The prize of my collection is *The Microcosm of London* which was published in 1808 by the German-born Rudolph Ackermann, the well-known art publisher of the Strand; it contains 104 aquatints by Augustus Charles Pugin, the French architect, and Thomas Rowlandson, the English artist and caricaturist; the history and topography are written by another Englishman—William Combe.

It was originally intended to publish the work in four volumes; each volume was to consist of six numbers, at seven shillings and sixpence each, and to contain twenty-five prints. After one volume containing thirty-two prints had been published, however, the price per number was raised to half a guinea, for new subscribers, and the work was completed in three volumes, the second containing thirty-two prints, and the third forty.

The work gives an immediate picture of London at that period, but the price, even of the 1904 reprint, puts it into the luxury class.

A few years ago I discovered the Third Edition of *Mornings at Bow Street*, a selection of the most humorous and entertaining reports which had appeared in the *Morning Herald*, by their Bow Street reporter, J. Wight, with twenty-one illustrations by George Cruikshank, published in 1825. A companion volume *More Mornings at Bow Street*, was published in 1827.

These little stories, and there are more than 170 of them in the two octavo books, give us word pictures of the underworld's small fry which might almost have been written last week. The forty-eight woodcuts, designed by George Cruikshank, are charming. Although, in a letter to a friend, he denied that his pictures were from sketches made on the spot, claiming that they came from his 'braine after studying and observing Nature', they are all the better for lacking a photographic touch.

It is not feasible to quote at length from these books, for anything short of a 'case' complete would inevitably fail to convey its full flavour. But I recommend them as perfect examples of police court reporting, which so exactly conduct the reader into the presence of the Majesty of the Law. However, I quote two shorter reports which are not in the book itself, but are contained in press-cuttings glued on to brown paper sheets and bound into it.

The first is from the *Sussex Express* of May 1862, and the other is dated November 1877:

'At Dover Police Court, the other day, John Collyer applied for assistance to regain possession of his Bath chair. He said that, at three o'clock on the previous afternoon, an order came to the chair stand for a gentleman to be taken up from a street at the back of St Mary's Church; he took the chair round, and found Dr Standen upon the door steps waiting for him. Not knowing that the people of the house had shut him out, and so got rid of a troublesome lodger, he assisted him into the chair, and had been driving him about ever since.—(A laugh.)—Magistrate: What, ever since three yesterday afternoon—all night? Applicant: Yes, sir, except for a little while. I can't get him out of the chair anyhow. I was wheeling him about from three in the afternoon until past two o'clock in the morning. (Laughter.)—Magistrate: I can't see how I am to help you; he has got possession of your chair. Where is he now?—Applicant: He doesn't know I've come here. I left him and the chair opposite Mr Elgar's, the butcher.—Magistrate: But has he had any refreshment all this time?—Applicant: Lor bless ye! Why I've druv him to nearly every public-house in the town—specially to Pier-end; he calls for something to drink, and then gives the best part of it away—(laughter)—'cept what he puts in a little square bottle he carries with him.—(Loud laughter.) After driving him to all these places, I was tired, so I said to him, "When do you mean to go home again sir?" "That's my business," says he, "you mind yours, and drive me back to the Pier-end."—(Laughter.) And there, sir, we went from one house to the other until it was twelve o'clock, and he couldn't get anything else served. Then I druv him about the town.—(Laughter.) Superintendent Coram raised a new roar of laughter by adding that, at one o'clock in the morning he saw the chair pulled up close to one of the public lamps, by the light of which the doctor was reading.—(Renewed laughter.)—Magistrate: How long did he keep reading? Applicant: Not long, sir. Soon afterwards he lit his pipe.—(Laughter) I was wery cold, and he said I might keep him "moving", so I pulled the chair until between two and three, and we'd been all over the town; and then I says to him, quite worn out, "Where are you going now?" "Where are you going to?" says he —(Loud laughter.) "Home", says I. Then he told me he hadn't any home to go to, and he asked me where I was going to put the chair. I told him in the coach-house, where I kept it. "Ah," says he, "that'll do very well—put me with it. I shall be just as well in this chair as in bed!" and so you know he would, sir.—(Loud laughter.)—Magistrate: And so you locked him up in the coach-house all night?—Applicant: I left him there about three, and looked in about five to see whether he was all right, and then he told me he had never slept more comfortably in all his life.—(Laughter.) At half-past six I took him a cup of coffee, part of which he drank, and told me he was quite ready to begin his morning visits when I was; but I ain't going to draw him about the town all day today.—(A laugh.)—Magistrate: Well, he can't make you drow him about; that's optional. What was he doing when you left him just now? Applicant: Reading, or writing or smoking.—Sergeant Bailey was directed to accompany applicant to the chair, and try the effect of his uniform and authority upon the occupant. A small crowd accompanied them, and in due time the chair was found where Collyer had left it. He received orders from the doctor to call at the Druid's Head, and after a craftily qualified cup at this hostelrie the doctor was "caught napping." Collyer then procured the service of a sturdy butcher, and the key of an empty room, attached to the Temperance Hall, having been obtained, Dr Standen was lifted from the seat he had stuck to for 22 hours out of 24, and deposited on the floor.—'

The second report is headed:

AMUSING NAUTICAL EVIDENCE

'At the Greenock police court, on Tuesday, a young woman was charged with having been disorderly in Longwell-close. She pleaded not guilty. Fergus Rodner, a sailor, was called for the defence.—The Fiscal (to witness): Do you belong to the Narcissus? Witness: No, sir; I belong to the Northampton, sir.—The Fiscal: Then tell us what you know of this case. Witness: Well, sir, I landed at Prince's Pier last night. Under a fair wind I made a course along by Hamilton-street, I think you call it, where I fell in with a fresh frigate—(laughter)—of the name of Jane Collins. (Renewed laughter.) I took her in tow, and we tacked about a little, and then steered for Longwell-close. There we met in with another fresh frigate—(laughter)—with barnacles on—(loud laughter)—and we got into collision with her. (Laughter.) She struck my frigate right across the bow. (Roars of laughter.) My frigate said it was a shame to do the like. I was on the look-out, sir, at the time my frigate was struck across the bows —(laughter)—and I sees two pirates (policemen) coming along. (Loud laughter.) They came alongside. (Laughter)—The Assessors:—Well, and what did they do? Witness: Well, sir, they brought my frigate to anchor. (Roars of laughter.) I have told the truth, and nothing but the truth. I never was in Greenock before, sir. (Witness was then allowed to leave the box.)—After hearing the evidence of the "frigate with barnacles on", accused was dismissed.'

I have two other books that fall into the same category: *Sketches of Life and Character: taken at The Police Court, Bow Street by George Hodder (Reporter to the Morning Herald) with illustrations by Kenny Meadows, Leech, Hine, Hammerton, Henning, and Newman.* published in 1845. And *Humours & Oddities of the London Police Courts from the opening of this century to the present time. Illustrated and edited by 'Dogberry.'* published in 1894.

Reporting one of the all too frequent husband-and-wife cases Dogberry reprints the following lines which formed part of the matter complained of in a libel action tried at the Court of King's Bench in the time of George the Fourth—

> Do come and help a poor old man
> A giddy wife to tame, sirs;

She's young and active, blithe and gay,
Whilst I am old and lame, sirs.
So lovely, handsome, plump and fair,
Her age is twenty-three, sirs,
That now I fear, in spite of all,
She'll be the death of me, sirs.
When I did go a-wooing her,
She smiled, and said—'Dadda!'
But now it's—'Disagreeable
And ugly old Papa!'
I wish I was a widower,
A widower I'd remain,
I would not have a young wife
To call me old and lame;
I wish I was a widower,
A widower I'd be,
I would not have a young wife
To tease and worry me.

But 'we must not make a scarecrow of the law . . .'

James Grant (1802–1879) certainly deserves an honourable mention among writers on the Londoners of his time: In 1836 (contemporary with Charles Dickens's *Oliver Twist*) appeared the First and Second Series (two volumes in each) of his *The Great Metropolis*; the books are easy to read, and convey a very clear picture of life in London at that day.

I have already mentioned my interest in an author's footnotes, which I liken to an old-fashioned stage aside, and I am interested in James Grant's note to the first chapter in Volume One of *The Great Metropolis* (Second Series) dealing with 'Almack's': 'It may be right to mention, that for much of the information contained in this chapter, I am indebted to one who has been for many years a member.' Presumably it was the same member who supplied the details of the fancy dress ball which ended the Season in July 1836: 'About 500 of the nobility and gentry were present', and the party lasted from ten o'clock, when the ball-room, 'illuminated by a profusion of wax-lights', was thrown open, until after five o'clock the following morning. 'At eleven o'clock, dancing commenced to the music of Collinet's fine quadrille band, led by Nadoud, and including Tolbeque, Remy, Rhode, Hatton, etc., from the King's Theatre.' 'La Remede contre le Sommeil' was one of the favourite waltzes 'finely played', as were 'others by Strauss.'

A long list of the company present was given, headed by:
'Princes—Galitzin and Wittycapstein.
Princesses—Wittycapstein and Galitzin.'

(There must have been something subtle in reversing the order of the names.)

And the list works down through Marquisses, Marchionesses, Earls, Countesses, Lords, Ladies, Barons, Foreign Counts, Sirs, Honourable Messieurs, Honourable Mesdames, and concluding with Honourable Misses.

Revelling in recollections of a time when London had nothing to learn in the way of luxury entertainment from any other capital in the world, I enjoyed this chapter.

There is a chapter on 'Literature' from which I cull the following sentence: 'Throw a string across any thoroughfare you choose in the metropolis, excepting of course such localities as St Giles's and the Seven Dials, and you may depend on it that out of every thirty or forty persons you catch, two if not more are authors. The mere circumstances of having written a book, good, bad, or indifferent, was at one time a mark of distinction of itself.'

Grant makes a charming, naïve remark in the chapter dealing with 'Authors and Publishers': 'Messrs Saunders and Otley are favourably known among literary men for the liberality of their terms to writers of celebrity,' and a footnote explains: 'This was written before the author was aware that Messrs Saunders and Otley were to be the publishers of his work.'

The same author's *Sketches in London* was published in 1838; I have the Second Edition, published in 1840, with twenty-four humorous illustrations by 'Phiz', and others. The twelve long chapters deal with such subjects as 'Begging Impostors', 'Debtors' Prisons—The Queen's Bench'—inevitably one thinks of Charles Dickens. There is a chapter on 'The Lumber Troop', which would appear to have originated as a frolic, but became an association of good fellows to which such illustrious persons as Hogarth belonged, as did several Members of Parliament, from time to time. It had its headquarters in Dr Johnson's old house in Bolt Court, Fleet Street—and boasted a Benevolent Fund. Their story is told in a lively style, which amuses at the same time as it imparts information of a bygone age.

One also reads about 'Penny Theatres', 'Lunatic Asylums', 'Bartholomew and Greenwich Fairs', and 'Courts of Request'—an early type of County Court—there were five of them in London— in which some 75,000 cases were tried every year; in none of them was a sum exceeding ten pounds in dispute!

Grant's *Travels in Town* was published in two volumes in 1839. Two years later followed *Lights and Shadows of London Life*, again in two volumes. Since no one can express an author's intentions better than the author himself, I quote his preface, which is dated October 1841:

'The interest which continues to be felt in everything connected with metropolitan society and manners, in conjunction with the remarkable success which his previous works on similar subjects has met with, has induced the author to present the public with two more volumes illustrative of London Life. The work, it will be observed, is formed on the same plan and written in the same style as "The Great Metropolis" and "Travels in Town"; to which six volumes, indeed, it may be regarded as an indispensable companion.'

In a chapter entitled 'Female Servants', in the first volume of *London Life,* Grant quotes 'an accomplished and highly-talented lady, in a private letter' to himself, as writing 'Reform marches everywhere but through our kitchens, where it is most wanted.' And the chapter is an illuminating revelation of the conditions of a class of worker who could, in Grant's words, 'exercise a very material influence on the comfort of families,' and who might expect to be paid a wage of six to seven pounds per annum in trades-men's houses; if she were over twenty years of age a servant of all-work could hope to receive ten to twelve pounds. 'In the middle ranks of society', wrote Grant, 'where a plurality of servants are kept, the wages of each vary from £15 to £20 per annum. The wages in the higher grades of society are con-siderably better, generally varying from twenty to thirty guineas a-year. In some instances they are higher still, but these instances are very rare.'

Those may have been happy days for the well-to-do, but one's imagina-tion boggles at the thought of the sum of human misery which the poor girls 'below stairs' had to put up with. And yet 'As servants receive much better wages in the metropolis than in the provinces, it will not excite surprise when I mention, that they dress much finer here than in country towns. Indeed, so smartly dressed are some of our metropolitan female servants, that on holidays they have all the appearance, so far as mere apparel can confer that appearance upon them, of perfect ladies. You may often pass in the streets the maid and the mistress of a family, living at the rate of £1000 or £1500 a-year, and be unable to say which is Mrs So-and-So, and which is Mary, her house-maid. This love of finery above their station, is the besetting sin of the female servants of London.' And they achieved this 'finery' on a *maximum* wage of thirty guineas a year.

I could continue quoting from these fascinating books, but I have surely written enough to confirm that I consider James Grant to have been a first class writer on his subject—probably because he was a journalist; and he subsequently became editor of the *Elgin Courier,* the *Morning Advertiser* and his own *London Journal.*

The World of London, by John Fisher Murray, a collection of articles which had appeared in *Blackwood's Magazine,* was published in 1844. I paid a shilling for my copy of the two volumes, bound into one, which, on any reckoning, was cheap for 598 octavo pages, containing thirty-two chapters on such diverse subjects as 'Of Vulgar errors concerning life in London', and 'The Stomachs of London'.

COSTERMONGERS IN HOLIDAY ATTIRE.

[*From a Photograph.*]

For a good thorough study of the dreadful hardships which the under-dog had to endure one hundred years ago I cannot too strongly recommend Henry Mayhew's *London Labour and the London Poor*—reproducing articles which had been published, serially, in the *London Chronicle* in 1851. I am not going to quote from any of its four volumes; my *The Street Traders Lot: London 1851*, published by the Sylvan Press in 1947, is a good introduction to the work, but I reproduce, by way of a literary-pictorial joke, the picture which appeared in 1852, in Volume Three, No. 79 with the caption 'Coster-mongers in Holiday Attire'. The two men on the outside appear to be of the rougher type, but the man in the centre, in his frock coat and top hat, would pass anywhere for a prosperous tradesman, whilst the bandage on the fore-finger of his right hand seems to add authenticity to the photograph. It is with mixed feelings that we find that in 1856 Mayhew reproduced the same picture in his work *The Great World of London* (which dealt with the prisons of London) with the caption 'Ticket-of-Leave Men'!

Such a substitution was not unique. In 1790 a portrait of Peter Pindar (the name under which Dr John Wolcot wrote) was published—but did not sell, whereupon 'Renwick Williams, the Monster' was substituted for the name of Peter Pindar, when the picture sold like hot cakes. There is an account of Renwick Williams's trial for an assault upon Miss Anne Porter (whose father 'kept a tavern and a cold bath' in St James's street) in Camden Pelham's *The Chronicles of Crime* or the *New Newgate Calendar*, which was published in 1840.

Similar books continued to pour from the press. Thomas Miller's *Picturesque Sketches of London, Past and Present*, was published in 1852. My copy cost me four shillings and sixpence. Its twenty-two chapters are, for the most part, reprinted from the *Illustrated London News*, but it is the illustrations which attract as much as the prose; of the forty-nine illustrations in the book I reproduce the one which I think the most entertaining. Hobson was the Cambridge carrier who hired out horses to the undergraduates, but gave them no choice of steed, so that they were obliged to ride whatever Hobson provided for them—hence 'Hobson's choice', and it is odd that, whilst Miller enthused about The Four Swans' Inn Yard, with its old fashioned galleries, he overlooked the implication of Hobson and his horses. The print is the only one I have seen illustrating 'Hobson'.

I have a copy of the Second Edition of the *Rookeries of London: Past, Present, and Prospective*, by Thomas Beames, M.A., Preacher and Assistant of St James's, Westminster, which was published in 1852, and for which I paid three shillings and sixpence. According to the author's preface it differs materially from the First Edition: 'large additions have been made, some of the antiquarian portions of it omitted or abridged, whilst the lighter and more satirical parts have also been left out.'

THE FOUR SWANS' INN YARD.

No entertainment is to be derived from reading this book, but it is a solid record of realities; it depicts the miserable conditions of St Giles, and Saffron Hill, Jacobs Island and Ratcliffe Highway, and describes the 'spivs' —The Crimp, the Broker and the Tallyman—the 'spiders' for whom these rookeries provided a never ending supply of 'flies'.

One of the strange facts recorded relates to the construction of New Oxford Street. It was cut through St Giles—one of the worst rookeries of London—and it was intended to assist in a clearing, and a cleaning up of the district. It would seem, however, that the architects of the scheme overlooked an important point: if you pull down old and overcrowded buildings you must find somewhere to house the people who are dispossessed. The result of the failure to grasp this obvious truth is clearly shown in the statement that in 1841 there were 277 people living in twelve houses in Church Lane, whilst in 1847, when New Oxford Street was opened, those same twelve houses harboured no less than 461 people.

A sordid book, but a useful contribution to our understanding of the social conditions of a century ago.

In 1853 Charles Manby Smith, author of *The Working-Man's Way in the World*, collected a number of papers, which he had during the preceding six or seven years contributed to various journals, and published them under the title *Curiosities of London Life: or Phases, Physiological and Social, of the Great Metropolis*. It is clear that Smith and Mayhew were working at the same time, on the same subject; but Smith contented himself with merely getting a story, where Mayhew became at all times analytical.

I like a remark which Smith makes at the end of his preface. After thanking 'those unknown but benevolent friends', who, having read in *Chambers's Journal* an account by him of some poor fellow's misfortunes, had sent him 'the means of ameliorating in some degrees the hard condition of his lot', he goes on, 'it is a pleasant task to return thanks for unsolicited kindness to an unfortunate stranger; and there is no valid reason why I should not couple it with another pleasure—that of returning my compliments to a coterie of "respectable" rascals who promised to break my head for exposing the villany of the "Knock-Out." ' I bought my copy of the book (I have never seen another) for five shillings and sixpence in Gloucester.

In 1857 the same author published *The Little World of London; or, Pictures in Little of London Life*—408 pages containing thirty-nine short pieces, reprinted from his contributions to the press, and including such subjects as 'Amusements of the Moneyless',' Confessions of a Picture-Dealer's Hack', and 'Fiddles and the Fiddle-Trade'. In the chapter on 'Pater-noster-Row and Magazine-Day' we read how, in the afternoon of the day of publication, 'carts and waggons begin to defile into the Row from the western entrance, to carry off the parcels to the carriers' depots. According to a very necessary regulation, well understood, the carts and vehicles performing this service enter the Row from the western or Ludgate Hill end, and draw up with horses' heads towards Cheapside. As a compensation for any trouble this rule may occasion, the carters have a small monthly gratuity allowed them.'

Charles Manby Smith gained no entrance into the *Dictionary of National Biography* or *Men and Women of the Time*; he deserved a mention.

If I had paid half a crown for the book, the name of which, according to the spine, was *Dens of London*, without looking inside, I might have had just cause to complain that the title was misleading. As a matter of fact before I bought the book I read the title page which clarified the situation, even if it gave the lie to the title on the spine. My copy—the Second Edition of *Notes and Narrative of a Six Years Mission, Principally Among the Dens of London* by R. W. Vanderkiste, late London City Missionary, was published in 1854—two years after the First Edition. And if the title page set out to convince me that the book was not to be taken in a light-hearted manner, some of the chapters—'The Professedly Infidel Population', 'Intemperance' and 'The Criminal Population', left me in no doubt as to the kind of book in which I was investing.

The book only just misses falling into the category of a religious work, but being, as the author himself points out, 'not a book of opinions, but of incident, narrative, and fact', it gives a first-hand picture of the London of a century ago.

I found it easy and interesting reading, generously interspersed with biblical texts, but with unexpected delights, such as this footnote to an extract from the *Illustrated London News* of 22nd May 1847, dealing with the 'Cow Cross District' of Clerkenwell, and some of the criminal dwellers in 'Jack Ketch's Warren' including, in particular, a reformed housebreaker: 'A thief once observed to me, gentlemen might do away with pick-pocketing —"Let them use cotton handkerchiefs, and it would not answer for us, they fetches a mere nothing." '

Practically every one of the book's 295 pages is given an informative running headline, such as 'Struggles for a Clean Shirt', 'Blood Money System', 'Socinianism not Popular Among the Poor', 'Evil Effects of Drinking Usages', 'Delirium Tremens', 'Bacchus and anti-Bacchus', and 'Absence of Parental Care', concerning which a passage from the Government Inspectors of Prisons' Introduction to their 10th Report on Home Discipline is quoted: 'It is well known that the principal causes which lead to the offences of criminal youth, may be traced to the absence of parental care and control. . . .' There is a modern ring about that which induces the thought that those responsible for the welfare of young people do not seem to have learned much in the past hundred years! Only one page is headed 'Den of Infamy', which is described as 'situated in W—H—C—, T—Street'.

There is an interesting account of a visit paid by the author to the sole survivor of the Cato Street Conspiracy of 1820; it appears that the man was warned by a government spy, of the name of Castles, to keep away from that fateful meeting on February 23rd, when a Bow Street Officer named Smithers was killed.

A quotation from a Treatise by Joseph Gurney, a friend of Wilberforce, and a relation of Mrs Fry, interests me because a label in the front of my book shows that it once belonged to John Henry Gurney of Catton Hall, Norfolk, whilst a transparent strip over his name carries that of S. Gurney Buxton. And John Henry Gurney may have been a son of that Sir John Gurney who procured the conviction of two of the Cato Street conspirators.

There are many poems in the book, one of them written by 'Knox', presumably Vicesimus Knox (1762–1821), the compiler of *Elegant Extracts*. It appears, surrounded by quotations from the scriptures, in the middle of a denunciation of the Philosophy of Atheism. It may well have provided the theme for T. E. Brown's 'My Garden'—that lovesome thing executed so many times in poker-work to adorn a myriad of walls. Although 'My Garden' was written between the 6th and 14th of July, 1875, it was not published until 1900.

Knox's poem is perhaps less well-known, in its entirety, so I give it below:

> The fool hath said, 'There is no God':
>   No God! Who lights the morning sun,
> And sends him on his heavenly road,
>   A fair and brilliant course to run?
>   Who, when the radiant day is done,
> Hangs forth the moon's nocturnal lamp,
>   And bids the planets, one by one,
> Steal o'er the night vales dark and damp?
>
> No God! Who gives the evening dew,
>   The fanning breeze, the fostering shower?
> Who warms the spring-morn's budding bough
>   And paints the summer's noontide flower?
>   Who spreads, in the autumnal bower,
> The fruit trees' mellow stores around;
>   And sends the winter's icy power
> To invigorate the exhausted ground?
>
> No God! Who makes the bird to wing
>   Its flight-like arrow through the sky,
> And gives the deer its power to spring
>   From rock to rock triumphantly?

No God! Who warms the heart to heave
    With thousand feelings soft and sweet,
And prompts th' aspiring soul to leave
    The earth we tread beneath our feet?

No God! Who fix'd the solid ground
    On pillars strong that alter'd not?
Who spread the curtain'd skies around?
    Who doth the ocean bounds allot?
    Who all things to perfection brought
On earth below, in heaven abroad?
    Go, ask the fool of impious thought,
That dares to say,—'There is no God!'

These poems make it easier to read about 'the stench' of that part of the Fleet Ditch which had not yet been covered in and which, although 'almost stagnant, possesses at times a current sufficient to turn a mill of forty-horse power.' On one such occasion 'a man ventured down on a ladder to draw water, whilst the stream was in rapid motion, and was swept away and perished'. Then we are told that 'after a heavy thunderstorm in 1847, the current became so rapid, that the arch to the Thames could not carry it off. It burst upwards with a terrific force, carrying away two houses and filling one street, Lower Bowling Street, and Bull's Head Court at the lower end, to the depth of seven feet, almost instantaneously . . . Heavy articles of furniture were washed away, and several persons narrowly escaped with their lives.'

Writing about the gambling houses of London (the 'hells'), the author tells us that 'Crockfords, in St James's Street, cost in erection nearly £60,000. The furnishing of this establishment cost in addition £35,000' whilst the cellar, which measured 285 feet in length, 'contained wines to suit every diversity of taste. It was kept by Crockford's son, and was valued at £70,000', and the author adds the 'melancholy reflection' that the total, £165,000, *exceeded by several thousand pounds, the whole sum in donations and subscriptions received by London City Missions for the evangelization of London during the whole sixteen years of its existence!'*

Vanderkiste, on the authority of *Chambers's Journal*, says that, according to the Post Office Directory for 1848, London contained:

    2,500   barbers
      990   buttermen and cheesemongers
    1,700   butchers
    3,000   grocers and tea dealers
      900   established dairy-keepers

400   fishmongers

1,300   greengrocers and fruiterers
_____

Total 10,790

And 11,000 public-houses.

And, as a final extract, I quote the following: 'On 1st January, 1852, the number of persons belonging to the Metropolitan Police Force was 5,549. One inspecting superintendent, eighteen superintendents, one hundred and twenty-four inspectors, five hundred and eighty-seven sergeants, and four thousand eight hundred and nineteen constables. The total sum paid for the police in the year 1851 amounted to £422,299. 5s. 4d. The City Police in 1850 numbered five hundred and sixty men.'

A book of a similar kind, only not so heavily charged with morals, or rather immorality, is *The Night Side of London* by J. Ewing Ritchie. My copy of the Second Edition, revised, for which I paid five shillings, was published in 1858.

In his introduction Ritchie gives us page after page of statistics—the number of men, women, and children, widows and widowers. He quotes Henry Mayhew as saying 'if the entire people of the capital were to be drawn up in marching order, two and two, the length of the great army of Londoners would be no less than 670 miles, and supposing them to move at the rate of three miles an hour, it would require more than nine days and nights for the average population to pass by.'

We are told how many streets there were in London; the length of gas piping under them; that the London General Omnibus Company paid £400,000 for 600 omnibuses, 'with horses and harness and goodwill,' and that, in the week ending the 31st October 1857, 595 of the Company's omnibuses ran in London not less than 222,779 miles, or nearly ten times the circumference of the globe, and they carried not less than 920,000 passengers.

Unfortunately there is no index, and one has to hunt through the introduction's thirty-three pages, aided only by their running headlines.

There are twenty-five chapters; they include accounts of visits to such well remembered resorts as 'The Cave of Harmony', 'The Canterbury Hall' and 'The Eagle Tavern'—commemorated in the old song:

> Up and down the City-road,
>   In and out the Eagle,
> That's the way the money goes,
>   Pop goes the weasel.

The Tavern was, as the author somewhat unkindly points out, 'situated in an appropriate locality in the City-road, not far from a lunatic asylum, and contiguous to a workhouse.'

He takes us into Ratcliffe Highway—'In beastliness I think it surpasses Cologne with its seven and thirty stenches, or even Bristol or a Welsh town.'

Ritchie was thinking—inaccurately—of S. T. Coleridge's little joke entitled 'Cologne':

> In Köln, a town of monks and bones,
> And pavements fang'd with murderous stones,
> And rags, and hags, and hideous wenches;
> I counted two and seventy stenches,
> All well defined, and several stinks!
> Ye Nymphs that reign o'er sewers and sinks,
> The river Rhine, it is well known,
> Doth wash your city of Cologne;
> But tell me, Nymphs! what power divine
> Shall henceforth wash the river Rhine!

He describes 'The Costermonger's Free-and-easy' and a public Execution.

The writing is somewhat wooden, yet I still recommend the book because it will help to recapture the flavour of the seamy side of London life a hundred years ago.

I have a recollection of a song about an animal shop sung in a musical comedy at the old Gaiety Theatre some forty or fifty years ago, and which began:

> If ever you're my way
> Quite close to Ratcliffe Highway
> Just look at my large stock in trade
>   I've everything on sale-o
> From a winkle to a whale-o

and, in *East and West London* 'being notes of common life and pastoral work in Saint James's Westminster and in Saint George's-in-the-East' by the Rev. Harry Jones, M.A., Rector of St George's-in-the-East, published in 1875, I read all about Mr Jamrach, and his shop in Ratcliffe Highway, 'always full of parrots and other birds'. Mr Jamrach kept his wild beasts in Betts Street, St George's, and he always had orders in his books for more than he could supply. He had no need to advertise, but from time to time 'announced' that 'such and such beasts were at Jamrach's', and he was so well known that there was no need to add his address.

The unopened pages following page 200 are evidence that the book's previous owners did not manage to get through its 303 pages.

But as proof that one can always find something of interest in a book

H. Adlard Sc.

Yours truly,

James Greenwood.

about London I quote the author's account of how he discovered 'the nearness of the East of London to the West':

'I lived close to the Langham Hotel, and on the occasion of my first taking Sunday duty at St George's I hailed a crawling cab in Portland Place and drove there. To my surprise it landed me at the gate of my new church in twenty-eight minutes. Of course, it being Sunday, the streets were clear, but I had not urged the driver to any special speed. The next week I got the jailor at the Marlborough Street police-court to go over my course with the fatal wheel which decides the disputes between cabmen and their 'fares'. The distance from the Oxford Street Circus to the iron gate of the church at St George's in the East turned out to be something under four miles—a verdict which several cabmen have since heard with much professional affectation of scepticism; but on my informing them of my authority they have shown by their acquiescence that they had drawn upon their faith in the vaguely exaggerated public conceptions of the remoteness of the East in attemping to decline half-a-crown for the journey.'

Mr Jones has a pretty story of a butcher who, ignoring the cheaper *Standard, Daily News* and *Daily Telegraph*, paid for the right to read *The Times*, after Mr Jones had finished it. Our author was congratulating himself on having inculcated a little culture into the worthy butcher only to discover that the latter's preference for *The Times* was in reality for the toughness of its paper—'material tenacious enough to hold small parcels of meat without bursting.'

I have three books by James Greenwood whose 'A Night in a Casual Ward' ensured the success in 1866 of *The Pall Mall Gazette*, edited by his brother Frederick, who had helped to found the paper in the previous year.

The first of these books was published in 1867, and was called *Unsentimental Journeys: or Byways of the Modern Babylon*. On the title page Greenwood is described as the author of *A Night In the Workhouse* (presumably the *Pall Mall Gazette* articles written up) *The True History of a little Ragamuffin, etc. etc.* I have not come across either *The True History* or any of the etceteras.

The *Unsentimental Journeys* wander pleasantly over the paths pioneered by Henry Mayhew, with eleven illustrations which look as if they were drawn by Alfred Concanen.

I could quote many extracts: one must suffice. Describing a trip on a paddle steamer, the author writes: 'You discover that it is all a mistake about Britannia ruling the waves; it is the waves that rule Britannia. Your birthright of freedom—of freedom to dress as you please, eat what you please, and go where you please—no longer avails you.' I decline to comment on these freedoms as enjoyed by modern Londoners.

A pleasant book for the bedside.

The second is entitled *The Seven Curses of London*. It was published in

1869, and contained, as a frontispiece, the portrait of the author which I reproduce. The Seven Curses, described with a wealth of detail, were Neglected Children, Professional Thieves, Professional Beggars, Fallen Women, Drunkenness, Betting Gamblers and Waste of Charity.

The first paragraph sets the tone: 'It is a startling fact that, in England and Wales alone, at the present time, the number of children under the age of sixteen, dependent more or less on the parochial authorities for maintenance, amounts to three hundred and fifty thousand'. A sad book.

The third book of Greenwood's for which I was happy to pay three shillings is *The Wilds of London*, which was published in 1874. Mine is the 1876 edition and it has the Earl of Portsmouth's book-plate in it with his motto, *En suivant la Vérité*. Its thirty-seven chapters are reprints of newspaper articles in which the author had delighted 'to do his humble endeavour towards exposing and extirpating social abuses, and those hole-and-corner evils which afflict society.' They make easy reading, reading made even easier by a dozen illustrations in tint by Alfred Concanen.

9

Some Foreigners Look at London

Many foreigners have from time to time come over to London and written about us. One of the best of the books of this description was published in 1853, when Otto Wenckstern translated *Saunterings In and About London* from the German of Max Schlesinger. This is a chatty description of London and Londoners of a hundred years ago, seen through the eyes of an intelligent German (although I have read that he was Hungarian), and 'intended for the profit and amusement' (as he tells us in his preface to the English edition) of his countrymen.

It also imparts some bizarre information: for instance, writing of Lincoln's Inn Fields as the largest of London's squares, the author tells us that it covers an area of twelve acres (a fact to be found in many books), but adds that the 'joint extent of all the London squares is one thousand two hundred acres', so the area of Lincoln's Inn, one hundred years ago, was exactly one per cent of the area of all the squares in London.

I like his definition of an English 'Gentleman':

'Imprimis, he must not be compelled to eat his roastbeef by the sweat of his brow; for he who has to work for his existence in England cannot, of course, be said to be independent. He must have made the grand tour; for to the English the continent is in a manner a social high school and academy. How miraculously is the innate indestructible kernel of English character developed in such a man! As he ripens in years, he breaks through that icy covering which in his earlier years surrounded him, and he shakes off the chains of etiquette or bears them with a grace which proves that to him they are not a restraint, but an ornament.

'A few years later, he eclipses the flower of the male part of society in Germany and in France; his jovial humour is restrained by an exquisite tact; his politeness acquires substance from a free and hearty manner. There is in him so grave and natural a manliness, that to oblige him and to be obliged by him is equally agreeable. He would seem that he becomes younger as he advances in years.

'And what code of family morals enact and prescribe? Thou shalt invite

BATHING IN HYDE PARK.

a gentleman to a good and solid dinner, the which consisteth of fish and roast-meat, and pudding and wine. But thou shalt not invite him to the eating of cakes and sugar-plums, and much less shalt thou tempt him to a *soirée dansante*, where he would have much labour and no sustenance. And at table thou shalt not, as the wicked do, make the said gentleman talk of politics, business, science, and divers other heavy matters, lest peradventure his attention should be diverted from the enjoyment of the various dishes which thou shalt set before him.'

The book has the advantage of a number of rather naïve prints by W. McConnel, engraved by Dalziel; its very readability helps one to become steeped in the atmosphere of the times.

Alltagsleben in London. Ein Skizzenbuch (Everyday Life in London) by Julius Rodenberg was published in Berlin in 1860. Dedicated by the author 'to his dear friend Emmanuel Deutsch' of the British Museum it well repaid my effort in ploughing through it, but I had to resist the temptation to spend valuable time reading the same author's *Ein Herbst in Wales, Land und Leute, Märchen und Lieder*, which (published two years earlier) is bound up with his London story. I have space to quote only one of the facts which he noted: writing about the reaction of lovers to St Valentine's Day he recorded that on 14th February 1857 the Post Office delivered 150,000 letters at 9 o'clock, 25,000 at 10 o'clock, 175,000 at 11 o'clock, 12,000 at noon, and a further

60,000 in the course of the afternoon; 422,000 in all, and which was between 200,000 and 300,000 more than were delivered on any other day in the year. An entertaining *Skizzenbuch*.

Another highly desirable book by a foreigner is *Palace and Hovel: or, Phases of London Life. Being personal observations of an American in London, by day and night. . . .*' The author was Daniel Joseph Kirwan, and the book, 662 large octavo pages, 'Beautifully Illustrated with Two hundred Engravings, and a finely executed Map of London', was published by Belknap and Bliss of Hartford, Connecticut, 'by subscription only', in 1870. It is, perhaps, a pity that the map shows Holborn Hill, as it was called, before it was improved into Holborn Viaduct in the previous year. But I have no cause to quarrel with the bookseller's description—'Spine poor, good inside'—of the copy I bought in Cheltenham for six shillings in 1961. Daniel J., as today's American would wish to be known, filled his pages 'with graphic descriptions of royal and noble personages, their residences and relaxations; together with vivid illustrations of the manners, social customs, and modes of living of the right and the reckless, the destitute and the depraved, in the metropolis of Great Britain'. And the author dedicated his book 'to Samuel L. M. Barlow, Esq., of New York City, a True Gentleman in Every Quality and Duty of life'.

In his Preface the author refers to the pleasure which he has derived, 'while acting as a Special Correspondent of the New York *World*, in London',

A BOHEMIAN CAROUSE.

BEFORE THE "LORD MAYOR."

in wandering among the 'Three and a Half Millions of people', inhabiting 'the greatest and most populous City of the Modern World'. Mr Kirwan leaned heavily on Henry Mayhew for some of his facts and illustrations, and in some cases, but not in all, he even named that author as his authority.

There is an account of a morning spent in the Lord Mayor's Court, and the entry of that dignitary 'in furred robe of heavy cloth, like one of Rembrandt's burgomasters, a blazing gold chain depending from his neck and covering his waistcoat', and who, having to sentence a convicted forger, 'plucked up a proper spirit, threw back his furred sleeves, put on a look of profound wisdom, consulted with the prisoner's counsel, and making up his judicial mind'—ordered him to be set at liberty! The illustration reproduced here shows him in the act of doing so.

The author was taken to one of the resorts of London's Bohemians, where were congregated 'every first and fourth class reporter in London, all the dramatic witlings and punsters, the great shorthand guns of the House of Commons, the book reviewers, and the dramatic and musical critics,' who were waited on by a pot-boy, who washed the pewter pots, and cleaned the table with a dish-cloth 'for a stipend of ten shillings a week in British coin'. I reproduce his illustration of the scene—with his own description of it.

He was asked 'what he would have to drink', adding, that 'this is an anachronism in English customs, for the people of this tight little island generally allow a friend to pay for his own drink, as a custom which has long ago been endorsed by the best authority. There is no such folly known here as may be seen in every American public house, where the free and independent electors stand at a bar each hour in every day, treating one and the other with a promiscuous and reckless generosity. But among Bohemians all over the world it is different. If they cannot pay for a drink, they will call for it and treat each other with a liberality which is, to say the least, a most praiseworthy trait.'

Meaningless lyrics, some of them imported, are not unknown in this country, but the author prints the following stanza, as sung by strolling minstrels, and which, he records, 'sound senseless to an American's ear':

> Button up your waistcoat, button up your shoes
> Have another liquor and throw away the blues,
> Be like me and good for a spree,
>> From now till the day is dawning.
> For I am a member of the Rollicking Rams,
> Come and be a member of the Rollicking Rams,
> The only boys to make a noise,
>> From now till the day is dawning.

There is a chapter entitled 'The Lungs of London', from which I extract the following list of the public parks and gardens, with their several dimensions, and the accompanying picture entitled 'Bathing in Hyde Park' indicates not only that the Lido in the Serpentine is no new thing, and that it was known nearly 100 years ago, but that topless bathing trunks for men was also the fashion!

Battersea Park, — — — — — —	200	acres.
Kensington Gardens, — — — — —	380	,,
Finsbury Park (in progress), — — — —	300	,,
Green Park, — — — — — —	71	,,
Regent's Park, — — — — — —	450	,,
Victoria Park, — — — — — —	290	,,
Primrose Hill Park (Cricket Grounds), — —	50	,,
St James's Park, — — — — — —	83	,,
Hyde Park, — — — — — —	395	,,
Southwark Park (not completed), — — —	120	,,
Kensington (*sic*) Oval (for Cricket Ground), —	12	,,
Cremorne Garden, — — — — — —	10	,,
Botanic Garden, Chelsea, — — — —	12	,,
Royal Botanic Garden (Regent's Park), — —	20	,,
Horticultural Gardens (Cheswick) (*sic*), — —	35	,,

Kew Gardens,	–	–	–	–	–	–	60 acres.
Buckingham Palace Gardens,	–	–	–	–			40 ,,
Temple Gardens,	–	–	–	–	–	–	7 ,,
Zoological Gardens,		–	–	–	–	–	18 ,,
Greenwich Park,	–	–	–	–	–	–	200 ,,
Richmond Park,	–	–	–	–	–	–	2,253 ,,
							5,006 ,,

Curious that there is no mention of Lord's, which has occupied its present site since 1814.

A fascinating book.

The World of London by Count Paul Vasili, not to be confused with Murray's book of the same name, was published in 1885. It was translated from the French, and its original title, *La Société de Londres*, better explains the subject matter of its twenty-five chapters, which under the guise of letters to a friend provide gossip on the personalities of the day. They must have been more interesting in the original, for a publishers' note informs us that the work was acquired 'blind'—unseen, that is, in reliance of the reputation of the French publishers, but with the right to use their judgement and discretion to suppress anything objectionable, 'And,' say the publishers, 'in the exercise of this discretion they now frankly avow that they have found themselves compelled to omit several passages which they can only regard as scandalous, if not libellous.'

The subjects of the letters include the Queen and the Royal Family, the Court, Politicians, Artistes, and the Middle Class, and ends up with Sport.

In his first letter the author tells his friend that 'When the Queen wishes to show her sympathy with any institution, she presents it with a copy of her *Journal of Our Life in the Highlands.*

Writing on journalists he records that 'In London the press enjoys unlimited liberty, but has the good taste and prudence not to abuse it. Only the "Society" journals are ever prosecuted, and to them the process is a good advertisement.'

And writing on sport the author reports 'At the last Derby, when the officers of the Horse Guards alone lost £75,000, the bookmakers won £225,000, by collusion with the jockeys, who, not being able to bet on their own horses, back the horses they are not riding, and keep back their own to make their favourite win. When the Jockey Club detects these frauds, they are punished severely; but it is very difficult to discover and prevent them.'

I paid half a crown for my copy of the book in Gloucester, and read its 300 octavo pages in the train coming up to London.

Another book of the same type *Society in London,* by a Foreign Resident, had been published a year or so earlier. It is perhaps a little more factual and rather freer with its anecdotes of the various personalities concerned; maybe the publishers may have had something to do with that. A couple of years ago I paid four Swiss francs for a German translation of the First and Second Editions (combined) which had been published in 1885, and shortly afterwards I bought for fourpence, the Ninth Edition of the original English version, which had been published in 1886. I will buy any book, even remotely connected with London and Londoners, at such a price! This book is worth more, how much more it is difficult to say; to the general reader on London perhaps not a great deal, but to the student of the Londoners of that particular period quite a lot more.

Some years ago I paid two shillings for a book entitled *Japanese Ideas of London and its wonders, Its Inhabitants, and their Manners and Customs; Described in a Letter to his Wife at Yokohama.* By A Japanese Scout. The book was 'Printed for Private Circulation', by G. Shield of Sloane Square, and my copy is inscribed in a flowing copybook style 'Mrs T. Garroway with the Author's kind regards. London Septr 1873.'

The letter is in verse—some 1500 lines in fifty pages. It is full of humorous references to Londoners—especially the ladies, and we can also learn from it; there is a reference to an accident which apparently happened to one of Queen Victoria's daughters. The author is describing the affected way our ladies dress—and walk. He goes on:

> Not to say anything of another vile imp
> That is called, I am told, the 'Alexandrian limp,'
> And which to acquire they make the one heel
> Much higher than t'other, in order to reel
> And stagger as if overflowing with drink,
> Just merely to imitate, —do only think—
> (The truth of the statement 'tis needless to blink)
> Just only to mimic an accident rare
> Which happened to Royalty's fairest of fair.

There are another 150 lines in a P.S. towards the end of which:

> Oh, England, thou blessed! the Queen of the Sea!
> Most generous of nations, most liberal and free,
> UNIVERSAL PHILANTHROPY here finds a home,
> And after thy doings—the Deluge may come!

And, history, proudly, shall blazon thy name,
Encircled by wreaths in the annals of fame,
The memory of which shall be *sweet* and *endure*,
While the 'Japanese Scout' shall be heard of no more!

I have the Second Edition of an unwieldy book entitled *Londres et les Anglais*, by W. H. Dumont and Ed. Suger, which was published in Paris some sixty years ago. A short preface by Hugues le Roux is followed by 312 jumbo quarto pages containing nineteen chapters, and eighty illustrations, mostly photographs. I do not know whether the book has been translated into English; if it has, I have not seen a copy. I like this book: to balance its excessive weight the text is light and easy to read.

There is a chapter on 'Games and Sports', which begins, 'The cockney (sic) is above all else the *Sportsman* (sic). But his favourite sport is *cricket* (sic), of which the hero, the Dr W. G. Grace, is the object of what may truly be denominated a cult in England. A national subscription opened by the *Daily Telegraph* in 1895 reached an enormous sum in less than a month'.

There is a splendid picture, captioned in French; 'Hero of the Day', showing W. G. Grace, fresh from the wicket, acknowledging the plaudits of the crowd, who, fully rigged in waistcoats and ties, are waving their boaters.

There is a photograph of the Lord Mayor's Show in Cheapside, but while it gives a good idea of the crowds, the view of the procession is very limited. Perhaps the most interesting thing about the picture is the sight of a man standing outside his office window in his shirtsleeves!

In contrast, there is the melancholy sight of a crowd of unemployed dockers waiting for work, and a sextet of photographs of poor children playing their traditional street games. In fact, there is something to interest and amuse a wide cross-section of readers.

Another book for which I have an affection is *London and Paris, or Comparative Sketches* by the Marquis de Verment and Sir Charles Darnley, Bart, which was 'inscribed', says the Dedication, to Mrs Opie, and published in 1823. As the title implies, the book consists of a series of letters, thirty-one in all, exchanged between the two authors concerning affairs in the two capitals, the Frenchman writing from London and the Englishman from Paris.

The letters are chatty and informative. The Marquis tells of his arrival in England. He is 'delighted with the rapidity of the posting' from Dover to London, 'the beauty of the horses, and the civility of the drivers—the excellence of the roads—the rich variety of the landscapes—the ornamental grounds and elegant villas of the gentry—the white cottages and neat gardens of the peasantry—the picturesque villages—the appearance of comfort so

generously displayed in the dresses and dwellings of all orders of the people—
and with the first sight of your renowned Thames, flowing majestically
between the counties of Kent and Essex, and so crowded with vessels that I
seemed to behold a forest of masts.'

The Marquis, as becomes, perhaps, an aristocratic gentleman, does not
seem to have moved very much among the lower orders; if he did, he failed
to write about the life led by the less fortunate. He does describe 'Mayday',
as affording 'an apology for idleness and dissipation,' but adds in a footnote:

'Mayday seems always to have been a period dedicated to gaiety in
England. Miss Benger (Elizabeth Ogilvy Benger, 1778–1827) in her late very
interesting *Life of Anne Boleyn*, tells us that on Mayday it was King Henry
the Eighth's pride to rise with the lark, and, with a train of courtiers splendidly attired in white and silver, to hasten to the woods, whence he bore
home the fragrant bough in triumph.'

He was more at home with gentlemen of his own class, even if they only
appeared to be so. He describes the dinner given by men, who can ill afford
them, firstly to make a display and assume 'the appearance of men of wealth
and appearance', and secondly, to repay those who have entertained them,
'and to challenge similar invitations from those whom they are ambitious
of visiting . . . after examining the *ledger account* in which they regularly enter
their parties, past, expected, and to come.'

He describes the '*first* and *second-hand* dinners which a host gives in the
same week; inviting 'the highest titled and wealthiest' of his acquaintance
to the first, and his poorer 'connexions' and country cousins to 'the second
(which is simply a hash of the former repast)'.

> If with limited means you would make a display,
> Come listen to me, and I'll show you the way;
> Pick acquaintance with persons of fashion and state,
> I mean such *as are*, or who *think themselves* great;
> For our folks of distinction, high rank, and high birth,
> Mix strangely with some of the basest on earth;
> And those counterfeit great ones pass current, I'm told,
> Just as pieces of paper *were* taken for gold.—
> Hire a house in the purlieus of *Tom*, and take care
> That it stands in a street near some *smart-sounding* square,
> Such as *Hanover*, *Grosvenor*, or *Portman* at least;
> Then make your arrangements for giving a feast.
> Of your room and your table first measure the feet,
> To see if a score of these *Dons* you can seat,—
> Wedged together like slaves in a ship,—for you know
> The object you aim at's not *comfort*, but *show*:

Next, send out your cards, and remember *their size*
Is a thing which by no means you ought to despise;
For a large printed card, like a thundering knock,
Announces a person of no vulgar stock;
And after inviting lords, *dandies*, and wits,
With some belles, and a few of the feed-giving cits,
Let your board, deck'd by *cuisinier françois*, display,
As per contract agreed on, *des plats raisonnés;*
And so having made on that day a great *dash*,
You may ask your old friends on the next to a hash;
For these Frenchmen a plan economic pursue,
And out of *one* dinner contrive to pinch *two*.
To be sure, it may happen that things may go wrong;
That the fish may be stale, or the soup not too strong;
That the sauces prove sour, and the creams rather acid:
But keep your own secret, dear Sir, and be placid;
Your second-hand guests (form'd of quizzes who dine
At home on boil'd chickens, roast beef, or cold chine),
In spite of wry faces will cram, and suppose
That all faults, are the faults of their taste or their nose.
And if the next morning their stomachs should rue
The honour allow'd them of feasting with you,
They'll think it a tax, though discover'd too late,
Which the *little* must pay when they mix with the *great*.

Most of these entertaining letters had previously appeared in the
European Magazine; they could be republished with advantage, for the book
was certainly cheap at three shillings and sixpence, which was what I paid
for it in Chancery Lane some ten years ago.

10

Maps, Prints and Illustrations

I wish it were possible to see a map of Roman London by a contemporary artist; it may well be that somewhere in the archives of the Vatican such a map exists; indeed, it would be strange if such a map had not been prepared by the direction of one of the Roman rulers of Britain and sent to Rome, but so far as this country is concerned no such copy is known.

Various imaginative antiquarians have tried to reconstruct London as it must have looked a thousand years ago, and the reproduction opposite, from Henry Thomas's 'Historical and Topographical Description of every object of Importance within the Boundaries of the City,' published, in 1828, under the title of *The Wards of London*, gives what is probably a fair description of the city and its environs. Since 1828 many more remains have been unearthed in various parts of London and the suburbs.

William John Loftie's *History of London*, published in 1883, contains, in addition to a map of Saxon and of Roman London of earlier date than Thomas's, a map or plan of London without any houses; it is, however, spoilt by the addition of modern names, with modern spelling, such as Parliament Hill, Dulwich Hill and the Isle of Dogs!

Actually the first contemporary map of London was not a map at all. it was a picture or Panorama of London, Westminster and Southwark, the work of Anthony Van den Wyngaerde, who is said to have come over from the Continent and executed this work between 1543 and 1550; it is now in the Bodleian Library at Oxford. Measuring ten feet by seventeen inches it is contained in seven sheets; there are tracings of it in the Crace Collection to be seen in the Prints Department of the British Museum and in the Guildhall Library.

The Panorama stretches from the Palace of Westminster in the West, with Lambeth Palace on the south side of the River Thames, to the Palace of Placentia, which lay to the East of Greenwich. In between these two points are some 124 buildings and recognizable places of interest.

Figures are scattered about the picture: men are rowing on the river; others are fishing from a punt just above London Bridge. A couple of

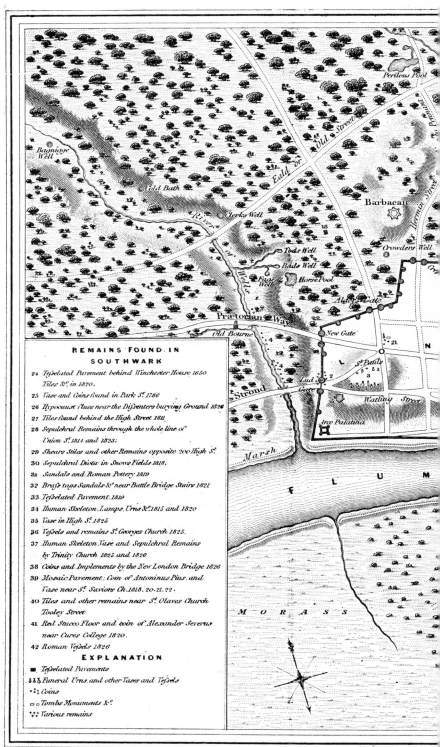

Perilous Pool

Bagnigge Well

Cold Bath

Old Street

Eald Str.

Barbacan

River or Wells

Clerks Well

Tods Well

Crowders Well

Bade Well

Fans Well

Horse Pool

Aldersgate

Praetorian Way

New Gate

Old Bourne

St Pauls

21

Strond

Lud Gate

Watling Street

Arx Palatina

Marsh

F   L   U   M

M   O   R   A   S   S

REMAINS FOUND IN SOUTHWARK

24 Tessellated Pavement behind Winchester House 1650
    Tiles &c. in 1820.

25 Vase and Coins found in Park St. 1786

26 Hypocaust Flues near the Dissenters burying Ground 1826

27 Tiles found behind the High Street 1811

28 Sepulchral Remains through the whole line of
    Union St. 1811 and 1823.

29 Shears Stiles and other Remains opposite 200 High St.

30 Sepulchral Diota in Snows Fields 1818.

31 Sandals and Roman Pottery 1819

32 Brass tags Sandals &c near Battle Bridge Stairs 1821

33 Tessellated Pavement 1819

34 Human Skeleton Lamps, Urns &c. 1815 and 1820

35 Vase in High St. 1825

36 Vessels and remains St Georges Church 1825.

37 Human Skeleton Vase and Sepulchral Remains
    by Trinity Church 1825 and 1826

38 Coins and Implements by the New London Bridge 1826

39 Mosaic Pavement; Coin of Antoninus Pius, and
    Vase near St Saviours Ch. 1818. 20. 21. 22.

40 Tiles and other remains near St Olaves Church
    Tooley Street

41 Red Stucco Floor and coin of Alexander Severus
    near Cures College 1820.

42 Roman Vessels 1826

EXPLANATION

■ Tessellated Pavements

ꝫꝫꝫ Funeral Urns, and other Vases and Vessels

∴∵ Coins

▭▭ Tombs Monuments &c.

∵∴ Various remains

Drawn by I.Thompson.

Publish

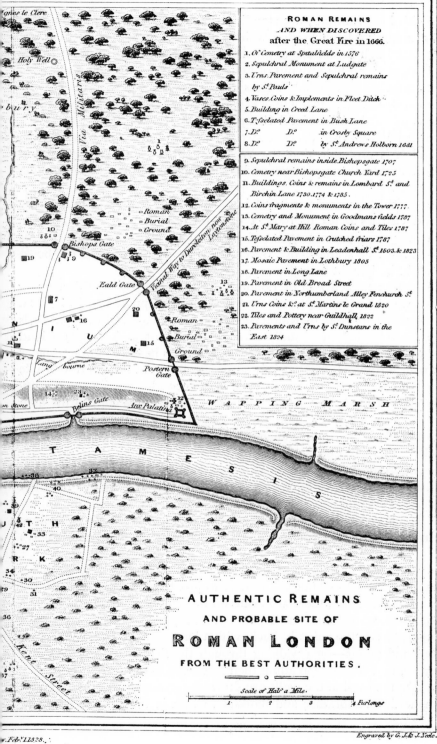

soldiers, with long ramrods, are standing beside the cannons guarding the Tower of London; a few travellers wait at Stargate Horse Ferry, and others in Southwark High Street are approaching London Bridge; a little to the south a horseman, on his way out of London, is passing a strolling musician playing a harp. If he intended to cross the Thames and play in the City he would probably have had to obtain a licence from the Fellowship of Minstrels, the 'Ancestors' of the Worshipful Company of Musicians.

Van den Wyngaerde concentrated on the City of London within the Walls, and it is probable that the Western suburbs, particularly around Clerkenwell and Holborn, were more densely populated than his Panorama would suggest.

The Panorama was reproduced in *Maps of Old London*—published by Adam and Charles Black in 1908. I paid thirty shillings for my copy in Brighton over twenty years ago, and it was marked by the bookseller as 'scarce'—it must be scarcer now. Seven maps are reproduced in the book, which should be bought on sight.

The earliest known *map* of London, according to George Vertue, an artist who was born in 1648 and died in 1756, is supposed to have been prepared secretly, in 1560, by Ralph Agas; it was to be used by the Spaniards after the Armada had successfully invaded this country. Agas was a land surveyor who, in a document dated 1606, claimed to have been practising as such for over forty years, so that it is not impossible that he was responsible for the map of which Vertue made a not very accurate copy for the Society of Antiquaries in 1738. In 1841 the Guildhall purchased a copy of the map at a sale at Messrs Leigh and Sotheby's for twenty-six pounds, and this was photographed by Edward H. Francis in 1874; copies can sometimes be found in secondhand bookshops.

It is interesting to compare Van den Wyngaerde's Panorama with the map. In the former, St Paul's Cathedral has its spire, but this does not appear in Agas's map although it was not struck by lightning until the following year. The Royal Exchange, which was opened in 1570, does not of course appear in the Panorama, whilst there is evidence of its existence in Agas's map.

The map which depicts London from St Margaret's Church, St Stephen's Chapel and Westminster Hall in the west to just beyond the Tower in the East, is an animated one: there are swans on the Thames, stags in St James's Park, and horses wading into the Thames at Dowgate and the Tower, whilst men fill the casks on the animals' backs with a long handled ladle. There are people out and about—men walking through the fields, cows grazing and dogs playing, and women spreading their linen out to dry in the open.

The suburbs outside the walls are shown in greater detail than in Van den Wyngaerde's Panorama; and Bankside, which in the latter is bare and desolate, is shown in Agas's map as the pleasure ground, with its bull-baiting and bear-baiting rings, in which the early Londoners spent their spare hours —and their spare cash.

An interesting feature in the map is a large tree standing on the Surrey Bank, due south across the Thames from the Savoy. It is depicted in the map reproduced earlier in the book (see pp. 16 and 17), and why this tree should appear in a number of maps, is not clear. Many years ago I tried to track down this tree. In the Third Edition of the *Ambulator* there is a reference to 'two remarkable Fig-trees' in the garden of Lambeth Palace. They covered 'a surface 50 feet in height, and 40 in breadth', whilst the circumference of one was twenty-eight inches, and of the other twenty-one inches. Fig trees were brought into England in the reign of Henry VIII, and the suggestion was that they were planted by 'Cardinal Pole, who had long resided in Italy, would be fond of cultivating these fruits to which he had there been accustomed', but as these fig trees were nailed against the house they cannot have had anything to do with the tree in Agas's map.

Examination of other maps has led me to believe that the tree might originally have been intended to represent something else. It is so big that it is out of proportion to the other trees, boats and figures in the map; perhaps it was a beacon to mark either the turn of the river or a collection of boats—spread out from the point at which they were tied up at a landing stage—there are several such points in this and in later maps. On the other hand it could have been a windmill, as indeed I have seen it marked on an old map.

Agas's map was engraved on wood, and is a little over 6ft ½ in. long and 2 ft 4½ in. wide. Only two copies of the original map are still in existence: one in the Guildhall Library; the other is in the library bequeathed by Samuel Pepys to Magdalen College, Oxford, but, having read in John Timbs's *Curiosities of London* that there was a copy of the map in the library at Lambeth Palace, I some years ago wrote to the librarian to enquire if it is still there. Alas, nothing is known of it, but Miss Irene Churchill, who was at that time the assistant librarian, courteously produced for me a copy of *Civitates Orbis Terrarum* in which is a map of London, magnificently coloured, by Hoefnagel.

The mysterious tree opposite the Savoy appears in the map, and whilst there are no people about there are a few cows—one of them sitting down— and there are horses in the field. An interesting feature is an archway or bridge connecting two buildings about three-fifths of the way down Fetter Lane.

Hatton's *New View of London* contains a copy of Hoefnagel's map in an identical size, but without the Latin headpiece, and in place of the four figures there is a decorative frame, in which there is a reference to the map and to Hatton's "Ye New Map of London" by which 'the prodigious increase of Building and other alterations of ye names and situation of Street etc., in this last Centry will plainly appear'.

In 1966 the Society of Antiquaries published *An Unrecorded Map of London* which had been previously communicated to its members by Martin Holmes, Esq., F.S.A.

The map, which is of sixteenth-century London engraved on copper, was recently discovered on the reverse sides of two paintings, one of which by Martin van Valckenborgh, was recently acquired by the London Museum, and the other by an unknown Italian-Flemish artist, is in private ownership.

Mr Holmes explains that it was the practice to sell engraved copper plates for scrap, and he conjectures that the Map may well have been engraved by Franciscus Hogenberg, who subsequently (in 1572) engraved the map designed by Joris Hoefnagel for the *Civitates Orbis Terrarum*, but its greater size enables it to be more detailed. However, after an interesting and learned disquisition he conjectures that Anthonis van den Wyngaerde, and not Hoefnagel was the artist who prepared the map!

In either event Mr Holmes is able to show that the map was designed before Ralph Agas's map of 1560, and which had been, previous to the discovery of this map, thought of as the earliest map of London in existence.

Mr Holmes pinpoints many of the interesting topographical features in the Map, which illustrate and help to bring Stow's *London Survey* to life; he is also able to trace some of the places mentioned by Shakespeare, pointing out, for instance, that when John of Gaunt spoke the lines

'This precious stone set in the silver sea
Which serves it in the office of a wall
Or as a moat defensive to a house
Against the envy of less happier lands',

his audience would have recalled passing Finsbury Farm, a moated house, which is shown on the map, on their way to the Theatre.

It is curious that not a single copy of this map has survived, and Mr Holmes has done splendid work by bringing it to light—and life—in his Communication to the Society of Antiquaries. His monograph, had it been available forty years ago, would have been of very material assistance to me. As it is I can only advise everybody to beg, borrow or otherwise, short of stealing it, to get hold of a copy.

John Norden produced maps of London and Westminster in 1593—within a few years of the publication of the First Edition of Stow's *Survey*—but they only measure $9\frac{1}{2}$ in. by $6\frac{3}{4}$ in., so that they can do little more than give a general impression of what London looked like at that date. The maps have been reproduced many times and cost only a shilling or two.

Next in order of date would appear to be a map of 'The Cittie of London' dated 1604, by Ryther, of Amsterdam. It extends from just beyond Smithfield, in the east, to Temple Bar, in the west. It does not extend further north than Islington, whilst Bankside, south of the River, is shown with two parallel rows of houses, but without the Globe or the bull- or bear-baiting rings. There are a few boats on the Thames, but otherwise no figures or animals. West of West Smithfield is a square, with 'Pennes', for the cattle brought to this famous old market.

The map, which is reproduced in Loftie's *London*, shows rather more clearly than the earlier ones the extent of unbuilt land in London. The archway or bridge in Fetter Lane shown in Hoefnagel's map has disappeared.

The last pre-fire map which I would mention was published in 1658. Prepared by Richard Newcourt (the elder) it was engraved by William Faithorne, by whose name the map is known.

It can be compared with the one prepared in 1677 by John Ogilby, assisted by his wife's grandson, William Morgan, and engraved by Hollar. This map was published to help those who were planning to rebuild the City after the fire of London, but it does not show the destruction which the City had suffered. The map is published as 'Ichnographically Describing all the Streets, Lanes, Alleys, Courts, Yards, Churches, Halls and Houses, Etc.' of the district extending beyond the bounds of the city, subject to the municipal authority, and there is a key which makes the map easy to read. Statistically-minded readers might care to note that the map contains twenty-five wards, one hundred and twenty-two parishes and liberties, one hundred and eighty-nine streets, one hundred and fifty-three lanes, five hundred and twenty-two alleys, four hundred and fifty-eight courts, and two hundred and ten yards.

The Fleet River is shown bridged in four places, although two of the bridges would appear to be for pedestrians only. There are boats on the Thames, the only other figures being a number of soldiers in the New Artillery Garden, pikemen, by the look of them, drawn up in front of their tents, and with banners flying.

There are a number of 'Gardeners Gardens' to the north-west of the City: the Charterhouse has a bowling-green, and the 'Pennes' in Smithfield would seem to have been enlarged.

John Rocque's post-fire map of 1741–45, includes all the outlying suburbs, and extends as far north as Edgware and Tottenham. The original, which is in the British Museum, is in twenty-four sheets and measures thirteen by six and three-quarter feet.

'Knock Fergus' is the curious name of the area which appears as a continuation of Rosemary Lane and Cable Street, and beyond which lies Bluegate's Fields.

A View of Stocks Market

Published according to Act of Parliam.t 1753 by

200

Veüe de la place nommé Stocks Market.

Unicorn the Corner of Queen Street Cheapside London.

Fletcher Sculp
N.° 39

The rather poor map in Ilive's *Survey*, published in 1742, also shows 'Knock Fergus', and it would be interesting to know which of the two maps appeared first. Before I discovered that there are towns of that name in Ireland I had endeavoured to find out the meaning of the name.

To the south of Cable Street—and therefore south-west of Knock Fergus is Wellclose Square. In that square the Danish church was built in 1696. To the east of the square and running north from Ratcliffe Highway was Denmark Street so, jumping to conclusions, I wrote to the Danish authorities in London in the hope that they might be able to tell me that Knock Fergus is a phonetic pronunciation of two Danish words. It is not.

I tried again: between Wellclose Square and Denmark Street lay Prince's Square. The Swedish church was in Prince's Square, so I wrote to the Swedish authorities—but with the same result.

Whilst on Ilive's map Knock Fergus would appear to have been a thoroughfare, in Rocque's map the name is printed above some buildings on the north side of the thoroughfare. And I evolved a theory that perhaps one of those buildings was an inn—kept by a generous Scotsman named Fergus— to whom thirsty but penniless sailors were referred with the advice to go and 'Knock Fergus'—upon the supposition that he was willing to give a poor sailor a drink at any time of the day or night.

More prosaically it might have been a meeting place for Irishmen. I was not so far out.

Further queries: although the first stone of Westminster Bridge was not laid until 29th January 1738–39 and the bridge was not opened until 18th November 1750, it already appeared in Ilive's map in 1742. The bridge also appeared in Rocque's map which also shows Blackfriars Bridge, the first pile of which was not driven until 7th June 1760. The first stone was laid on 7th October in the same year; it was passable as a bridleway on Wednesday, 19th November 1768, and was finally opened on Sunday, 19th November 1769. How came these bridges to be shown on maps published in the early 1740s?

Within a week of the fire of 1666 both John Evelyn and Sir Christopher Wren had produced plans for the re-building of London. There was a third plan, however, which the historians (other than Walter Bell) have ignored. It was prepared by Valentine Knight, who proposed to construct a canal which, leaving the Thames at Queenshithe, was to wind its way round the north side of the City, and enter the Fleet near Clerkenwell. The object of the canal was to be strictly commercial, and Knight pointed out to King Charles II how he could gain revenue from the transport of cargoes on the canal, whereupon, much to his astonishment, no doubt, the King clapped him into the Tower, explaining, in his wrath, that he did not propose to make money out of his people's misfortunes, and that it was several sorts of offence to suggest that His Majesty was capable of doing so!

A few years ago I paid a few shillings for the Fifth Edition of Carey's *New Itinerary or an Accurate Delineation of the Great Roads, Both Direct and Cross Throughout England and Wales*; it was published in 1812, dedicated to the Earls of Chesterfield and Leicester, and contained more than 9,000 additional places. In 1946 I paid six Swiss francs in Zurich (and felt a touch of patriotic pride in bringing it home to its native country!) for the Ninth Edition, 'with improvements', published in 1821, and dedicated to the Earl of Chichester and The Marquis of Salisbury (Post Master General). Of interest in these books is the 'List of all the Inns throughout the Metropolis from which the Mail and Other Stage Coaches depart', and the 'List of the Stage Coaches going from London to all the circumjacent Villages etc'. The number of these old time transport services is astonishing: In 1812 there were 422, and in 1821 there were no less than 795 different routes operating from London, and on some of them the coaches ran daily.

It is interesting to find that the first patent for an invention was issued on 2nd March 1617 to Aaron Rapburne, gent., and Roger Burges, who were 'granted a privelege for the terme of XXI yeares of the sole makeing, carveing, describeing, and graveing in copper, brass, or other metalle, alles suche and soe manie mappes, plottes or descriptions of Lond., Westm., Bristolle, Norwiche, Canterbury, Bath, Oxford, and Cambridge, and the towne and castel of Windsor, and to imprint and sette forthe and selle the same'.

Studying a map stimulates speculation: I have Agas's map before me: I wander through the City and reach Cheapside, turn up Foster Lane, pass Barber Surgeons Hall on my right, bear to the right through Noble Street into Silver Street—and on my left is Muggle Street—and I am standing opposite the house, at the corner of the two streets, in which Shakespeare lodged with a family named Mountjoy from 1598 to 1604 and further up Silver Street is Bacon House.

There are those who have thought that such plays as *Much Ado About Nothing, As You Like It, Twelfth Night, Julius Caesar, Hamlet, Troilus and Cressida, Othello* and *Measure for Measure* were written during those years; that Shakespeare and Bacon were neighbours is surely not without significance for those who claim that the Voice was the voice of Bacon, though the Hand was the hand of Shakespeare.

And in what circumstances, one asks oneself, did Shakespeare come to be Bacon's neighbour? In 1598, when he went to live with Mountjoy, he was playing at 'The Curtain' in Moorfields. Could he not have found accommodation nearer to the theatre, and so saved himself a walk through streets which, certainly when there was no moon, must have been dark and difficult, particularly when he would have been tired after the evening's work?

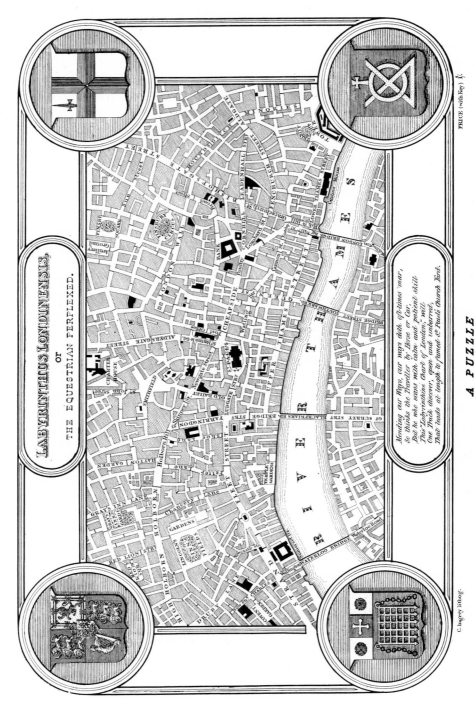

LABYRINTHUS LONDINENSIS,

or

THE EQUESTRIAN PERPLEXED.

Mending our Ways, our ways doth oftimes mar',
So thinks the Traveller by Horse or Car,
But he who scans with calm and patient skill
This "Labyrinthine Chart of London", will
One Thirck discover, open and unbarred,
That leads at length to famed St Pauls Church Yard.

C. Ingrey lithog.

A PUZZLE

Suggested by the Stoppages occasioned by repairing the Streets. The object is to find a way from the Strand to St Pauls, without crossing any of the Bars in the Streets supposed to be under repair.

PRICE (with Key) 3/.

Mountjoy was a wig-maker; he also made ladies' headdresses. He *may* have made wigs for Shakespeare's theatrical company, and Shakespeare *may* have met him in the way of his profession, and gone to live with him because he liked his company. On the other hand he may have made wigs for the legal profession—including Bacon; and Bacon, hearing that Mount-joy had a spare room, and was looking for, or willing to accommodate a lodger, *may* have arranged the tenancy in order to have Shakespeare near at hand whenever he should feel the mood for collaboration come upon him!

In those days, when a man settled down to work after dinner he could do so without the irritating interruptions which we have to put up with. The condition of the streets was not such as to make it worth a man's while turning out on the off-chance of finding a friend at home; so if Bacon sent for Shakespeare he knew that it was unlikely that they would be interrupted by chance and unwelcome visitors.

It is a pity that Robert Southey the poet did not record to which map he was referring when he wrote: 'I begin to study the map of London, though dismayed at the sight of its prodigious extent. The river is no assistance to a stranger in finding his way. There is no street along its banks, and no eminence from whence you can look around and take your bearings.' But Southey might have been less dismayed, and found his study made easier if he had peopled his London, as he might quite well have done, with the shades of departed Londoners.

I reproduce a map (for which I paid a few pence), because a lot can be learnt about Georgian London in trying to solve the puzzle posed by the map maker, whose effort is a kind of elaborate Hampton Court Maze. The copy of the map in the Crace Collection in the British Museum was dated (presumably by Crace) 1820, but has no key; my solution is on page 218.

The map reminds me of that old song, 'The Lord Mayor's Coachman; or, The Man who knew how to Drive'. It was written in 1896 by Harry Hunter and composed by David Day, and I reproduce it here as the (relatively) modern counterpart of old John Lydgate's London Lyckpeny.

THE LORD MAYOR'S COACHMAN;
or, *The Man Who Knew How to Drive*

The Lord Mayor had a Coachman, and the Coachman's name was John,
Said the Lord Mayor to the Coachman, 'Take your wages and be-gone,
I want a better driver, for I'm going to see the Queen',
Said John, 'I am the finest Coachman that was ever seen,
And if you'll let me drive today I'll show I can't be beat,
For I'll drive to Buckingham Palace and I won't go through a street'.
'You must be mad', the Lord Mayor said, 'but still I'll humour you,
But remember that you lose your place, the first street you go through.'

(Chorus)

The Coachman gave the Lord Mayor, the Lord Mayor, the Lord
    Mayor,
The Coachman gave the Lord Mayor a curious kind of treat,
He drove him from the Mansion House, the Mansion House, the
    Mansion House,
From the Mansion House to Buck'n'am Palace and didn't go through a
    street.

The Coachman jumped upon his box and settled in his seat,
And started up the *Poultry*, which we know's not called a street,
Then up *Cheapside* he gaily went, the bobbies cleared the course,
To the statue of the Bobby who first organized the force,
'Why you're going into Newgate Street', the Lord Mayor loudly bawls
But John said 'Tuck your tupp'ny in, I'm going round *St. Paul's!*'
'Well, round St Paul's means Ludgate Hill, and Fleet Street, John!'
    said he,
But John said, 'No! down *Ludgate* Hill and up the *Old Bailey*.'

Up to Old Bailey then he goes on to the *Viaduct*,
Up *Holborn* and *High Holborn*, there was nothing to obstruct,
When 'Now you're going up Oxford Street', the Lord Mayor shouts again,
But John said, 'I don't go that way! I go down *Drury Lane*.'
Down Drury Lane, *Long Acre*, and *Saint Martin's Lane* he drives,
And thus to keep out of a street he artfully contrives,
And when they reach Trafalgar Square, the Lord Mayor in a pet,
Said, 'Dash my wig and barnacles! I think he'll do it yet.'

John nearly drove into the Strand, then stopped as if in doubt,
And the Lord Mayor said, 'I'm not surprised to find that you're put out.
Through Parliament Street you must go, or else cross Cockspur Street,
It's very hard, but still you must acknowledge your defeat,'
But John turned back and said 'My Lord, I don't much think I shall
If you ask me, I think you'll find I'm going down *Pall Mall*',
Then round the Square the coachman goes and drives at racing rate,
Goes through *Pall Mall*, into the *Park* to Buckingham Palace straight.

It is not possible to do justice to London Maps in a single chapter, and
it would be impossible to write a complete book about Pictures of London—
and, of course, Londoners.

I reproduce a rough woodcut of a statue of Charles II from Robert
Burton's *New View*, A New Edition, published in 1720, concerning which he
records that '*St Mary Woolchurch*' one of the six churches in Walbrook-Ward

206

destroyed by the fire in 1666) 'the Church-yard, and *Stocks-market* are pull'd down, and made a very handsome Market-Place, in the Front whereof towards the street, is a Conduit, and the statue of King *Charles* II on Horse-back, placed thereon, with a Turk or Enemy, under his Feet; which was erected at the Charge of Sir *Robert Vyner*.'

But the statue is—or rather was—of greater interest than Burton implied, Charles II has been commemorated in at least twelve statues, and this statue has the most curious history of them all: Sir Robert Viner, a wealthy goldsmith, who was Lord Mayor of London in 1674, wished to show his loyalty to the king by erecting in the City a statue of him in the act of trampling Oliver Cromwell underfoot.

At the same time the Polish Ambassador in England had ordered a marble statue of *his* master, John Sobieski, on horse-back, trampling a Turk underfoot. But when the statue was finished the Ambassador could not afford to pay for it, and Sir Robert Viner, hearing of this through his agent at Leghorn, bought the statue, paid the sculptor Latham to change John

Sobieski's head into Charles II's, and brought it to London in 1677, and there it remained, in the Market Place, until 1738 when both the statue and the conduit referred to by Burton, were removed to make room for the Mansion House.

The *Stocks* Market referred to has nothing to do with Stocks and Shares! Stow relates how, in 1282, '*Henry Waley* Mayor caused divers houses in this City to be builded towards the maintenance of London Bridge: namely one void place neare unto the parish church called Woole Church, on the north side thereof, where sometime (the way being very large and broade) had stood a payre of Stocks, for punishment of offenders, this building tooke name of these Stockes, and was appoynted by him to be a market place for fish and flesh in the midst of the City. . . .'

That the market changed its character is clear from the print made in 1745, which I reproduced on page 200 and 201. The picture is an animated one, and whilst 'fish and flesh' are still being sold, other street traders have appeared on the scene.

The church on the right is St Stephen Walbrook, considered, after St Paul's Cathedral, to be Wren's masterpiece.

The Sun Fire-plate (dated 1744) affixed to the building on the left is a reminder of the time when each of the various fire insurance offices kept its own body of firemen, dressed in a distinctive livery with a silver badge, ready to fight fires at the buildings which were insured in their office. About the year 1825, the Sun, Union and Royal Exchange formed a brigade, which was followed, in 1832, by an alliance of eight insurance companies for assisting each other at fires, the process of amalgamation being completed by the 'London Fire-Engine Establishment', which began operations in 1833.

The distant steeple, to the left of King Charles's statue, is that of St Swithin.

But the artist has made a mistake: in his view the Turk is leaning on his left elbow with his right arm outstretched; in Burton's he is leaning on his right elbow stretching out his left arm. A photograph in Walter Bell's *Unknown London* of the statue at Newby Hall, the Yorkshire seat of the head of the Viner family, proves Burton's crude picture to be correct and the elaborate view to be wrong!

Many intriguing hours can be spent trying to catch out old artists.

Satirical poems greeted the erection—and removal—of the statue, and they were reprinted in *Unknown London*.

London's Open Air Statuary, by Lord Edward Gleichen, published in 1928, is another book which may be read with pleasure and profit.

Whilst on the subject of statues I reproduce from *The Town and Country Magazine; Or, Universal Repository of Knowledge, Instruction, and Entertainment*, February 1771, a print of a statue of the Duke of Cumberland, which was

Ridiculum acri fortius et melius.   Hor.

erected in Cavendish Square on 24th November 1770, by Lieut. General William Strode.

In 'An Account of New Books and Pamphlets' in the Magazine is the following notice of a recently published pamphlet, *Critical Observations on the Buildings and Improvements* of LONDON. quarto. Price 2s. 6d. Dodsley:

'This very ingenious performance has been ascribed to Mr Horace Walpole; but it is really written by Mr Stewart, a young gentleman, who is going to India in the company's service. It abounds with judicious observations and just satire (see p. 85).'

Underneath the print on page 85 is the following communication:

To the Printer *of the* Town *and* Country Magazine.

SIR,

On the perusal of a pamphlet just published entitled, 'Critical Observations on the Buildings and Improvements in London,' I was struck with the ingenious reflections and shrewd remarks to be found in every page of that performance. The author's strictures upon the new erected statue in Cavendish Square, excited my curiosity so strongly, that I resolved immediately to go and view this extraordinary erection. While I was reading his Observations (page 18, 19, which I have flung into a note) I distinctly heard the following Dialogue, which I have sent you as accurate as I could take it down, together with a sketch of the equestrian statue, to be cut in wood; hoping it will afford as much entertainment to your readers as it has done to me.

I am, Sir,

Your constant reader

And admirer,

CURIOSUS.

A Dialogue *between the* Antique *Horse in Cavendish Square and its* Modern *Rider.*

Rider. What's the matter, Antique, why this foaming and blowing?
    Thou seems't for some reason, d-mn'd ready for going.
    Thou would'st not unhorse, sure, the statue *equestrian,*
    And reduce me, disgrac'd, to a figure *pedestrian!*
    I'm no *asinine* statue, however bely'd,
    If thou'rt hard of Belief, turn thy head but aside,
    And read, in small compass, my title and name:
    For my *virtue* and *kindness,* refer to the same.
    You too, an't you stirrup'd, and housing'd, and holster'd;
    And my belly and shoulders in equipoise bolster'd;

Don't thy erst flowing tail in ribbon'd-knots linger?
Han't you veins on your flanks as big as my finger?
When C——, Str——, and I, have done all this to please ye,
One wou'd think, poor Antique, you'd be placid and easy.

Horse. The devil you wou'd! what in my situation!
Thus expos'd to the gibes of the wits of a nation,
(I who carry'd the Caesars from Julius to Nero,)
Between such a *pedestal* and such a *hero*?
One cued, lapel coated, triangular hatted,
Having both paunch and pate beyond all meaning fatted;
The *other* a mason-hewn stone monumental,
With a *one-ear'd* inscription at which eyes are bent all;
And you now astride a Mezentian rhebus,
As fiery a courser as ever drew Phoebus,
I suspect, and whoe'er in your history dips
Will believe you had rather have stuck to *Eclipse*.
I will not submit then, I declare sad and sober;
For your general, you see, has abrig'd my OCTOBER.

Rider. Nor am I content, in the pride of my soul,
To be coupled with St——, and pass cheek by jowl,
As Milton and Benson hang in the West-Minster;
Tho' I know I look smart in the eyes of a spinster.
And imperial statues, as I have been told,
Were compos'd oft' of silver, and sometimes of gold;
Yet St——, with pretended precision, has said,
His Hero should be represented in *lead:*
But he splendidly gilt us, to make us go down,
And has mounted aloft on a quarry of stone.
So, horse, I'll *dragoon* ye, if thus you alarm me;
And *ride* ye, by G-d, as I once did the a-my:
To your back will I stick, like perpetual blister,
With my breech to the town, and face to my s-ster.
On this ruinous spot a grand guard I keep,
To perquisite varlets, and 'tend a few sheep.'
Here my post I'll maintain in spite of bad weather,
In defiance of *Saxe* and *D'Estrees* put together;
Of the *ancient* and *modern* a motley *hotch-potch*,
And victor of taste too, as well as of *Scotch*.

I reproduce the note 'Curious' refers to in his letter, in explanation.

'In Cavendish square is erected an equestrian statue. An officer, in the exact *modern* uniform of the Guards, is mounted on an *antique* horse all very richly gilt and burnished. The figure, both in features and proportions, is extremely like the original; and so, I am told, is the hat. The general encomium bestowed upon it is, that it is *mighty natural*; but in my opinion, the resemblance would be much stronger, were it, in place of being gilt, to be painted in proper colours, the coat scarlet, the facings blue, and the lace to remain as it is. This would not only make it more *natural*, but also render it of use as a pattern suit for the regimental taylors.

'The character of the inscriptive style is brevity, perspicuity and force; and there is also a system of contraction established, different from those of law bill. The reader will be able to judge how far his character is retained in the following inscription: I have distinguished it with Italics in some particular parts:

W——D—— of C——

Born 15th April, 1721, died 31st October 1765,

This *Equestrian Statue*

was erected by

Lieutenant General

W—— S——

In Gratitude

for *his private Kindness*

In honour

To *his* publick Virtue.

November the 4th *Anno Domini*, 1770.

'The possessive pronoun *his* is very happily introduced here, because it may be applied to either of the antecedent persons, and will no doubt create subject of learned dispute some ages hence. If this fashion should prevail among great men and rich, of erecting public statues, to those who have been *kind* to them in *private*, it is not warriors in compleat uniform, bestriding gilded steeds, who would be most frequently seen in our streets and squares, but beauty simple, *unadorned*, like the Venus of Medicis, and (could art do justice to nature in this country) finer forms than every Grecian chizzle graved.'

The statue was removed 'for repairs' in 1868, but was melted down instead—and the proceeds of the metal, amounting to £23. 3. o., were handed over to the Treasurer of Cavendish Square.

The Grangerised Pennants contain thousands of examples of the print-sellers' productions. There are more than 5,000 in the Crowle Pennant alone. John Timbs, in *Historic Ninepins A Book of Curiosities*, records that one of them, a German print, is 'the oldest existing representation in existence of the Tyburn gallows'. It represents Henrietta Maria, Queen of Charles I, kneeling in penance, the chaplets in her hands, and praying beneath the triple tree.

It was Sir William Waller who asserted in his *Recollections*, published after his death in 1668, that the queen's confessor once compelled her to walk in penance to Tyburn, 'some say barefoot,' seemingly for some kindness towards heretics. Although Charles I believed the story the queen denied it, and it would seem to be generally discredited. The full story is in Timbs's book.

Another indefatigable collector of prints was John Gregory Crace, an architectural decorator, whose 'kind and genial disposition gained him a large circle of friends' (says the *Dictionary of National Biography.*). Born on 3rd June 1779, he died on the 18th September 1859. His magnificent collection was acquired by the British Museum in 1880, and in 1898 there was published *A Catalogue of Maps, Plans, and Views of London, Westminster and South-wark*, 'collected and arranged by Frederick Crace', his son. The catalogue runs to 696 pages, and records some 20,000 items, contained in nineteen portfolios of maps and plans and thirty-six portfolios of views. There are, in addition, eighteen large rollers with maps and plans, three volumes of maps and one volume of Frost Fairs on the Thames.

In the preface to the catalogue Frederick Crace relates how, following his father's profession, John Gregory Crace was extensively employed in the decoration of the Royal palaces and other important works, and that during the last thirty years of his life he collected systematically and with a definite object, his ambition being 'to illustrate every building of note', and, his son adds, the 'catalogue will show with what diligence and success he followed up his task'.

Included in the collection is 'A Geometrical View of the *grand Procession* of the *Scald Miserable Masons* Design'd as they were drawn up over against Somerset House in the Strand on the twenty-seventh of April an° 1742. A. Benoist *del. et sculp*, 1771'. A pencil note adds 'Drawn by Paul Whitehead'.

This is topographically interesting, showing the north front of Somerset House as it then appeared, together with the buildings on each side, from the sixth house eastward, to the neighbourhood of the Savoy towards the west.

Brayley produced an abbreviated—and mutilated—copy of this print in his *Londiniana;* I deprecate imperfect reproductions, and I refer those who share my view to the original in the British Museum.

One tends to think of illustrated journalism as, relatively, a modern innovation, but the print of the 'Ruins of the Houses burned down . . .' which I bought a few years ago in Brighton for half a crown, and reproduce here, is evidence to the contrary; for the print appeared on 5th April 1748—eleven days after the Fire of 25th March which was a Friday. There were thus two weekends between the Fire and the production of the print. Incidentally, it was the worst fire since the great fire of 1666.

The fireman's accoutrements are interesting: an engine with leathern pipes for quenching fires was patented in 1676, previously the several parishes were provided with leathern buckets, ladders, pickaxes, sledges, shovels and

A. Mr Eldridge's House in Exchange Alley where ye Fire began, NB. Mr Eldridge has Wife, two Children, &c a Journeyman perished in ye Flames.
B. St Michael's Church where it Stopped to ye eastward.
C. The White House opposite ye Royal Exchange where the Fire stopped to ye Westward.

An exact View of the Ruins of the Houses
burned down by the late dreadful Fire in Cornhill
the 25th of March 1748.
taken from Sam's Coffee House in Exchange Alley.
Published according to Act of Parliament May 14th 1748.
Printed & Sold by I. Giles Printer in Catherine Alley Pudding London.

D. The George & Vulture Tavern in George Yard where ye Fire Stopped on that side.
E.E. Cornhill.
E.F. The Ruins of two Houses in Birchin Lane.
G. The Jamaica Coffee House.
This Fire Consumed 82 Houses.

Pr. 6. d

brass hand-squirts. About 1720 two Germans were manufacturing in Bethnal Green a water-tight seamless hose.

A few years earlier—in 1716—John Gay in his *Trivia* had thus described the scene at a fire:

> Now with thick crowds th' enlighten'd pavement swarms,
> The fireman sweats beneath his crooked arms;
> A leathern casque his vent'rous head defends,
> Boldly he climbs where thickest smoke ascends.
> Mov'd by the mother's streaming eyes and prayers,
> The helpless infant through the flame he bears,
> With no less virtue than through hostile fire
> The Dardan here bore his aged sire.
> See forceful engines spout their leveled streams,
> To quench the blaze that runs along the beams;
> The grappling-hook plucks rafters from the walls,
> And heaps on heaps the smoky ruin falls.

In addition to illustrations in which figures are merely incidental to the 'scenery', whether landscape or building, there are innumerable pictures in which the buildings were added as background, and the figures were the main preoccupation of the artist. William Hogarth's 'Gin Lane', painted to enforce the attack on gin drinking in the same way as he painted the companion piece, 'Beer Street' to glorify beer, is an example. The church in the background is St George's, Bloomsbury, the architect of which was Nicholas Hawksmoor—one of Sir Christopher Wren's pupils—who made himself ridiculous because, to please a wealthy brewer in the parish, he placed a statue of George I at the top of the steeple, which occasioned the following epigram:

> The King of Great Britain was reckoned before
> The 'Head of the Church' by all Christian People
> But this brewer has added still one title more
> To the rest, and has made him the 'Head of the Steeple'!

The brewer was Mr William Hucks, the Member of Parliament for Abingdon and Wallingford, who is said to have paid for the statue.

Horace Walpole presented to the world the more popular version of the epigram:

> When Henry the Eighth left the Pope in the lurch,
> The Protestants made him the Head of the church
> But George's good subjects, the Bloomsbury people
> Instead of the Church, made him head of the steeple.

And shortly afterwards Charles I's equestrian statue at Charing Cross addressed George I on his pinnacle:

No longer stand staring,
My friend at Cross Charing
Amidst such a number of people;
For a man on a horse
Is a matter of course
But look, here's a man on a steeple.

I would like to go on, but when I started to expand the few short articles which had appeared some years ago in the *Antique Dealers' Guide* I did not set out to write an exhaustive study on the subject. And having read—and re-read—this book, I swing between two extremes.

On the one hand I realize how very far short of anything like completeness falls my effort, and on the other hand I experience the pioneer's exhilaration at having essayed something which so many far more qualified people than I am have omitted even to attempt.

I know that my references to books are, in so many cases, incomplete: of some I have given the sizes, of others the prices at which they were published—or bought, whilst others are only referred to in passing. But despite its numerous shortcomings I am satisfied that nearly everyone who has read the book will know a great deal more about London than he did before, and that he has acquired that knowledge more speedily and more entertainingly than he could have done had he been left to grope without guidance for the proverbial needle in the apocryphal haystack. And the references in the Index to the several 'Lives' included in the *Dictionary of National Biography* provide the enthusiast with reading matter for many a long day. And, to quote Stow after he had given a somewhat detailed account of an apparently unimportant procession of Skinners on the afternoon of Corpus Christi day: 'Thus much to stop the tongues of unthankful men, such as used to ask, why have ye not noted this, or that? and give no thanks for what is done.'

What I have done is to make a beginning, and the reader is very welcome to anticipate outstripping me with every step forward which he takes. Bargains can still be found—in the most unlikely places. It is unnecessary to add that if I should be informed of some of those facts and fancies I shall be the better pleased; maybe they will justify a new edition—or even a *new* book—I have a sufficient number of *old* books to justify one!

'. . . much might have beene said, and shall be hereafter discoursed more at large, when I have more spacious ground to walke in, and other helpes (thereto belonging) can more conveniently be had'—is a sentence in the 1633 edition of Stow's *Survey*.

And I cannot think of a better sentence with which to finish my book than the one with which Stow finished his: 'And so I end, as, wanting time to travel further in this work'.

Engraved by H. Adlard.

BEER STREET AND GIN LANE.

GIN LANE.

From the Original Design by Hogarth.

Jones & Cº. Temple of the Muses Finsbury Square, London.

APPENDIX

I offer the following key to the 'Puzzle' reproduced as endpapers and on page 204.

You must forget that he who runs may read,
Nor think you only have to mount your steed;
To reach your journey's end no simple ride is;
To follow up your nose no certain guide is;
You must twist left and right—skirt several walls,
And after many miles you'll reach St. Paul's.

To leave the Strand turn up Newcastle Street, take the fourth turning on right, first on right, second on left, second on right, first on left and straight through to Chancery Lane. Turn down Chancery Lane and turn left into Fleet Street, take the second turning on left (up Fetter Lane), first on right, veer to the right and ahead, first on left, first on right to Shoe Lane. Turn right and first on left to Farringdon Road, down Farringdon Road and right into Fleet Street. Take the first turning on left, second on left into Bridge Street, turning right down Bridge Street, take first on left, second on left, second on right, third on right, first on left, third on left, second on left and (exhausted) into St. Paul's Church Yard.

BIBLIOGRAPHY

The following bibliography lists the books about Old London mentioned in the text. Unless otherwise specified, all titles were published in London. Individual editions mentioned are not listed below.

Abbott, John William — *A History of London, from the Earliest Period to the Present Time.* 1821

Ackermann, Rudolph — *Microcosm of London,* 1808–9

Addresses presented from the Court of Common Council to the King, on his Majesty's Accession to the Throne ... 1778

Allen, Thomas — *The History and Antiquities of London, Westminster, Southwark and Parts Adjacent.* (4 vols) 1827; new edition (5 vols) 1839
The Panorama of London, or Visitors' Guide. 1830

Ambulator; or, the Stranger's Companion in a Tour Round London within the Circuit of Twenty-five Miles. 1878

Beames, Thomas — *Rookeries of London: Past, Present and Prospective.* 1852

Bell, Walter George — *Unknown London.* 1920

Besant, Walter — *London.* 1892
Westminster. 1895

Black, A. & C. — *Maps of Old London.* 1908

Brayley, Edward Wedlake — *London and Middlesex, etc.* (5 vols) 1810
Londiniana. (4 vols) 1828

Burton, Robert — *Historical Remarques on London and Westminster,* 1681
A New View and Observations on the Antient and Present State of London and Westminster. 1730

Chamberlain, Henry — *A New and Compleat History and Survey of the Cities of London and Westminster, etc.* 1771

'Citizen, A' — *A New and Compleat Survey of London.* 1762

219

Civitates Orbis Terrarum

Clinch, George — *Bloomsbury and St Giles's.* 1890
Marylebone and St Pancras. 1890.
Mayfair and Belgravia. 1892

Combe, William — *The Microcosm of London.* (3 vols) 1828

Crace, Frederick — *A Catalogue of Maps, Plans, and Views of London, Westminster and Southwark.* 1898

Craik, George Lillie — *The Pictorial History of England.* (4 vols) 1838

Crosby, Benjamin — *A View of London; or, the Stranger's Guide through the British Metropolis.* 1803–4

Crouch, Nathaniel — *A New View, and Observations on the Ancient and Present State of London and Westminster.* 1730

Cunningham, Peter (ed.) — *Hand-Book of London, Past and Present.* 1849

Darnley, Charles and Verment, Marquis de — *London and Paris, or Comparative Sketches.* 1823

Dictionary of National Biography

Dobie, Rowland — *History of the United Parishes of St Giles in the Field and St George, Bloomsbury.* 1829

'Dogberry' — *Humours & Oddities of the London Police Courts . . .* 1894

Downes, Thomas — *A Copious Index to Pennant's Account of London.* 1814

Dugdale, William — *History of St Paul's.* 1753

Dumont, W. H. and Suger, Ed. — *Londres et les Anglais.* Paris, *circa* 1907

Entick, John — *A New and Accurate History and Survey of London, Westminster, Southwark and Places Adjacent.* (4 vols) 1766

Fabyan, Robert — *The Concordaunce of Historyes.* 1542.

Faulkner, Thomas — *An Historical and Topographical Description of Chelsea and its Environs.* 1810
An Historical and Topographical Account of Fulham, Including the Hamlet of Hammersmith. 1813
History and Antiquities of Kensington. 1820
The History and Antiquities of the Parish of Hammersmith. 1839.

Fitzstephen, William — *Description of London.* 1698.

'Foreign Resident, A' *Society of London.* 1884

Gadbury, John *London's Deliverance Predicted . . .* 1665

Gleichen, Edward *London's Open Air Statuary.* 1928

Grant, James *The Great Metropolis.* (3 vols) 1836
Sketches in London. 1836
Travels in Town. (2 vols) 1839
Lights and Shadows of London Life. (2 vols) 1842

Greenwood, James *Unsentimental Journey: or Byways of the Modern Babylon.* 1867
The Seven Curses of London. 1869
The Wilds of London. 1876

Harben, Henry A. *A Dictionary of London.* 1918

Hare, Augustus, J. C. *Walks in London.* 1878

Harris, J. *London.* 1806

Harrison, Walter *A New and Universal History etc.* 1776

Harvey, William ('Aleph') *London Scenes and London People.* 1863
The Old City, and its Highways and Byways. 1865

Hatton, Edward *A New View of London.* 1708

Hodder, George *Sketches of Life and Character . . .* 1845

Hodges, J. *A Present for an Apprentice.* 1747

Hughson, David *London; Being an Accurate History and Description, etc.* (6 vols) 1806

Hunt, James Henry Leigh *The Town; Its Memorable Characters and Events.* (2 vols) 1848
A Saunter Through the West End. 1861

Hunter, Henry *The History of London, Containing an Account of the Origin of the City.* 1811

Hutton, Laurence *Literary Landmarks of London.* 1885

Ilive, J. and Lyne, S. *A New and Compleat Survey of London.* (2 vols) 1762

'Japanese Scout, A' *Japanese Ideas of London and its Wonders, its Inhabitants, and their Manners and Customs.* 1873

Jenkins, Elijah, *see* Mottley, *Literary and Historical Memorials of London.* 1847
Jesse, J. Heneage *London and Its Celebrities.* 1850
London: Its Celebrated Characters and Remarkable Places. (3 vols) 1871

Jones, Harry *East and West London.* 1875

Kingsford, Charles Lethbridge,
  see Stow, John

Kirwan, Daniel Joseph   *Palace and Hovel: or, Phases of London Life.* Connecticut, 1870

Knight, Charles   *London.* (6 vols) 1841–4

Lambert, B.   *The History and Survey of London and its Environs from the Earliest Period to the Present Time . . .* 1806

Lexicon Balatronicum. 1811

Loftie, W. J.   *History of London.* (2 vols) 1883

                       Kensington Picturesque & Historical. 1888

                       London City. 1891

London and its Environs Described. (6 vols) 1761

London Before the Great Fire. 1818

London History and Topography. (Members' Library Catalogue of the Greater London Council). Vol. I, 1939

Lowndes, William Thomas   *Bibliographer's Manual of English Literature.* (4 vols) 1834; new edition (6 vols) 1857.

Luffman, John   *The History of London and its Environs.* 1793

                       The Charters of London Complete. 1793

                       Elements of History and Chronology from the Creation of the World to the Close of the Year 1804. 1806

Lyne, S. and Ilive, J.   *A New and Compleat Survey of London.* (2 vols) 1762

Lysons, Daniel   *The Environs of London.* (4 vols) 1792

Mackay, Charles   *The Thames and its Tributaries: or Rambles Among the Rivers.* 1840

Maitland, William   *The History of London from its Foundation to the Present Time.* 1756

Malcolm, James Peller   *Londinium Redivivum; or an Antient History and Modern Description of London.* (4 vols) 1802

                       Anecdotes of the Manners and Customs of London etc. (3 vols) 1811

Mayhew, Henry   *London Labour and the London Poor.* (Issued serially) 1852

                       The Great World of London. 1856

Meteyard, Eliza   *The Hallowed Spots of Ancient London.* 1870

Miller, Thomas   *Picturesque Sketches of London, Past and Present.* 1852

Mitton, G. E.   *Maps of Old London.* 1908

Montague, Baron	*History of England.* 1771
Morley, Henry, *see* Stow, John	
Murray, John Fisher	*The World of London.* (2 vols) 1844
'N.B.'	*The Antiquities of London and Westminster.* 1722
Nelson, John	*The History, Topography, and Antiquities of the Parish of St Mary Islington.* 1811

A New History of England. 1790

Nightingale, Joseph	*The Dictionary of London*
Noble, T. C.	*Memorials of Temple Bar.* 1869
Noorthouck, John	*A New History of London, Including Westminster and Southwark.* 1773
Parton, John	*Some Account of the Hospital and Parish of St Giles in the Fields, Middlesex.* 1822
Pelham, Camden	*The Chronicles of Crime.* 1840
Pennant, Thomas	*Some Account of London.* 1790
Pepys, Samuel	*Diary.* (Many editions)
Pinks, William J.	*The History of Clerkenwell.* 1865
Pratt, A. T. Camden	*Unknown London.* 1897

The Present State of Britain. 1736

Riley, Henry Thomas (trans.)	*Liber Albus: The White Book of the City of London.* 1861
	Memorials of London and London Life. 1868
Ritchie, J. Ewing	*The Night Side of London.* 1857
Robinson, William	*The History and Antiquities of the Parish of Edmonton.* 1819
Rodenberg, Julius	*Alltagsleben in London. Ein Skizzenbuch.* Berlin, 1860
Rubinstein, Stanley J.	*The Street Trader's Lot: London 1851.* 1947
Ryan, W. P.	*Literary London, its Lights & Comedies.* 1898
Schlesinger, Max	*Saunterings In and About London.* 1853
Seymour, Robert	*Survey of London.* (2 vols) 1734–5
Smith, Charles Manby	*Curiosities of London Life: or Phases, Physiological and Social, of the Great Metropolis.* 1853
	The Little World of London; or, Pictures in Little of London Life. 1857

Smith, John Thomas	*Antiquities of London and its Environs.* 1791
	The Streets of London with Anecdotes of their More Celebrated Residents. 1846
Stow, John	*Survey of London.* 1st ed. 1598; 2nd ed. 1603; 3rd ed. 1618; 4th ed. 1633; 5th ed. 'Brought down from the year 1633 . . . to the present time' by John Strype, 1720.
	1st ed. reprinted, with additional notes by William John Thoms, 1842; 2nd ed. re-edited by Henry Morley, 1889.
	Completely revised ed. of 1st and 2nd eds with additional notes by Charles Lethbridge Kingsford, 1908
Stow, W.	*Remarks on London.* 1722
Strype, John	*Survey of the Cities of London and Westminster.* 1720
	see also under Stow, John
Suger, Ed. and Dumont, W. H.	*Londres et les Anglais.* Paris, *circa* 1907
Thomas, Henry	*The Wards of London.* (2 vols) 1828
Thoms, William John, *see* Stow, John	
Thornbury, Walter	*Haunted London.* 1880
	see also under Walford, Edward
Thorne, James	*Handbook to the Environs of London, Alphabetically Arranged.* 1876
Thornton, William (ed.) *et al.*	*The New, Complete, and Universal History, Description, and Survey of the Cities of London and Westminster, The Borough of Southwark, and the Parts Adjacent.* (issued serially) 1785
Timbs, John	*Curiosities of London,* 1855
	London and Westminster: City and Suburb. 1868
	Historic Ninepins: A Book of Curiosities. 1869
Tomlins, Thomas Edlyne	*Yseldon, a Perambulation of Islington.* 1858
A True and Faithful Account of . . . the Late Dreadful Burning of the City of London. 1667	
Trusler, John D.	*The London Adviser and Guide.* 1786
Vanderkiste, R. W.	*Notes and Narrative of a Six Years' Mission, Principally Among the Dens of London.* 1852
Vasili, Count Paul	*The World of London.* 1885
Verment, Marquis de and Darnley, Charles	*London and Paris; or Comparative Sketches.* 1823

Bibliograpy

Victoria County Histories

Walford, Edward	*Londoniana.* (2 vols) 1879
with Thornbury, Walter (eds)	*Old and New London: A Narrative of its History, its People and its Places.* (6 vols) 1873
Waller, William	*Recollections.* 1668
Wallis, John	*London, being a complete guide to the British Capital.* 1810
Weever, John	*Epigrammes.* 1599
	Ancient Funerall Monuments within the United Monarchie of Great Britaine. 1631
Wheatley, Henry B.	*London Past and Present.* (3 vols) 1891
Wight, J.	*Mornings at Bow Street.* 1825
	More Mornings at Bow Street. 1827
Wood, Anthony	*Athenae Oxoniensis.* (2 vols) 1691

Newspapers, Magazines, Journals and Pamphlets mentioned in the text

The *Annual Register*
The *Antiquary*
The *Antique Dealer's Guide*
Blackwood's Magazine
Chambers's Journal
The *City Press*
'*Critical Observations on the Buildings and Improvements of London*'
The *Daily News*
The *Daily Telegraph*
The *Eclectic Review*
The *Elgin Courier*
The *European Magazine*
The *General Magazine*
The *Gentleman's Magazine*
The *Globe*
Good Words
The *Illustrated London News*
The *London Chronicle*
The *London Journal*
Men and Women of the Time
The *Monthly Review*
The *Morning Advertiser*
The *Morning Herald*
The *New London Magazine*

The New Spiritual Magazine
Notes and Queries
The Pall Mall Gazette
The Pall Mall Magazine
St James's Gazette
The *Spectator*
The *Standard*
The *Sussex Express*
The Times
The Town and Country Magazine; Or Universal Repository of Knowledge, Instruction and Entertainment
The Universal Magazine

GENERAL INDEX

Page numbers in italics refer to illustrations. For titles of books not listed see Bibliography.

BIOGRAPHICAL INDEX

Page numbers in italics refer to illustrations. Dictionary of National Biography *volume and page numbers are given in the right-hand columns.*

Biographical Index

239